*Journeys with a Real
Jack in the Pulpit*

Journeys with a Real Jack in the Pulpit

For Betty Hills and Carola my Best Friends in Duxbury
Helen Philbrick

Helen L. Philbrick

Copyright © 2005 by Helen L. Philbrick.

ISBN: Softcover   1-4134-9419-6

All rights reserved. No part of this book may be reproduced or transmitted in any form or by any means, electronic or mechanical, including photocopying, recording, or by any information storage and retrieval system, without permission in writing from the copyright owner.

This book was printed in the United States of America.

To order additional copies of this book, contact:
Xlibris Corporation
1-888-795-4274
www.Xlibris.com
Orders@Xlibris.com

28380

Contents

Introduction: About John and Me 9

Chapter 1: Early Childhood—
  Bristol Ferry and Providence, RI 11
Chapter 2: Middleton, Massachusetts 14
Chapter 3: Danvers, Massachusetts 21
Chapter 4: Silversmithing 35
Chapter 5: From School Days to Silversmithing 50
Chapter 6: A New Haven Prelude to Brightwater 57
Chapter 7: Brightwater, My True Love 70
Chapter 8: Partridge Manuscript 74
Chapter 9: Marriage and Groveland 81
Chapter 10: Over the Threshold 89
Chapter 11: Weymouth to Duxbury 92
Chapter 12: Stone Bridge/ Faith
  Homestead/Peterson House 103
Chapter 13: Biodynamic Gardening 114
Chapter 14: Roanridge 1949-1957 138
Chapter 15: The National Town-Country Church Institute
  (NTCCI) and the Roanridge Demonstration
  Homestead 148
Chapter 16: The Three Churches 160
Chapter 17: Duxbury Madras 178
Chapter 18: Ashfield—1957-1962 184

Chapter 19: Wilkinsonville—Arrival, 1963 208
Chapter 20: Holy Humor—From the Bulletin of the Sutton
    Historical Society—About John's Ministry 219
Chapter 21: Duxbury II—Retirement 1972 231
Chapter 22: Memory—1985 251

Index 257

"In breathing there are two blessings! Draw in the air, release it again. The first compresses, the second refreshes. Thus, marvelous is the mixture of life! Give thanks to God when He presses you and thank Him when he releases you."

—Goethe

Every Once in a While
A Page for Meditation

You cannot find yourself
In the mirror of another's soul.
The force of your own Being
Must strike its roots deep into world foundations.
Would it transplant authentically heights
The beauty from the spirit
Into the depths of the earth.
Make bold to be yourself's own being
That you, as strong soul form,
Can sacrifice yourself to cosmic powers.

from *The Soul's Probation*
by Rudolf Steiner

Introduction

About John and Me

Everything has to start somewhere, and these stories start right now, while memory still brings back sounds and places and names which good fortune has let me share.

First of all, a good word for the Rev. John Philbrick, a truly holy man with a predominant sense of humor, who was my life's companion and husband. Rather, I tried to be his companion and helper without myself being too pious or too involved in parish doings.

The following pages should be not necessarily my story, but my pictures of some of the individuals I have been privileged to know over quite a long lifespan.

Chapter 1

Early Childhood—
Bristol Ferry and Providence, RI

When one is born to elderly parents, one is already in an uncharted and perhaps unenviable situation. In the first place, there were no living grandparents but because Mother and Dad had many friends, there were pseudo-grandparents springing up whenever Mother took her new baby anywhere.

After a few months of being trundled around in a large and ornate baby carriage this young, defenseless spectator expected every adult in sight would stop and coo and speak nonsense without ever making any kind of real sense.

As I grew older and wise enough to know there was a difference between cooing and any real sense, I began to realize that Helen Saunders Lathrop was really a person worth knowing. When the time was right, she taught the baby how to turn a somersault. Another session of infantile lessons was the Lord's Prayer—or at least the sounds, but not much about the meaning.

Helen Lathrop was Mother's beloved friend—so much beloved that Mother had made her a grandmother without benefit of even husband or children. Mother used to say that Helen was Helen Louise's "grandmother," but when the older Helen passed away from tuberculosis, there was still an older lady (her mother) who sort of automatically assumed the role of another grandmother. For the first few years that was inevitable and acceptable, but with expanding years and increasing insight there began to be questions with unexplainable answers.

Anyway, "Grandmother Lathrop" filled the need for a grandmother and we often used to visit this kindly old lady in Providence who wore her thin wispy white hair wound in a tiny knot tied somehow to the back of her head. She presided at the dining table in her basement dining room where the cook sometimes burst in from the basement kitchen.

The meals were very formal with the old lady dressed in gray silk, presiding at the head of the frugal table. Aunt Lucy, her elderly daughter, sat prim and silent and, I noticed, always disapproving of whatever was happening. Or perhaps she was perpetually in mourning for her deceased sister—"Grandmother Helen." There are many odd and unexplainable occurrences that never make sense to a small child. No wonder I had trouble with arithmetic, which seemed to me just another unexplainable mystery!

The food at the Lathrop table was memorable for its simplicity and its scarcity. Even the bread was sliced thin, and each slice was cut in half. My father was once heard to whisper to my mother, "Sometimes I am almost tempted to walk downtown to get a square meal."

Back in those days, between the Victorian era and the First World War, if one was wealthy one never "let on." Old and almost shabby clothes were quite acceptable. If there was an occasion one might wear one's "best dress," but then the dress was put away in safekeeping to have it ready for the next occasion.

The Lathrop family in their daily life style never indicated that they had any connection whatsoever with the Gorham Silver Manufacturing Company right there in Providence. But now that I am grown up with a little more insight I cannot express deeply enough my appreciation of Grandmother Helen's Gorham stock, which paid for my college education. No more somersaults, but I do still value the Lord's Prayer.

Discipline

Discipline of young children in the early nineteen hundreds was strict even for a timid only child, the little girl who didn't really mean to cause trouble. But there was an element of curiosity that prompted deeper investigation which often commenced with "I wonder what would happen if . . . ?"

The first time that sequence was performed was very early in the Bristol Ferry days, so long ago that the details have vanished. The wood fire burning down into grayish ashes must have looked inviting, and I had my little broom close by. Why not sweep the ashes out of the fireplace over the floor to see what would happen?

Mother happened! Fast! I don't recall what she must have said (or done), but that must have been the earliest episode of the Victorian tirades that seemed never ending.

Although there is no record of the scolding, I still keenly remember closely studying the patterns on the old cashmere rugs while they scolded. Even today an unusual geometric design on the edge of an oriental rug awakens a misty feeling that there should be a thunderous voice somewhere, making very positive statements and demanding my equally positive promises not to do it again, whatever my crime had been.

Father was worse. There was no proclamation—just a quick ascent up the back stairs to the back bathroom where the strap hung on a hook on the wall. The speech was always the same, and it never made any sense to me: "This hurts me more than it hurts you." Why did they always have to talk nonsense if it was such a serious occasion?

But that was how it was in the early nineteen hundreds.

In a Rhode Island Cemetery

One memorable day, my father was waiting to take a street car into Newport on West Main Road, just across from an old cemetery. Two men drove up in an automobile, stopped the car, and walked over to the cemetery fence. One man pointed to a gravestone. The other man looked, and looked again. Then he reached for his wallet. He handed something green to the other man. They both burst into loud laughter, got back in the car, and drove away.

The name inscribed on the gravestone was "PRESERVED FISH."

Chapter 2

Middleton, Massachusetts

Getting acquainted with a new world

Middleton, Massachusetts was a very small town when Mother's friend Ethel Manchester Perkins suggested that the Porters, with a growing child who would soon need schooling, should move to Middleton from the even smaller town of Bristol Ferry.

We had no car, so I'm not quite sure how we arrived at the wharf to take the Bristol Ferry from the island side to the town of Bristol. We watched its walking beam as it directed the ship toward Bristol. (This was before Mount Hope Bridge had been thought of.) In Bristol we passed the Herreshoff Boat Yards where the famous sailboats were and still are built.

From Bristol we took a steam train to the Providence railroad station. From Providence we took the train to Boston, to the South Station. Across Boston to the North Station we rode the elevated train where we could look down along the shore to Rowe's Wharf and the boats out in the harbor. Trains from the North Station naturally served towns and a few cities north of Boston. The train to Lawrence would go through Middleton, and that was the end of the long expedition.

Visiting with Aunt Ethel

"Aunt" Ethel's house was large and commodious, and "Uncle" Frank greeted us with a warm welcome. Two sons, Alfred and Little Frank, probably accepted the inevitable and waited to see what would happen next with an unexpected girl "cousin."

Mother said, "Who lives in that house across the street?" And Aunt Ethel answered, "That is the house we hope you will buy." And we did. Until we could move into the house across the street, we stayed at the Perkins house. To a four-year-old, the buying and selling of houses was nothing to bother one's mind. There were places to explore and adventures to invent. There was a great stand of tall pines for walks, and swamps, and a fine clear brook that one might fall into—and did, one day, wearing a heavy dark brown sweater which grew slowly darker brown as the water saturated the wool.

I loved Aunt Ethel's pantry. It was a long narrow room with a window on one side. The walls were lined with shelves that were filled with china and glass. When the door was opened at the end one was enveloped in the delicious scent of home-baked bread—and one's mouth watered! Why and how, after all these years, do I suddenly recall that breakfast at Aunt Ethel's table always meant oatmeal with cream, in a cereal bowl of the Blue Onion pattern?

The two boys in the family gradually accepted my presence, and we played the usual games with trains on tracks and whatever outdoors play was appropriate to the season. We also sailed boats in the bathtub.

I always felt that the apple tree in the Perkins's yard was my own tree because it was a Porter Apple tree with mellow pale yellow apples.

One day it was my turn to wield a full-size shovel over my shoulder for some undecided project. I went to the front door to speak to Aunt Ethel. As she opened the door, I stepped back and put the shovel through the window behind me. Oh dear. Spanks!

In those days, many housewives followed the pattern of their mothers and grandmothers. The big iron cook stove that burned coal was too hot to use in the summer, so there was also a summer kitchen where they used a three-burner kerosene stove. It was an adventure to drop in at a neighbor's house to see what was going on, or perhaps to beg for a cookie. The summer kitchen always smelled of kerosene. One of the summer chores was to make soap out of the year's excess fat "drippings" and lye or potash. There was often a cardboard box of soap scored into cakes drying out on a shelf. The combined smell of kerosene joined with potash in the soap is still memorable. It was good soap too, and whitened the clothes well. It was rubbed by hand over the clothes up and down the washboard. But it almost broke Mother's long-suffering back to bend over the tub.

Alfred was a lot older and his talents were more mature. Little Frank had musical abilities far beyond mine. There was a big celebration for all of us when he sat down at the piano and played by ear one of the favorite John Philip Sousa marches. The one I now remember best is "And the monkey wrapped his tail around the flag pole." Frank's talent later led him to Hollywood for his lifetime.

Uncle Frank worked in the Five Cent Savings Bank in Salem. (There were only four FCSBs in all of Massachusetts: in Salem, Plymouth, Boston and a town I don't remember.) He was used to riding the train every day to go and return. It was a long trip by public transportation, but there was change in the air. One unforgettable day he drove home in the first automobile to be owned in Middleton. He had safely maneuvered the 20 miles of good and bad roads from Salem. When he finally reached his own house, he turned into the driveway and knocked down the fencepost.

The next "first" was a telephone right in our own house in about 1915, on the wall in the Silversmith's workshop. One called the operator by ringing with a crank.

That year, my father taught me to tie a bowknot.

War going on

About then we began to realize there was a war going on in Europe. I was about four years old. It was called the First World War. Several neighbors put on khaki uniforms and went away.

We learned songs and sang whenever a group of people were together: "There's a long, long trail a-winding, till the time when I'll be coming down that long, long trail with you." Another favorite was "Keep the Home Fires Burning."

Times were hard. Food was scarce. We made our own soap from "drippings." We baked our own bread with wholewheat flour. Mother used a cake recipe called "Butterless, eggless, milkless cake," and Father teased her about it.

There was no radio, no TV, and people made their own entertainment. Beside our house was the Town Hall. Before the invention of television, the Town Hall was the center of community life. There were regular meetings of the Grange, the Odd Fellows, the Improved Order of Red Men, and all the other local clubs, which had their own special meeting nights. These were serious service organizations.

The building's identity was made clear by just two words above the front door: "Town Hall." From our house so close by on Sunday afternoons we could hear the tourists out for a ride in their new cars, shouting out "Taowhn Hall" as they passed by in the accent they imagined we must use. They thought Middleton was a hick town. It was.

But there were also clever people who loved entertainment. Some groups produced a play every year. Or several entertainers would present several skits in an evening. There were magicians and singers and readers, and once in a while, a serious speaker.

Some afternoons we had dancing school, where we learned to sit politely with hands in lap and ankles crossed. We watched the dancing school teacher and her helpers put on a performance of Stravinsky's *Petrushka*, the floppy dancer whose floppy doll was her smaller double. We never dreamed that fifty years later Displaced Persons from Russia would teach us, as we pulled store-bought greens out of a grocery bag, chanting "Petrushka, Petrushka," that *petrushka* is the Russian name for parsley. That's why the floppy dancers were named for the floppy green herb.

The Town Hall inspired amateur performers to perfect their talents to present plays and musical shows of infinite variety and skill. Mr. Pfeiffer presented himself as a One Man Band with drum and banjo and other unnamed musical instruments, topped by a harmonica geared to lip level. My favorite was Cousin Alfred's

Impersonation of a Piccolo Player at Five Miles Distance, using a bona fide piccolo but making no sound.

Cousin Alfred was in his teens, old enough to be influenced by World War I, which was by this time a strong part of our lives. Uncle Frank was an officer and was in Europe during the War. It was the custom then to put a gold star in the window if a member of the family was in the service. Our mothers used to go to meetings where they made bandages and filled khaki cloth tubes full of milkweed floss. Everybody called this "the war to end all wars." I remember at night watching a light in the sky moving rapidly, and I snuggled deeper in the bed in fear that that airplane would blow up something. Uncle Frank came home again, a sick man because he had been gassed, and died shortly thereafter.

Alfred had a "dugout" down in the lower part of the back yard. He rigged up some kind of communication and called it a "wireless," but even though it was contemporary with the trend in those days, it did not attract my interest. What fascinated me more was Alfred's total devotion to everything in nature. There were gardens and hens and a big red dog. And there were squirrels and mice and rabbits and rats. We took everything apart! One memorable display was Alfred's Market: a neat arrangement of cuts he must have seen in a butcher's shop, where liver and heart and kidneys were labeled with fictitious price tags. How much for a mouse's liver?

There were dog-tooth violets to pick on Howes Hill, and Howes's cows used to scratch their backs as they rounded the lignum vitae hedge around the village church.

Perhaps the most daring thing my mother ever did, being a newcomer in that little town, follows. There was a sick lady who lived in a house next to the church. Mother heard someone say that on the night before the Fourth of July, the boys would peal the big bell in the church tower. Without a word to anyone, my very proper mother slipped out of the house, walked the mile or so to the church, found a door unlocked and stepped inside. She located the stairway up, and then the ladder, and climbed to the belfry. Up there, in the belltower, all alone she figured out how the ropes made the clapper strike the bell. She disconnected the ropes so the bell would not ring. She walked the long mile back home, confident that Miss Stiles could sleep through the night before the Fourth.

Our milkman drove a small wagon with a black horse, and my joy was to accompany him every morning as he delivered the pint or quart milk cans to his customers along the route, picking up the empty cans they kept for him to fill next day.

One day his sister gave me a grape basket with four or five baby kittens to take home. I sorrowfully returned them the same day: Mother's orders. Not too bad, just a little grief.

School in Middleton was conducted according to educational customs of that era. The one schoolhouse contained eight classes, with two classes in each of the four rooms. This was a good system for the smart pupils because they could hear the teacher teaching the second grade while they were still in the first grade.

A sad occurrence happened when we were in the first grade. Virginia Merrill, a little girlfriend of mine, was skipping her way to school when the big trolley car was coming along the track and down the hill. She was running along the track and fell, and was run over.

Every day, according to the custom, our teacher, Mrs. Henderson, read from the Bible and we all said the Lord's Prayer, but that morning I had a deep solemn feeling for all of us, and I still remember Virginia's long red curls, and how we missed her.

Second grade, same room, same teacher, and harder arithmetic. Third grade teacher caught me eating a peach during Geography. Not advisable. Fourth grade. Not memorable. Fifth grade: fractions and panic. When we moved to nearby Danvers, school was much worse. My childhood in Heaven had ended.

Father was working hard at his silversmithing against insuperable odds. Mother donned a big apron and set up our front room as a Tea Room. People came in to drink a cup of tea and to look at Dad's silver in the glass china cupboard. There were several loyal "clients" who left orders for the silversmith. My parents were a good team, but the income was small. In those days a craftsman was a lone operator who had to make a go of it without much experience or training in marketing. It was one life's work to be a craftsman but a totally different life's work to be the salesman. Father decided we should find a helper.

They decided to adopt a lad to be apprenticed to learn silversmithing. Around my fourth birthday, he arrived. An eighteen-year-old boy was available from Saint Andrew's Boys' School in Barrington, R.I., highly recommended by the Headmaster, Dr. Chapin. Edward's father had died and his mother was in the hospital. Taking an open street car to visit his mother, he had an accident to both legs. Doctors saved one knee, but the other knee was gone. After his mother's death, he was welcomed into Dr. Chapin's school, where he was an excellent student.

It was only right for him to be adopted into our family. Surely he was meant to be a companion for a four-year-old girl! Those well-intentioned Victorians were more romantic than realistic! Fortunately we all survived, but I still can feel Brother's cane crooked around my neck in some disciplinary struggle.

He came into our family, adopted legally with a new surname, two gentle parents, and a meddlesome little sister. Edward entered high school and excelled in all subjects. He commuted to school in Danvers by trolley car every day.

Eddie learned silversmithing and was a good fellow. Insurance from his accident enabled him to go to college. While at the boys' school he had learned the trade of printing. At Boston University he was editor of the college yearbook. There were fewer euphemisms back then. No polite words like "prosthesis." He wore his "artificial legs" and had to visit the Artificial Limb and Brace Company to get new ones. He sometimes developed a squeak in one knee joint, for which he carried a small oil can in his pocket. He never went anywhere without his cane, but the story is that at school one day he broke the cane trying to bat a prune sandwich in the lunchroom. He also held up his socks with a boxful of tacks and a hammer.

Eddie became an apprentice in the silver shop, and the volume of silverware increased, but not enough. There was still the mortgage. Father found a job at a big company named General Electric, in Lynn, where he could earn more money as a Master Mechanic. Father contracted typhoid fever from raw milk. When he was well enough to work again, he took a job as "Master Mechanic" at the Champion Lamp Factory in Danvers, where we soon moved.

Chapter 3

Danvers, Massachusetts

They must have had to sell the house in Middleton. Quite suddenly, I was whisked out of the fifth grade in Middleton and landed in the fifth grade in Danvers. No wonder mathematics came hard. Brother went to Boston University and with the use of trains and trolley cars we survived as a family of four, living simply and making do as best we could.

Our new house was a "flat," a second floor apartment in a house with another family living below and above us. When we moved in, the owners of the house lived below us with their bedrooms on the third floor. They were a well-educated Irish family, Mr. Timothy Lynch and his wife and three schoolteacher daughters.

Mrs. Lynch's sister, Mrs. Kerans, lived in a huge old house on the same street. She had six daughters and five sons. She was stately and beautiful, with silvery-white hair, and her family called her the Queen of Conant Street. The daughters were each specialists in their own skill. Rebecca was a dancing teacher, and Rachael, with the smooth creamy voice, was the school singing teacher.

Often in the afternoon we would all gather at Rachael's proclamation, "Let's knock over a cup of tea." Our tea parties were hilarious. Rebecca, the mistress of the kitchen, put on the kettle to boil the water for the tea. One sad day I was helping her in the kitchen, slicing her beautiful homemade bread. She suddenly cried out, "Oh my poor little cream pitcher." It was a small pewter pitcher that she had set down on the hot stove and it was melted into a small puddle of melted pewter. (Parenthetically, the low melting point of lead is one reason why our modern pewter no longer contains lead. Another reason, of course, is its toxicity.)

There was always a high-spirited and hilarious atmosphere about the tea parties. No news was overlooked, and we polite and proper products of Providence, Rhode Island, were surprised and delighted to be let in on an Irish trait we had never seen before: nicknames! No malice, just fun!

They had funny nicknames for everyone. Of course, I was "The Infant Terrible." They called one schoolteacher Syringa Bush. They loved my father, and I can hear Rachael now chanting in her creamy voice, "Father, dear Father, come home to me now, The clock in the steeple strikes one," a song or poem from *Ten Nights in a Barroom*. She trained us in school music. Rebecca, our dancing teacher, was more quiet but had deep love for us all. She always made the tea and served her fine homemade bread. They were born teachers, and we all learned about the gentler arts from them. Public schools in those days lacked time and incentive to bother with culture. It was a shy but appreciative childhood.

There were two deaths while we lived there. Typical Irish wakes, which were sad but beautiful, involved all the affection and traditions they had brought from the old country. Everyone wore their best clothes to honor the wake, and the refreshments were sumptuous.

When Mrs. Lynch died after a long illness, her husband took over the preparations for a great wake with huge containers of food, and enough provisions to feed the crowds who came to the house to pay their respects. The wake for the Queen of Conant Street was beautiful, with everyone in full dress.

In the Porter family we were totally inexperienced and uninformed that people coming from another country would always band together as neighbors. We Porters were privileged in those years to be included in this charming little Irish community, where we shared not only their loving generosity and their hilarious humor, but also their exquisite appreciation of the fine arts, in their music and their house full of fine paintings and sculptures.

They also had in the upstairs front hall a family Prayer Space with life-sized holy figures near the top of the front stairs. Other Irish neighbors naturally were familiar with the shrine. They were reverent toward the beautiful statues, but with that typical Irish humor, they could not resist asking with a twinkle, "Do they always have to stand there all the time? Don't you ever let them out?"

These friends were likely to be unexpectedly frank about their involvement with religion. One day, I remember Rebecca's mother telling us all about her own prayer. She said, "I was there on my knees talking to God, [this is absolutely verbatim as I heard her story] and I said, "Now you know my daughter, Rebecca, and you know how good she is, attending Mass early every morning, and she is so patient and so kind and so forgiving—well, I am just like her . . . . !"

Humor makes holiness palatable.

When one of the sisters complained to the priest in the confessional that her attic room rocked in the wind, she told us that father "Flat Hat" had told her if she was afraid the house would blow down, she must "just keep in a state of Grace!" Good advice for all of us.

Summer Sojourns in Boxford

For the family confined to a second floor flat in a small town, it was refreshing to spend a few weeks in a much smaller town. Boxford was sparsely settled, an unspoiled rural area with unlimited fields and woods to explore.

Father used to rent a cottage on Stiles Pond for perhaps two weeks, probably the length of his vacation from the lamp factory. A rowboat went with the cottage. From somewhere there appeared fishing poles, saplings culled from nearby woods. There was always some string available. Fishhooks and pieces of red flannel completed the equipment. We caught bullfrogs. With embarrassment I now confess that I thought frogs' legs made a delicious breakfast, and in those days we were unaware that nature's bounty could ever be diminished.

Sunday afternoon was for a walk in the woods. Mother carried along Mrs. Dana's book *How to Know the Wildflowers*, and specimens we found were duly noted in the book. Some that were not illustrated were drawn in on the margins, and Mother painted them with watercolors. The same book had been in the family for many years, and it still bears records of wild flowers that grew in Providence or in Bristol Ferry.

There was a hermit in Boxford whom we used to visit. He lived in a tumbledown shack, which was next to a fresh spring of cold water. We used to walk over and ask the hermit for a drink of water. That water was indescribably clear and cold and sparkling, unforgettable, brilliant, icy. Why do I still recall it? Is it perhaps because water is one of the four elements of infinite value to our world?

The hermit himself was a mild-mannered man with a kindly face and a rather haphazard appearance. He used to identify himself in a sing-song tuneless tune: "my name is Henry Chick Chick Kimball . . ." Perhaps we visited him to buy eggs. I don't recall. But what made the greatest impression was a big patch of clover, tall plants with rich dark green leaves, and practically every one was a four-leaved clover. Does anyone nowadays ever attribute good luck to finding a four-leaf clover?

At the end of the short stay "in the country," we packed our bags and boarded the train at the Boxford Railway Station to return the twenty-five miles back to the larger town of Danvers.

Grace before meals

Some folks may be able to remember when this little bit of ceremony was commonly used as we sat down to dinner. Before the "official fork" was lifted, there was a pause. Then someone expressed thanks for the food that sustains us.

Grace means gratitude.

My husband John's Grace was traditional and very brief:

> Grant, O Lord, that our companionship may be the Revelation of Thy Presence, and so turn our daily bread into the Bread of Life, through Jesus Christ our Lord. Amen.

In my childhood, meals were always blessed by our Irish blessing:

> O God, be giving us thy Blessing
> And have the thanks
> And give us Peace
> For Christ's sake.

The German philosopher Rudolf Steiner wrote:

> The plant-seeds are quickened in the night of the Earth
> The green herbs are sprouting through the Might of the All,
> And all fruits are ripened by the power of the Sun.
>
> So quickens the soul in the shrine of the Heart,
> So blossoms Spirit-power in the light of the World,
> So ripens Man's strength in the glory of God.

Another grace from my childhood:

> O God, our great companion, lead us day by day ever deeper into the mysteries of Thy life and ours, and help us to be interpreters of life to our fellow men, through Jesus Christ our Lord. Amen.

Now that many things are speeding up, we cherish this very brief moment, holding hands in a circle and speaking a deep thought in only four words : "Blessings on the meal."

Doctors

Medical doctors in those early years were, from my childish point of view, set apart from all other men because they were mysterious and formal.

My first encounter was with Dr. Ewing in Middleton, who drove me in his own automobile all the way from Middleton to the J.B. Thomas Hospital in Peabody to remove "tonsils and adenoids," which was the custom in those days. Ether was applied using a large snow-white fabric, which looked like Mother's best linen table napkins. My only other memory of this occasion was watching Dr. Ewing unwrap a "stick of chewing gum" and stooping to hand it to me before we boarded his automobile for the long trip home.

The doctors in Danvers were different, or perhaps I was a few years more mature. Doctor Baldwin lived near us, and we used to encounter him frequently. He seldom spoke a word, whether in greeting or in prescribing. His greeting was a grunt. On a professional level he might grunt twice or three times, but his only other communication might be an abstract-sounding mutter like "grunt, oil, grunt, of peppermint."

But our favorite doctor was red-haired Irish Doctor Moriarty, who would burst into the Kerans's house with a loud proclamation, "Glory be to God, Rebecca, you're not going to have the flu again this year, are you?" Every diagnosis was prefaced with "Glory be to God," or that might be the preface to his hearty "Good morning." We always loved to see him coming. "Glory be to God." He was a good influence and possessed that mystical Irish trait of saying something backwards intended to mean the opposite, as in his statement to Rebecca, "You're not going to have the flu this year," when he really meant, "Glory be to God, Rebecca, are you coming down with the flu?"

A favorite bit of advice given to me in my childhood by a beloved Irishman was: "Never tell a lie when the truth will do. Never tell the truth when a lie will do better."

Neighbors and Other Delights of Danvers

There was a sort of half-adopted young man in the Lynch family who had a beloved dog named Rex. The lad's name was Frank and he had some kind of aphasia that made his speeches come out backwards. "Mrs. Porter, have you got anything in the house you want uptown?" He said once, "I saw a car with a back in the door and those lights in the front are good because the car behind can see you coming." And one day he told us about a new dog. "We thought he would be a Spaniard but he turned out to be a moodle." Mother kept a notebook of Frank's upside down speeches.

The larger town presented more opportunities for broader experiences. Father left the house to walk three miles to work in the morning. My adopted brother stayed in Boston to attend Boston University with the money he received after his legs were amputated in the streetcar accident. I walked to school under protest. The fifth grade in the larger town was very threatening. (One morning I panicked and walked back home and told Mother the door of the schoolhouse was locked. Mother took me by the ear and walked me back to that horrible fifth grade.) After school that day the teacher, whose name was Miss Obst, held me in her lap with what I'm sure she intended to be comforting words. But they didn't feel that way to me. She had cold blue eyes—but she meant to be comforting.

The best cultural experience ever to hit the small town of Danvers in the 20th century was Chautauqua, a cultural fair that traveled the countryside, and we eagerly anticipated its arrival. Every summer the trucks rolled into town and the big tent was erected. At the appointed time all of us who were children gathered for the morning session. We learned songs. Almost on the eve of my 91st birthday I have just recalled this song, which they must have taught us when I was about ten years old, living in Danvers.

The Chautauqua song follows:

> "I am proud of my town
> Is my town proud of me?
> What she needs is citizens
> Trained in loyalty.
> When we work, when we play
> With our fellow men
> Good citizens we will be
> And I'll be proud, be proud
> of my own town
> And I'll make her proud of me."

This recollection, complete with a catchy tune, has "come back" suddenly to add to another rather silly story about Chautauqua.

One night a speaker had finished the serious part of his lecture on human relationships. He was talking about the person who "gets your goat." For a bit of variety in the program he stopped and asked, "Does anyone know where that phrase came from—to get one's goat?"

My hand went up, in spite of my shyness. "In horse country they have goats in the pastures to keep the horses company. If the goat is taken away, the horses are unhappy." And the lecturer loudly proclaimed "Here is a silver dollar for that little girl who could give me the answer." My proper parents were amazed.

Our Troubleshooter and Master Mechanic

Dad was a troubleshooter and master mechanic in the Champion Lamp factory. It was a new experience to visit the factory and watch the glass lamp bulbs go through the processes of manufacture, ending with the glass being heated and the little glass tip being flipped off the top of the bulb. On a windy day the pendulum clocks on the fifth floor used to stop because the building swayed so much in the wind. Mr. Jasper Marsh was the owner of the factory. His brother Francis lived in Danvers on Sylvan Street. He, too, manufactured lamp bulbs, and he called his factory Sylvania. That was the origin of two famous names we still hear today, Champion and Sylvania.

One of the men in charge was reputed to have quite a vocabulary. Father came home one day with the latest story. The little boy asked his mother, "What did Daddy say about God last night when he tripped over my fire engine in the dark?"

Mother began to blossom in this new town. She made friends with everyone she met. Of course we walked to the stores "Uptown" and she carried on lively conversations with all the storekeepers. Mr. Lovelace of the Butter and Eggs store was a favorite. But there were also those casual meetings with friends on the sidewalk, and the long, long conversations while I tugged at her skirts to no avail.

The Danvers Women's Association and Maria G. Kimball

Mother joined the Danvers Women's Association and became corresponding secretary as well as a member of the DWA Glee

Club. They sang familiar old songs in the Glee Club before the advent of radio, and occasionally they would visit a neighboring women's club to sing for them. These clubs were rather small, and several had been recently assembled. The gatherings were rather formal, expressing the new self-assurance blossoming among these groups of women. Programs were serious and educational and friendly.

The whole idea of a Woman's Club was so new that there were many kinks to straighten out. Some towns would call it a Woman's Club and others preferred Women's Association, and there were long telephone conversations about the pros and cons of each. As a matter of fact, one conversation was so long that our new little puppy chewed the phone cord in half, perhaps with the hope of attention and dog's supper. Mother was talking with the lady we all called "Talkative" Clark. She lived in the house across the fields where Tituba and the little girls started the witchcraft delusion of 1692.

As Corresponding Secretary, Mother found herself handling much of the Club business. She said that in her correspondence she refused to refer to the Danvers Women's Association as the Danvers Women's Ass. While the Women's Clubs and other affiliations were brewing all around Essex County, the Porter family had a chance to move to the Judge Samuel Holten House (of which more elsewhere), which made us neighbors of Mrs. Maria Grey Kimball (pronounced Mar-EYE-a—not Maria, no hint of softness.) Maria was President of the Danvers Women's Association, which in a way made her a bit higher than Ethel Porter, Corresponding Secretary.

Our houses were a stone's throw apart and both of these women recognized that they belonged together. Maria suddenly had a thought: to gather all the neighboring clubs together into a Federation. This was the birth of the idea, and like all new ideas, it had to be suggested and explained and promoted until the Clubs all around gradually accepted the idea. It took days and days to sell the plan, first in our county and gradually all over the state.

History has shown that an idea that begins to work in one locality often spontaneously develops somewhere else at the same time. Maria's idea was beginning to grow in other neighborhoods too. The final proof was a very large assemblage of all the women's clubs, who met at one large meeting place in a hall connected with a large hotel in Swampscott, Massachusetts.

Maria and Mother drove home in Maria's car, flushed and radiant over the success of an assembly of over one thousand women willing to cooperate in the creation of the Federation of Women's Clubs. Maria gave me her orchid—the first time I had ever even heard of an orchid.

Too late to make this a short story, but the Federation continued to grow in various parts of North America until the great climax many years later when an enormous Federation meeting in Portland, Oregon, proclaimed Maria G. Kimball the inventor and instigator of this thoroughly worthwhile Federation. This special meeting was celebrated with sterling silver ship pins made by Franklin Porter, using the design of the good ship Leander, which he had first developed for the 250th anniversary of the City of Salem.

Maria was behind another famous drive to promote World Peace called the Maria G. Kimball Peace Fund, but that was before the Second World War. Where is that peace now? Maria and her husband John moved from Danvers to a loft on T Wharf in Boston. Loft 25 was their address and when the tugboats returned from a towing job, they often bumped the poles under T Wharf, which made all the dishes rattle in the kitchen. Maria had so many friends from all over the country that her guest books looked like encyclopedias. She made friends everywhere. The tipcart merchants gave her rides. Ship builders named their ships for her.

She volunteered to work in the Seaman's Library not far from T Wharf. The books were brought in from the ships just as the sailors had left them. It was Maria's job to examine the books for whatever she might find—perhaps drugs tucked into the loose binding on the back of a book. She would often find a big square hole cut into the book pages, large enough to hide a watch to be smuggled in, invisible at any angle from the outside of the book.

When the time came that the shoreline of old Boston was about to be changed, Maria was the last one to give up the fight to keep the old T Wharf. In her old age, this was one battle she could not win. After a valiant fight she capitulated and moved to a retirement home in Magnolia, Massachusetts, still to be near the ocean she loved. And T Wharf became part of Boston's shoreline.

The Judge Samuel Holten House

When the Daughters of the American Revolution offered the Judge Samuel Holten House to my parents to live in, our whole family rejoiced. The house, although it was old, was large and commodious. Everyone had his own room. There were no complaints, and Dad had a shorter walk to the Champion Lamp Factory. But it was not very many months before his fifty-fifth birthday when he was laid off without even any talk of a pension, in 1924. How fortunate that we were settled in the Holten House. Day by day we muddled along.

Making the best of our situation, we studied the style of the house and tried to learn all about its history. It was built in 1670 and restored in 1760. The Holten House attracted visitors, and we were always prepared to lead them through it and explain that Samuel Holten was a judge in the very early days of our country. He may also have been a doctor. He probably attended the Continental Congress and, it used to be rumored, erroneously, that he had nominated George Washington for the presidency. Holten was buried in the small cemetery on Holten Street, and his name was applied to lend an air of authenticity to many things in Danvers Highlands.

The Holten House was of the saltbox style so often built on the North Shore. In olden times, some people kept their kitchen salt in a salt box. The box was really a pottery bowl with a wooden cover raised at one side and hinged to slope down on the other side.

When the early settlers built their houses north of Boston, they studied the prevailing winds and observed that the strongest winter wind blew down from the north. That observation was incorporated into the plan for building the houses. The plan was to build the long roof sloping from a high ridgepole all the way down almost to the ground against the north wind. The south side of the house had windows to let in the sunshine. Because the sloping roof reminded them of the sloping saltbox cover, the final structure was given the name of a salt box house.

The front of the Holten House was broad, with a large door in the center flanked by two windows on the right and two on the left. Upstairs above the front door was a small window, with two larger windows on either side above the ones downstairs. There was an enormous central chimney (9' x 18') with fireplaces on three sides. The roof started from the front eaves to stretch up to the ridgepole at the center. From that height the back roof swept the longest distance, sloping almost down to the ground at the back of the house. There was just room for small windows and a strong storm door. The roof faced north, to baffle the north wind from the back of the house and send the cold wind up over the roof. On the right hand side was a Beverly Jog.

According to *A Field Guide to Salem's Architecture* by Mark Lorenz (2004), it is " . . . not entirely clear where the name came from or . . . what purpose they served. Many of the 'Beverly Jogs' enclose stairways to a second floor to free up room inside the main house. Some people believe that because there is no living space attached, there were no additional taxes as a result of the addition." It may have been intended to separate the service stairs from the main stairs, or to keep tenants out of the main part of the house.

The "other side" of the house consisted of a large meeting room with a big fireplace and plenty of space for DAR meetings and activities. The last room, built onto the house in 1888, was known as the Garden Room. Correctly so, because two sides of the room had windows looking out onto our garden.

Sometimes there were lectures on various subjects. Our family always attended. The ladies of the DAR used the Holten House for all kinds of social occasions and special meetings. One way to gain a little revenue, they decided, would be to invite friends every Wednesday afternoon to a feast of hot tea and waffles. Several waffle irons were installed on the big kitchen stove. There were special assignments among the ladies. Some set up the tables with tablecloths and centerpieces with flowers and silverware and maple syrup. The room took on a festive look and many guests came to enjoy the gatherings. After awhile, though, people tired of the waffles and the clientele wavered.

What could be done to restore their appeal? Why that would be simple, just change the flavors. Let's make crispy waffles. They would surely attract people, especially if we advertise them.

The ads went out and some devotees came for crispy waffles. Other people still wanted plain ones. Both the customers and the cooks were divided into two camps. By the end of the summer, there was no reconciliation and that was the end of the waffles.

It was not the end of the general good times, however. People will always come for a party. The evening parties drew as many guests as the rooms could accommodate. One special dinner honored the member whose husband was a hunter who provided venison, with all the proper accompaniments. The speaker that evening told stories about nature and about the behavior of local wild animals.

One evening the speaker was Henry Beston, a New England author most famous for *The Outermost House* on Cape Cod, who told us about the historic house he lived in in Topsfield. With my little girl's eyes, I beheld this tall, dark, kind man with a profound admiration. So much so that as we said good-bye that night I said to him, "Sometime I will write a book and will dedicate it to you." We were brought up on the saying that "A promise made is a debt unpaid." This book will have to be payment of my debt after all these years.

We used to take people around the house, showing the different rooms and talking about various building features. Foremost was the privy in the back yard, once used by several families who all lived in the house at once. The privy has recently been spruced up and repainted by the DAR. The magazine *Early American Homes* ran an article in 1997 entitled "A Tool Shed with a Past." A photograph dated 1938 shows the fine proportion of the double privy with its curved roof corners and its elegant finial carved of wood. There is a suggestion that one could build a neat tool shed by following the classic dimensions of the original building, which belongs to the 1832 Greek Revival period.

When we lived in the Holten House, the outbuilding still fulfilled its original purpose and everyone was grateful. Next to it is the usual woodshed with one side to store wood and the other side for tools. Obviously, my father accepted the wood shed to be his workshop and named it Saint Dunstan's, after the patron saint of silversmiths. There is even a verse about this connection:

> Saint Dunstan, so the story goes
> Once seized the Devil by the nose
> With red-hot tongs
> Which made him roar
> That he was heard a mile or more.

Father always spoke with a sweep of his hand, calling the two buildings Saint Dunstan's and Saint Mary's. I am pleased to say that the DAR has in recent years restored these two historic buildings.

Chapter 4

Silversmithing

Little did Father realize that as the years wore on and he worked into his own style of silversmithing, he would become famous. When Dad was laid off from Champion around 1924, he was delighted to have the time and the tools and the workshop to become a full-time silversmith at the age of fifty-five. More than that, our living in the DAR house brought many people to see the silver he was already producing. His old clients from the Middleton days came back and the workshop was humming again. It was not long before the little old glass-fronted bookcase became his silver display case again. First and foremost was the mayonnaise bowl with spoon, and a plate under the bowl. He chose to make a bowl first, to give his visitors a demonstration of the process. A bowl is hammered continuously to create its curved shape. A fact almost unknown: the name Smith is derived from "he that smiteth."

The silver Brig Leander pin Dad made for the 250th anniversary of the City of Salem brought more customers, and he was busy. Mother and I were busy, too, except that I had to finish high school. His reputation caught fire and more people came to buy, and he was busy and happy.

There was Porter silver all over New England, especially in areas like Salem and Marblehead and Hamilton and Wenham. The Essex Institute in Salem (now the Peabody Essex Museum) has always featured him as a 20th century Paul Revere, because he used the same tools and the same processes as his earlier model. The majority of his pieces are in the Peabody Essex collections. The National Cathedral's Resurrection silver, used in the Resurrection Chapel and always admired and appreciated by those who see it, is his greatest accomplishment. I have been tracking down pieces in various museums, including the Boston Museum of Fine Arts and the Yale University Gallery of Art. Dad's silver still occasionally comes up for auction.

The High School "Masterpiece"

High School was a little more challenging, but some of the challenges were congenial. Not Algebra! Nor was our Algebra class congenial to the teacher we nick-named Cape Cod Crocker. It was a day to remember when she flung the algebra book wrathfully the length of the aisle while she snapped with venom, "RATS!" We wondered who the rats could be. The pupils? The algebra examples, or perhaps it was herself. She named it!

There was another teacher who helped us express our thoughts in writing, Miss Frances Wadleigh. She was tall and gentle and kind, not only understanding, but more than that, she was encouraging. She was the one who made the school magazine a goal which some of us aspired to achieve.

Under her understanding guidance I produced an imaginative legend about life on the high seas in some kind of sea-going vessel which of course I had never really seen. To see the story in print was a moment of triumph. Perhaps this success might be a hint of a future vocation when I should grow up. The title was "Blood and a Plank."

We were all so proud of the printed story that doting parents distributed a few copies among their contemporaries to show what a future genius their child was destined to become. Aunt Ethel and Uncle Frank got the first gift copy. Their son Alfred—the one with the five-miles-away piccolo—several years older than I, felt required to "take me down a piece" and he wrote me a letter, which I quote below.

> Dear Madam:
> Enclosed please find literature which is forwarded to you on request of Mrs. Albert R. Plant of Providence,

R.I., also an illustration by our staff artists for your recently published story, "Blood and a Plank."

Our artist has never heard of sailors splicing ropes while running to and fro, nor is it customary, so far as we have been able to determine, for them to do any very great amount of running while scrubbing or sweeping down decks. This being, therefore, a rather unusual situation, we feel that it should be recorded in art as well as in literature.

Should you be unable to use this illustration, the matter might be easily rectified by punctuating your story by inserting a comma after the word "fro" in the sentence, "Below him the sailors were running to and fro (,) splicing ropes and scrubbing decks."

We trust that you will pardon us for taking this action.

With kindest regards to you and your colleagues at the Holten House, which, we understand, is being torn down or something of the sort, we are,

Very truly yours,
ALF REDD'S ATTRACTIONS, INK-OPERATED.
Per D. Onald
1st ass't. attraction.

(His younger brother)

The Holten House was in no danger of being torn down.

Summer Youth Conferences

During our teen years, several very wise leaders of the Episcopal Diocese arranged summer youth conferences to be held at St. Paul's Boys School in Concord, New Hampshire. Along with the customary formality of religious groups in those years, there was a deep experience of warm fellowship among the teenage boys and girls. Suffice it to say that in those early days there were also some strict rules of behavior. Along with a couple of weeks of serious study and good times we also had a lot of fun. Several contemporary young men later went into the ministry (including John Philbrick, whom I had admired from my shy distance.)

After several years of the summer conference, I was invited to come back as a leader. This was a serious undertaking, and I felt quite inadequate. But the more seasoned adults were wonderfully kind and my affection and appreciation grew. The conferences developed through the years their own characteristics, and we all enjoyed the good humor that prevailed, along with the appropriate attitudes of reverence and respect for the serious aspects of religious study.

Many of our most reverent and devout clergy have also an appreciation of the real value of humor in our daily lives. More than one thorny debate has been tranquilized and rescued by a bit of humor that could gently ease the tension. So we also learned that even in holy places, humor had its welcome.

What I in my inexperience was not prepared for was the first gathering of all the leaders to plan the arrangements for the upcoming conference. We planned and discussed until all the details were covered. It was time for prayers. All of a sudden everyone slipped out of his chair and suddenly knelt against his own chair. It was so sudden and I was so surprised (and tickled!) that it was hard not to snicker right out loud.

Many years later when the Rural Workers' Fellowship was meeting in Salt Lake City, we leaders held a serious meeting in the Mormon Hall where we were staying. Time to pray for the RWF conference, only this time there were six or seven pious members suddenly all kneeling around the same hotel bed. Now I find in the book *Paul Revere and the World He Lived In* reference to prayers in an early kitchen in Boston. The visitors arrived in the middle of prayers but "the leader did not look up. When he had finished they turned round and knelt on chairs or benches . . ." So perhaps it was wicked of me to have been amused at what was really a time-worn and utterly accepted custom.

Practical jokes? A neat one came during the conference one summer at St. Paul's School. Miss Eva D. Corey, a most dignified Bostonian lady and one of the Directors of the whole conference, made a speech at dinner that there were not to be any watermelon seeds thrown on the ground at St. Paul's. The next morning she was presented with a long, long necklace made of watermelon seeds.

Danvers—32 Conant Street, 1915-1919

Returning for a bit to my early years, let me write of my little neighbor Frances Bates, who lived in the house next door. We were "chums" for a number of years. We rigged up a rope between our respective bedroom windows. With a small box on the rope we could exchange messages and even some doll's clothes. Between us we explored everything and everybody in the neighborhood. We knew who made chocolate doughnuts on Saturdays, and where the fiercest dogs were likely to chase us away. We also knew that the family named Davenport lived nearby, and we chatted about funny people who were named for a sofa. They lived next door to Frances, and the folks had a handsome apple tree, which was so big some of its branches leaned over her yard and in season dropped the biggest apples I ever saw in my life. We ate a lot.

Years later, when John and I lived in Wilkinsonville we often visited the Worcester Horticultural Hall. Mr. Davenport's daughter worked in the horticultural library. She told me about her father's famous collection of old varieties of apples. For every county or state occasion the Davenport apples were always on display. On Sunday, August 24, 2000, *The Boston Globe* wrote: "The Davenport Collection of 110 antique apple varieties, propagated a decade ago from trees previously maintained at Old Sturbridge Village, is growing into a handsome and important orchard. Tasting tours . . . will give visitors an opportunity to experience varieties their great-grandparents loved and that have never seen the inside of a supermarket."

From the ancient apples at our Duxbury home, Faith Homestead, we brought samples to the horticultural librarian, and Mr. Davenport identified them and recorded their names. These are still bearing fruit: one Tolman Sweet, two Rhode Island Greenings, two Roxbury Russets, one Baldwin, and another tree whose fruit we never could reach.

The history of the apples continues. From these trees, which are at least 200 hundred years old, scions were taken to the Waldorf School in Viroque, Wisconsin, where the children learned how to graft the trees already there. In years to come, those children, grown up, may eat apples with ancient names which they helped to grow in their school yard.

"To Be Happy in New England"

Recently, I discovered the following unidentified newspaper in the archives of my local historical society. It seems to help explain why traditional New Englanders must sometimes appear rather odd. I quote verbatim.

"You must select the Puritans for your ancestors. You must have a sheltered youth and be a graduate of Harvard. You must know Emerson. You must live within two hours' ride of Boston. You should have a professional or literary calling. You must speak low, be a conservative in politics and a liberal in religion. You must drop your r's, be fond of the antique, eat beans on Saturday night and fish balls on Sunday morning. You must tolerate the Jew, respect the Irish, and love the Negro. You must wear glasses, be fond of tombstones, and, man or woman, carry your parcels in a green bag. You must be a D.A.R., a Colonial Dame, and S.A.R. or belong to the Mayflower Society. You must be neighborly to the unmarried. You must read *The Atlantic Monthly*. You must shudder at the West, but go to Europe frequently. In old age you must live on Easy Street with a little Boston and Albany preferred. You must make sure in advance that your obituary is in *The Boston Transcript*. There is nothing else."

The above lines, which have appeared many times in print, were written by the Reverend Joseph P. McCarthy, then pastor of the Unitarian Church in Waltham, and appeared first in the *Christian Register* as a "Letter to the Editor."

The author of this quote could not have written it had he not observed over and over that that was what New Englanders really were like. There were no questions and there were seldom any deviations, except I must confess that my mother, the wife of the Silversmith, did carry his silver pieces to Boston to be polished, not in a green bag but in a purple corduroy bag, which she had made herself. Aside from this almost unforgivable deviation, she was in general a talented and well-beloved lady, except that sometimes my father hinted that she had been vaccinated with a phonograph needle, because she always had so much to say.

The above tells almost everything, but when one adds the American echo of Queen Victoria's rules regarding gentility one really has to toe the line. For instance, there were those rules we had to observe. Don't speak until you are spoken to. Keep your voice soft, and retreat if anyone ever challenges you. Children kept out of sight, even if they were deeply involved in all kinds of indescribable mischief, such as when I made Hallowe'en decorations in the cellar out of rat poison because someone told me it was fluorescent. Don't speak to anyone unless you have been introduced. Worse than that, remember the rule to introduce the lady to the gentleman or the younger woman to the older woman. Never introduce an older person to a younger person. Do it the other way around and don't forget and get it mixed up.

There were rules about money. Don't talk about how much money you have, and never ask how much anything cost. I recall with shame the cataclysm that ensued when I asked what the Flexible Flyer Sled cost when my father hauled it from under a couch by the Christmas tree and presented it to me with a gracious flourish. When I, with 12-year-old innocence, asked "what did it cost?" the sun went in and the thunder roared, and I was in the doghouse.

Another prohibition was never to speak of a lady's dress—directly to her, that is. Behind her back you could say what you thought, of course. Compared with today's custom, it was a good old rule and gave us freedom for real conversation. Conversation today is full of comments like, "What a pretty sweater!"

Women's Educational and Industrial Union— Around 1928

The Women's Educational and Industrial Union had existed on Tremont Street in Boston for many years. There was a new director and she had a new idea. Wouldn't it be interesting to have a big assembly of craftsmen all together in a big hall, with each one working on his own craft? Her name was Miss Ethel Brown. She canvassed everyone, even came to visit Franklin Porter, and gathered them all in one large hall in Boston.

Topmost was the sculptor Cyrus Dallin, who also brought Native Americans from the Southwest. There were weavers and knitters and spinners and painters. There were men and also women who worked with wood to make furniture. There were stained glass window craftsmen and bookbinders and there were all kinds of shoemakers and leather workers.

The Native Americans came to the WE&IU show with two purposes. One was to demonstrate their Navajo artifacts in the show. The other was to bring corn pollen from their crops to scatter on the waters of Plymouth Harbor. They accompanied Cyrus Dallin when he came to Plymouth to bring his statue of Samoset, which to this day stands overlooking the harbor. That same day they scattered the corn pollen on the water with ceremonies related to their hopes for a good corn crop the following year.

The Navajos made pictures with colored sand on the floor of the exhibit hall. They were so skillful and so deeply respected that they seemed to elicit a deeper appreciation and respect than ever before. And to continue their example as time went on, Cyrus Dallin made the statue at the Museum of Fine Arts, Boston, the Appeal to the Great Spirit.

Although my father was rather a shy man, inclined to be in the background observing whatever was going on, this contact with the craftsmen's show had a magic effect on him. The attention he received from all his admirers was like a tonic to his ego and he grew in self-confidence from the experience.

Among the work of dozens of other workers, his craft did not go unnoticed. The mere fact of having a big wooden block with a steel anvil embedded in it meant that his hammering on a silver bowl did attract a lot of attention. Also, the capacious blue poplin smock and the Windsor tie that he wore made him stand out visually, and he improved his line of salesmanship.

One never knows what is going to influence one many years in the future. But I suspect that weaving became my favorite craft because of the influence of Miss Estes, a quiet, mousy little lady who was a weaver without flaw. When I learned to weave in

Occupational Therapy School, I selected one of her original patterns and tried to be as accurate as her work.

The show was very expansive and lasted a long time. It was long enough to give the craftsmen a chance to meet each other and exchange not only information but bartered goods. My father took great delight in swapping a six-inch silver bowl, which he hammered out while Mrs. Shurcliffe was making a small wooden bench to exchange for the bowl. We also made a friendship that lasted for years. We used to visit her on Beacon Hill on Christmas Eve. She also led a troupe of bell ringers.

Christmas on Beacon Hill

Beacon Hill back in those days was largely residential, and several old families had been neighbors for many years. Before the days of the ubiquitous automobile, many people had open house on Christmas Eve. We were warmly welcomed at one house in Louisburg Square. Another friend whom we frequently met was my dear old "Uncle Sumner," Mr. Appleton of the Society for the Preservation of New England Antiquities. Opposite his house, across the iron-fenced square, were the Sisters of Saint Margaret, Episcopalian nuns. In all probability, they were inside in their beautiful chapel celebrating Christmas according to their own devotional practices.

I can still feel the magic of the evening, the dark sky above, and the happy melody of the bell-ringers. There were no automobile horns, no rowdyism—just a busy happy exchange of friendly greetings. The festivities for many people ended with midnight Mass in the churches.

Salem/Brig *Leander*

In 1926, Salem celebrated at a house on Chestnut Street the early ship builders and sea captains who had brought thousands of dollars into the Salem Custom House manned by Nathaniel Hawthorne. The most famous ship was the *Brig Leander*. Someone on the Committee asked my father if he could make a sterling silver brooch to look like the *Leander*. Of course he could! They needed twenty-five or thereabouts, and they should cost something like $1.50. He studied the pictures and sketched the outline of the two-masted ship with eight square sails plus a third mast with a triangular sail. There was a flag on the stern and there was a bowsprit and ten portholes, or perhaps they were apertures for cannons.

Between the sails there was daylight, and the sails were hammered from the back to show they were "bellied out" by the wind. In all, there were 17 holes to be outlined and pricked and punched and sawed with a jeweler's saw about the size of a human hair. Dad and I used to compete to see who broke the first saw. My spare time was filled to the limit. We made them in groups of ten to help speed the work. The back of the pin was stamped "Sterling" and "F Porter."

After the front was shaped and hammered, the piece still had to be equipped with a safety catch, hinge, and pin. For a craftsman who specialized in large tools and heavy hammers and anvils, to have to fumble with these miniature fixtures was a torment. It took his very dry sense of humor to express his real private opinion when he wrote out a ribald parody on a famous contemporary song which began with the line "The hours I spend upon my knees." Dad's clumsy fingers struggled with the tiny catches, and we both learned all kinds of tricks to keep those tiny bits in place under the melted solder and the hot blowtorch. Dad said, "They jump like bugs!"

The Committee requested a total of one hundred pins. They were all sold and more were ordered. My spare time was commandeered to work on the Leanders, and more orders came in every day. A pin sold for $2.50 and it came in a neat white box bedded in white cotton with a card which said "Simplicity and Service" and extolled the skill and versatility of the silversmith.

"The piece of silver which is accompanied by this card was made in one of the oldest houses in the United States, it having been built in 1670 and for many years the home of Judge Samuel Holten, one of the staunchest of the New England patriots.

Like the house in which it was made, this piece is constructed of the best materials obtainable, by methods older than the house itself, and is intended for a century or more of service. Embodied in this piece of silver, as in the old House, are the ambition and love and some of the life essence of the craftsman, and it is offered to you in the belief that by its daily use and association, your artistic sense will be nourished and the gospel of its maker, Simplicity and Service, be extended.

Franklin Porter
Judge Samuel Holten House
Danvers, Massachusetts

Persons interested in the Judge Holten House or in my silver are always welcome, but appointments should be made for the evenings, Sundays and holidays. Tel. Danvers 975-W."

There was also another card in the cover of the box describing the ship itself.

> The *Brig Leander*.
> One of a fleet of eighty-three vessels built or owned between 1790 and 1844 by Captain Joseph Peabody of Salem and freighted by him from Salem.
>
> Launched from the yard of Benjamin Hawkes, July 25, 1821. 223 tons burthen, 91 ft. 4 in. long, 23 ft. 5 in. beam, 11 ft. 81/2 in. depth, 156 tons present scale carried thirteen men all told.

And also in that same little white box only 2 3/8 by 1 5/8 inches, with matching white cardboard cover, was yet another card, 3/8 by 1 1/8 inches:

"Made by
Franklin Porter
at
Judge Samuel Holten House
Danvers, Mass.
Guaranteed Hand Made"

This of course was tiny, but it supported all the other evidence that the former master mechanic had now become a hardworking, thoroughly discriminating artist in his own chosen field of labor. Actually, he was also greatly stimulated by his eager customers, whose admiration he quickly absorbed, and whose good suggestions were often incorporated in his silver creations. Those ship pins launched the silversmith and made him famous. Stories came back to us of two women on Tremont Street in Boston, strangers speaking to each other simply because each was wearing a *Leander* pin.

In 1929, three years later, when the Great Depression began and money was scarce, we were still filling orders for Leanders, sometimes an order for ten at a time, boxes and all! By that time, we had perfected the routine and we turned them out dozens at a time. Dad, with his usual taciturnity, called them "pot boilers," and we as a family were thankful that the pot was still able to boil.

It is my intention in mentioning my father to praise the accomplishments of a quiet, impecunious gentleman who blossomed in the late 1920s into a skilled artist and craftsman. His meager background, starting work at 12 years of age in a factory in Providence 12 hours a day, with little schooling, was balanced and expanded by his voracious desire for education. He learned Latin from the titles of the Psalms in the 1789 Book of Common Prayer: *Dominus regit me.* The Lord is my shepherd.

In those days, we lacked the omniscience of graphs and charts and specialists trained to interpret their wisdom. We had to be content with knowledge of local conditions, and to learn skills to use whatever opportunities were presented. Our advisor and counsel was real life and we had to make the best of it.

Here is Dad's entry in the *Directory of American Silversmiths*, third edition:

> Franklin Porter's early artistic training was at the Rhode Island School of Design, followed by technical training at Browne and Sharpe in Providence. For many years his artistic inclinations took second place to the need to support a family. All the while though he made brass and copper pieces and occasionally silver when he could afford the raw material. In 1924 when he reached his fifty-fifth birthday he was released from his factory job without a pension. On that date, May 9, 1924, he purchased a copy of Bigelow's *Historic Silver of the*

Colonies and its Makers and joined the ranks of American silversmiths. In his journal, Porter wrote "January 1, 1925. Beginning this date, I began the practice of attaching my mark to every piece of work executed by me on which it is practicable to attach same, together with 'F Porter' and 'Sterling' in order to distinguish my work, should any of it survive, in years to come, from that of F. Porter, Pewterer, of Connecticut."

This was a choice bit of Dad's humor. The idea of "should any of it survive!" Silver is practically indestructible. And how could anyone fail to distinguish sterling silver from a piece of pewter, which in those days was mostly lead! Of course, modern day pewter has no lead in it because lead is so toxic.

William Sumner Appleton

One of the visitors to the 1926 celebration of early ship builders and sea captains at the Chestnut Street house in Salem, was a friendly gentleman who chatted with my father and turned to speak to me. His first words were a bit of a shock: "When you are through with the dress you are wearing, would you please give it to me?" He then explained that he had a collection of antique dresses. He was William Sumner Appleton, the founder of the Society for the Preservation of New England Antiquities, now familiarly known as SPNEA. (Dad irreverently mixed that title with another and it came out "Prevention of Cruelty to New England Antiquities).

"Uncle Sumner" became a great favorite of my family and was a delightful escort. I was always ready to accept his invitations. I believe he always hoped he could lure the Porter family out of the Holten House into one of the old houses owned by the Society for the Preservation of New England Antiquities. His technique consisted of occasional dinners at Boston restaurants, with theater afterward. On our part, we used to invite him to come to the Holten House in Danvers for Christmas.

He and I used to meet in Boston years later, when I was in occupational therapy school. We would go out for a meal and he would unfold a newspaper page to search for a show we could take in that evening. He always blue-penciled the approved Boston shows. One evening he invited me to go with him to the Boston Pops in Symphony Hall. We went first to the Russian Bear restaurant. As we got out of the taxi, the Russian doorman came to attention and Mr. Appleton said to him, "Are you really Russian, or did you come over from South Boston this morning?" From the way Mr. Appleton spoke to him, I think they were probably old friends.

The dinner at the Russian Bear was late, and we arrived by taxi at Symphony Hall with no time to waste. Mr. Appleton strode up to the ticket office and requested a table on the floor.

"We are very sorry, sir, but every table has been taken."

His reply was gentle, but it was firm, and he was not fooling. "No tables left? That is ridiculous. Why, just put in another table!"

The lady in the ticket office said, "Why, yes, of course, Mr. Appleton!"

When we reached the front of the front row, the added table was already there, and the Boston Pops Orchestra was right over our heads.

Uncle Sumner lived in Louisburg Square across from the Saint Margaret's Convent. We used to visit him in his apartment to admire his collections of white marble statues and multitudes of other treasures, which were the beginning of the famous collections of the Society for the Preservation of New England Antiquities.

By now the silversmith was really in business and orders came in from clients all over. The Essex Institute collection of Porter silver is featured as the work of a 20th century Paul Revere. In 1969, the *Danvers Herald* wrote: "Danvers silversmith Franklin Porter, whose work is rated by the Metropolitan Museum of New York along with the work of Paul Revere, is little known in print. This has prompted his daughter, Mrs. Helen Philbrick, a native of Danvers, to write about her father and his craft. Her recollections will constitute the July issue of the Historical Collections of the Peabody Museum of Salem. They were also the basis of a talk she gave at the annual meeting of the Danvers

Historical Society last week, marking the 100th anniversary of the birth of Porter."

The time had come for the Porter family to leave the Judge Samuel Holten House, so with characteristic simplicity and directness, they bought the house next door and business went on as usual until 1929, when I entered the Northfield School for Girls. The most memorable moment of my career there was when Miss Boak told my parents that my Latin was sketchy. I went on to Wheaton, graduating in 1932.

Chapter 5

From School Days to Silversmithing

There was work for the new graduate to do in the silversmith's workshop and one just had to buckle down to the realities in the outside world. Even though the market had crashed in 1929, there were some loyal clients who still ordered special silver pieces because they recognized that Franklin Porter "At the Sign of the Hammer" was as unique as Paul Revere.

The work in the shop was as grimy as it always had been. Father was glad to have help in the shop and we quickly fell into the same old routines. When we were both sawing little bits out of filigree handles at the same time, we raced, not to finish first, but to see who would break his jeweler's saw first. They would snap broken at a slightly wrong angle.

Dad's dry humor sometimes enraged me. When I was deep in the complexity of some construction problem, he would look it over and ask, "Do you think you can save it??" That question always made me mad! But then it was time for a cup of tea and he never knew. Besides, he was only quoting an old New England question.

When customers came—he called them clients—he was always ready to open the made-over bookcase with glass doors that served as a showcase (which had a homemade burglar alarm) to show them the beautiful silver pieces. Silver bowls of all sizes, and sometimes a bowl and spoon and a suggestion of mayonnaise as the use (always pronounced as *my*onaise). There were sets of teaspoons and dessert spoons and forks, all orders ready to be delivered to some bride. Very little jewelry except the *Leander* brooch.

The prize piece was the Queen of Siam Tea Infuser, a set consisting of a beaker, inside of which was a tapering infuser with holes, and a wooden handle. On top was a silver cover because some lady had been "offended" at the sight of wet tea leaves. To be used, the infuser was set into the teacup after the cover had been removed. And the boiling hot water was poured into the infuser. When the cup was full, the infuser was put back into the beaker and the silver cover was put back. The handle on the cover was a silver pineapple, symbol of hospitality, which was making its first appearance in Porter silver in those early days. Now we see pineapples everywhere.

The piece was named Queen of Siam because the royal couple of Siam, both "horse people," had come to the Myopia Hunt Club to visit in Hamilton and Wenham and the tea infuser had been presented to Her Majesty Queen Rambai Barni and His Majesty the King of Siam as a gift. Father shone with pride when he told his clients the story—and as he hoped, they often would order one for themselves for a gift.

Because of all the publicity, we could not keep them in stock. Mother wanted one but it would be sold before her first cup of tea. Finally, she demanded that one be engraved with her initials to make sure. The initials were ELBCP, for Ethel Louise Borden Chase Porter. (Some friends called her Ethelalphabet.) That was the teamaker that served our family for years, and is now in the Porter Collection at the Peabody Essex Museum in Salem.

Back in the workshop it was grubby again. There was always the whole sizzling red hot silver heated with a gas blow torch, which we pumped with one foot while we were touching the hot silver with silver solder. Silver melts at 6000° F, but there was no thermometer, only experience to tell us. The next step was to drop, with wooden tweezers, the whole hot piece into a crock of "pickle" to take off the oxide from the soldering. Pickle was a mixture of sulphuric acid and water and when the hot silver hit the pickle, there was a splash, and every drop of pickle that hit anything burned a hole right through. That is why the silversmith's apron is always a network of tiny holes.

It wasn't always a soldering job. Father's favorite process, which he always did, was like singing a song. He loved to "raise a bowl" from a flat piece of silver. He started by cutting out a circle with a huge pair of metal shears. He leaned the circle on a steel anvil and began to shape the flat piece into the beginning of a bowl shape. Each time he went all the way around the circle, first with mallets, and then with various hammers to create the bowl shape. His strike with any hammer was always the same rhythm—one, two, three, four, five, six, stop, and turn the bowl for the next six blows. Wherever one was in the neighborhood in summer, one could hear the song of the hammer striking against the silver against the steel anvil. It was a kind of musical hallmark. When the bowl was raised, it was time for the "Maker's Mark." This consisted of "sterling" first, then "F. Porter," and "P," his maker's mark.

If any one asked him—and people often did ask, "How long does it take you to make a bowl?" he would answer that it took forty years. "Frankly," he would explain to us in the bosom of the family, "If I really told them the real time, they would never feel they should pay as high a price as twelve dollars for a hand made solid silver bowl." Prices and values have changed since those years! Today, the same bowl would cost $75 to $100.

Even though the finished bowl was a beauty, there was another, not so pleasant process: to polish it until every hammer mark shone. The polishing wheels, made of layers of cloth, were fitted on to the lathe and spun at a high speed. The first wheel carried some heavy abrasive in tallow that smoothed down the edges of the hammer marks. The next several wheels carried other material to clean and polish. But the final polishing wheel was red and unquestionably a very fine, final abrasive named Rouge. By the time he had worked the polishing wheel for awhile, no matter how many baffles he wore, he would emerge from the polishing with face and neck and ears and hair and hands powdered with all these polishing powders. Polishing jobs were always followed by baths.

People who bought exquisitely beautiful silver with a flawless patina never knew of the ugliness of the processes, but only of the charm of the finished piece. And the silversmith's responsibility was to make the bad parts a bit romantic and oddly enjoyable.

When I tell my friend I was once a silversmith, she hears me and she will smile and nod, but speak as clearly as I am able, I never can make her see the whole sizzling mess of the red hot silver exploding when we dropped it into the saucepan of sulfuric acid to dissolve the oxide from the soldering process. Nor can I explain the tiny holes in my apron which was sprinkled with acid from the "pickle." There was also the strong smell of the acid, and the acrid smell of the floor sweepings we burned to retrieve every scrap and filing of silver to send back to the refinery for credit. These are the realities of being a silversmith.

Words cannot convey another ever present feature of silversmithing: pound, pound, pound, six times on silver metal against the steel anvil with the hammer, which shapes the silver blow by blow—perhaps a thousand blows to create a silver bowl. A quick, sharp, musical ring that told the world something of beauty was being created.

Today, silver has largely been replaced by silver plate, and other things of even lesser value, but silver itself is as worthy of respect and veneration as it was when Paul Revere and his contemporaries made silver into vessels ranging from kitchen saucepans to silver tea services and Church chalices. Even though stainless steel is now popular, silver and gold are still known as "noble metals," and will be forever. No other metal can come near them for beauty and versatility, or purity of content.

To polish silver, put it in an aluminum pan with one teaspoon of bicarbonate of soda (baking soda) and two teaspoons of table salt. Pour in boiling water and the tarnish will disappear instantly from the silver that touches the aluminum. This is a galvanic action that doesn't harm the silver and will not damage plated silver. You may have to turn the silver over to take the tarnish off each side.

When we moved, the workshop in the new house was in the cellar, and it was a happy change to climb the cellar stairs to greet friendly clients in the living room admiring what had been created, or perhaps describing something special they wanted the silversmith to invent.

One lady said, "I want a bigger serving spoon. All my serving spoons are too small." So, Father went to work to invent a larger spoon bowl with a flat handle with a pineapple soldered to the end of the handle. The whole spoon had a pleasant balance, and the bowl was large and had a hospitable feeling. He named it The Salem Spoon because the woman who commissioned it lived in Salem. It became justifiably popular. One woman bought so many Salem Spoons for her friends and family that she would call on the telephone to my father, and all she would say was "please send my usual order to So and So, who is the next bride in our family."

Franklin Porter had an assignment to make a Memorial Eucharist Set of silver which was to go to the National Cathedral in Washington. He was almost overwhelmed with the enormous compliment paid to him by the Washington architect, who had placed the order. Father was a devoted churchman and a lay reader, but also a modest craftsman. He could hardly believe that his work had attracted that spectacular an assignment.

For weeks and weeks, as he was making other orders for his clients, he was turning over plans for the communion set which was to be used in the Norman-style Resurrection Chapel in the huge cathedral, which is used by all denominations.

We spent hours in the Boston Public Library, traveling in those days by train and subway. He took out dozens of books and studied pictures of churches. One day I sat opposite him at a library table. Suddenly he turned the book upside down, pushed it across to me so I could see the picture and said, "Here is the ciborium," the name of the covered box that holds the wafers for communion. It was a picture of an old church tower in the round in Little Saxham Church in Suffolk, England. It had been built in the twelfth century in the Norman style, with a circle of small rounded arches like a crown around the top of the church building.

With that pattern in mind, he went about designing all the other pieces in the set. There was a large chalice (which, confidentially, had capacity of one quart!). The paten was appropriately large. There were to be six pieces in all, two cruets, a large flagon, chalice, paten, and ciborium. Each piece was designed with the Norman-style arches circling the top and a Norman-type cross on the cover of each piece. The set is used in the Resurrection Chapel of the Cathedral every year during the post-Easter season. Friends who have gone there to attend a service, or even just to see the silver, report that the Resurrection Silver is the most exquisite of all the Cathedral silver. It is possible to see it by asking at the information desk.

After we were married, John Philbrick and I traveled to Washington to visit the Cathedral and to see if the silver was being used. John's classmate from the Seminary was the Canon Precentor of the Cathedral, and he wanted us to see the Ring of Bells in the Bell Tower. While we were up there admiring the new bells, we told him about the Porter silver and he said, "We'll find it."

We searched and searched in all the safes and all the hidden spots. Our friend even sent for one of the vergers, and he led our search. I was distraught, because Father had always said that when he passed away that silver would be all the memorial he would ever need. What a sad situation if we could not find it! We spent a troubled night.

The next day, we found out that the famous silver was in the Altar Guild rooms; the whole set was being used every day in the Resurrection Chapel and sometimes on the high altar—another neat compliment to the silversmith.

Sanctuary Lamp

Father loved especially to make silver pieces for churches that needed special creations. The needs were often unusual and required special treatment. One such assignment was from Charles Mason Remey, a Washington architect who was searching for the right silversmith to make a suitable memorial piece in honor of his father, the late Rear Admiral George C. Remey U.S.N., of Washington, D.C. and Newport, R.I. Admiral Remey had been captain and correspondent of Portsmouth Navy Yard, and during those years Mr. Remey's family attended St. John's Church in Portsmouth. Father designed a sanctuary lamp. We all attended the dedicatory service presided over by Bishop Dallas, the bishop of New Hampshire. It was a bit of a feat to get the lamp to hang from the ceiling.

The lamp belongs to the Georgian Period of design, with a double anchor. It is notable that it's suspended by silver anchor stud chains, a replica of the stud chains used on anchors. A "stud" is a rivet or crosspiece in each link of a chain cable. If there is an extremely strong pull on the anchor cable, the studs will prevent the anchor chain links from collapsing.

Several years later, Father happened to meet Bishop Dallas, and with his typical modesty and self-effacement, he said to Bishop Dallas, "You don't remember me." The Bishop grinned and said, "Of course I remember you. We hung lanterns together." Father was delighted.

By the end of summer, there was not enough work for another silversmith, so I needed something to bring in a little money. The market for hand-made sterling had already begun to dwindle. We were in the depths of the Great Depression. The next step was to find a job. Wasn't that what everyone did following graduation?

Chapter 6

A New Haven Prelude to Brightwater

Volunteer in New Haven

I was fresh (and I really mean superlatively fresh, meaning naive) out of Wheaton when the college could look back on itself as Wheaton Female Seminary, a graduate with a rolled-up diploma and a pair of overwhelmingly proud middle-aged parents. My major had been in the fine arts, and I was still dreaming of travel on "the old continent" for further study of the Renaissance paintings and ancient Greek sculpture, which we had been copying in the college studio. (Like one half of Michelangelo's *David*'s head—to learn how an eyeball and a nostril are put together!)

My adopted brother, Edward, had become a teacher in the New Haven Commercial High School. (He claimed to be teaching men who would be the best truck drivers in the world.) He told me about an opportunity at a new organization in New Haven called The Religion and Labor Foundation. I was too much uninformed to know that a volunteer was not a wage earner. It had been founded by Professor Jerome Davis, who was a teacher at Yale Divinity School. The purpose of the organization was to assure the newly growing labor movement that it could depend on the churches of America to support the demands of labor. Dr. Davis had an office staff and two office workers, but they needed a volunteer to help with the office work.

I volunteered and was accepted by Dr. Davis for the job. I never told him how little experience I had had, and he obviously didn't care. The office work was way over my head, but I tried to do what my bosses asked me to do.

This was in the 1930s when the labor movement was beginning to take shape. Dr. Davis was a champion of many causes, sometimes getting himself into trouble because of his sympathies. He had set up an office on the third floor of the Young Men's Hebrew Association Building. We were to handle publicity and correspondence related to the labor movement, and for another new organization called the NAACP. The third aspect of the foundation's work represented religion.

There were two lively young men who ran the office, which was very small and hardly large enough for three people. I was green and ignorant both of office operations and of the process of development of large social movements. My job must have been reduced down to sharpening pencils and emptying wastebaskets. They did teach me to file documents. I had to handle the mail and send out reams of correspondence, much of which I was too uninformed to understand. We worked happily there together, but I was not then really conscious of the importance of the labor movement or the NAACP, not to mention the religion aspect.

I was aware that there were three very important gentlemen who were founders of The Foundation, but aside from handling their mail, I rarely saw them. Their names have gone from my mind, but they were important leaders of American thought in the very early stages of the labor movement. One was a rabbi and the other two were leaders of public thought.

Dr. Davis came sometimes to talk about the work, and to tell us about his yearly trips leading groups through Russia. Many people in those days were shocked at the mere mention of Russia. One day when Dr. Davis came, he brought up a huge poster, predominantly red and orange, with a title in Russian. I couldn't read the text and I wasn't quite sure whether it was friendly or not. It was so big it took up a whole wall. The custodian of the building never spoke to us, and we had no way to encourage him to speak to us. But after that poster was put up on the wall of our office, every time the custodian saw any of us, he would shake his fist and yell "Bolsheviki!"

It was stimulating to be so close to Yale University, when Harvard University had been my former source of general culture. Yale had fine free concerts and excellent libraries and museums. Yale Divinity School on the hill was always cordial and welcoming, and there were many friends there among the students studying for the ministry.

Best of all, Dr. Jerome Davis became my friend. He and his wife were almost like parents to me, and it was good to have a family to visit with. Their little girl, Patty, and their adopted son, Wilfred Grenfell Davis, provided friends and family relationships that year.

I had gone to the Foundation as a volunteer, but each month they paid me an honorarium of fifteen dollars, and I remember whittling down lunch to twenty-five cents a day. I learned to survive on a fifteen-cent sandwich at the Waldorf every noon. My brother lived in a boarding house run by a Miss Pratt, which had a spectacular restaurant decorated on all four walls with birdcages inhabited by live birds. This was obviously before any rules about health in a public restaurant. He finagled me a tiny room there, and we had our meals in the restaurant downstairs. The best feature of that whole job was living in the boarding house with several Yale students, where we had constant music and games and even fencing lessons for the boys.

One morning at breakfast time, one of Miss Pratt's favorite birds was not well, and she was so frantic that she could hardly wait on her guests. My brother and a fellow school teacher tried to think of something that would finish off the bird so that Miss Pratt could come back to wait. They solemnly assured her that whiskey would restore the bird, hoping that it would not. She tried whiskey on the bird, the bird recovered, and food service was restored.

It was a fun community in that boarding house. I used to eat supper with my brother Edward and his friends, one of whom was obviously going to grow up to be a brilliant musician. With a mechanically superior phonograph, we sat on the floor and listened to classical music. The "Liebestod" from *Tristan und*

Isolde was our favorite, and we sat and wept over it so many nights that the steel needle wore out the wax record. We could never hear it often enough. Then someone told us that Walter Damrosch's son was a Yale student and that he was directing Gilbert and Sullivan's *Pirates of Penzance*. We were all in the front row at the next rehearsal, and joined the group.

One of the boys studied fencing and his equipment was hung on the wall. Our favorite password was "foiled again." We had games and scavenger hunts and all kinds of homemade entertainment, which cemented our group. We even followed one lad who worked on the top floor of a New Haven skyscraper. He had the key, and in the middle of the night we climbed to the top floor to watch the sunrise.

Becoming an Occupational Therapist

By the spring of 1933, New Haven had lost its charm for me, and I went back to Danvers to look for a more promising career. How about Occupational Therapy? There were only four schools in this country that taught it at that time, and the best school was right here in Boston. That was enough to know. The course was one year in the school and two years to be spent in various hospitals applying the knowledge we had learned.

I entered the Boston School of Occupational Therapy and commuted from Danvers. When one traveled by trolley car from the small town of Danvers to a much smaller town of Middleton, Massachusetts, there was a spot halfway there where the conductor always shouted as the car stopped, "Hathorne, Hathorne, the nearest point to the hospital." It was really a long walk up hill to the hospital.

For many years these shouted words meant nothing to me. But there came a day, in the second year of training for Occupational Therapy in 1935, when several of us were assigned for field training, and our assignment was the Danvers State Hospital.

Those huge buildings on the very top of the highest hill were a landmark, visible from many places. When we landed up there, we could see all those same places from our own elevation. It took several days to learn one's way around the buildings and to learn how to adjust to what was called familiarly the Danvers Insane Asylum. There were seven other State Hospitals in Massachusetts.

From a distance this great structure on the top of the hill looked like a series of battlements, and one could imagine there were turrets and towers and even some steeples. But really the structures were brick exteriors with the usual assortment for a state building of flagpoles and weather instruments and other paraphernalia.

In the Occupational Therapy Department we wore a blue poplin uniform with a stiff white collar and stiff white cuffs. The uniform buttoned down the front, and there were two generous side pockets. My closest friend in the class was Grace Wright Tinkham, born in Edinburgh, Scotland. She was older than I, a weaver of great accomplishment, with a terrific sense of humor. She had two nicknames used interchangeably—one was "Righto" and the other was "Tink."

When Tink and I arrived with the other members of our Boston School of Occupational Therapy class, we were given a general tour of the buildings. The men's wards were north of the rather impressive center reception area which led to offices and doctors' chambers and all the official professional rooms. Located in the main offices, there was also a large assortment of all kinds of weather instruments and other technical and astronomical instruments to locate our position on the earth. It was so fascinating that we returned there again and again. The current weather situation was part of our daily visit for information.

To the south of this entrance extravaganza were the women's quarters. The personnel situation was arranged according to the condition of each patient. It seems now almost heartless that those human beings were placed in the institution according to their degree of insanity. The most reliable inmates were called "Trusties" and were generally free to come and go as they chose, as long as they did not run away. The next best ones were housed on the "Front Wards," which were enormous rooms, each holding about 90 persons. There were intermediate wards next. Finally, the sickest patients were in the so-called "Back Wards." As soon as we had had some indoctrination, we were each presented with a big bunch of keys heavy enough to sink a small ship, with severest instructions how to conduct ourselves.

There were strict rules. The one that affected us OTs the most was the stricture that, before leaving a ward or the OT workroom, we had to take complete inventory of every tool. It only happened once that a chisel was missing when it was time to go to lunch from a men's ward. A ward full of hungry men getting hungrier by the minute was anything but a happy place until we found out what another OT had done with the chisel. That never happened again.

At first one wondered how one could possibly work all day with people in an insane asylum, but in no time at all we made friends and found the surrounding population really not too different from our own neighbors on the outside. The Trusties were actually delightful to talk with.

One big husky fellow would be walking out on the paths around the hospital. He had a very important message to tell to the world, and would speak with complete conviction whenever we asked him. He would tell us all about the great hill where we were standing. He said the mountain (as he called it) was riddled through and through with great corridors and terraces and balconies which were all filled with rubies and emeralds and diamonds. He spoke with earnestness and serious conviction about the jewels and treasures he knew about down there. He spoke so seriously that we knew he believed every word, and he almost convinced us all. Sometimes he was even invited to various professional gatherings to tell his story. He was charming, and always a dependable reporter.

Another Trusty used to meet us on the paths. He was a fairly young African-American, who was friendly and cheerful. He had one special talent, which we often asked him to demonstrate to us. If we asked him what day the tenth of March 1986 fell on, he would immediately give the name of the day. Of course, we tried this over and over, and he always had the right answer.

On the Back Wards, everything was quite different. Working to teach a simple handcraft project to Back Ward members was a real challenge. We did have access to a wall telephone, and one day I recall making a phone call while someone was going through both my pockets.

Sometimes even the Back Ward people had a bit of charm. One lady had cut the box of Vick's VapoRub to get the title, which she pinned to the neck of her dress. She may have been trying to get a bit of color, but on the turquoise blue cardboard were the words "Use Vick's for a clear head." She never knew she had made a bit of a joke.

One other woman on that ward had been in a catatonic stupor for months, but on Friday the 13th, when we were all a bit apprehensive, she picked up a glass of water and threw it to hit another patient in the eye. But in the OT workroom there were many patients who had special talents and who found fulfillment of their own lives in the projects they worked on.

One gentleman came to the workshop regularly every day. He spoke to no one. He was a sculptor and was making a model of a special horse that had won all the races that year. On the day the horse was finished to his satisfaction, he relaxed and talked with all of us, a delightfully contented man who had found his niche in the State institution that gave him a home.

All of us OTs who worked in that workshop benefited from a man who had come from Canada, where he was employed in a woolen mill. He taught all of us weavers a rather technical skill which we have never seen elsewhere: how to set up a wooden block with four long nails and how to tie string over those four nails to make "heddles" through which the threads go for weaving—a technical bit taught by the patient to the OTs, who are forever grateful.

Some of us felt very strongly that it was a sad day for humanity when our State closed its eight working State Hospitals and turned out onto the streets so many people who still needed help. Perhaps this step seemed justifiable, considering the cost of repairing the old hospital buildings, but the losses were borne by many people who were sadly incompetent and who needed the help of a large organization.

We often admired how the Danvers State Hospital gathered together all the angles, and made everything work in a kind of desperate harmony. The patients worked in the gardens. Those who were able, raised the food that was served in the cafeteria-type dining rooms at every meal. The men who were able to weave wove the blue denim to make the clothing for the men who did the work. Everyone had a bed—perhaps not quite ideal in a ward with 90 patients. But it was a time of patience and caring for helpless citizens, and the loss of the good system is deplorable.

Every morning there was a staff meeting of the doctors and workers and OTs who were making it run smoothly. The number of patients was in the thousands even in a single hospital. Now, at the beginning of the millennium, we seem to be in a period where machines are dearer to us than people—I even heard an ad on the radio today starting with the idea that an automobile is like a person. This is a dangerous kind of thinking. Machines are so magical, and so immediately manageable, that they seem to work better than people. But they are not people, and it is a dangerous precedent to think of them as human beings. An automobile does not have a soul. Human beings have souls, and I believe it is the prerogative of every human being to find and cultivate his own and other people's souls.

During the time I studied occupational therapy, I moved in with the family of John Philbrick, whom I had met many years earlier. I graduated as an occupational therapist in the spring of 1936. By luck, Dr. Jerome Davis invited me to spend the summer with his family at Brightwater on the New Meadows River in Maine and take care of the two children.

Jerome was a lively gentleman. He moved fast and strode around always whistling or singing words from an old song: "Little drops of water, little grains of sand, make the mighty ocean, and the beautiful land."

We met and headed north toward their summer place. Patty was a very gentle ten-year-old, both serious and playful. Wilfred Grenfell Davis, about four years old, had been adopted and named for Dr. Davis's friend, the famous physician who had established a medical missionary work near Labrador. Many doctors used to give time on their vacations for the missionary work there.

As we drove northward, Dr. Davis became less formal. He started to tell me about his own history. He had been born in Japan, where a large group of missionaries worked. They must have gone over in the 1800s, and one of them was a trained medical doctor from Maine, where we were heading. His name was Dr. John Berry, one of the first medical missionaries to go to Japan. Others came to join the work, and in the summertime they all gathered together, living in Japanese tents and enjoying their companionship in the mountains.

Dr. Davis, who was driving, explained that we were going to a place in Maine that had once been the farm where Dr. John Berry grew up. Now in his old age, Dr. Berry was once again living in the little old farmhouse on the hill. Around his farmhouse there were several buildings, and two of his daughters lived there. Miss Katherine lived in summer in a small cabin where she kept the missionary tents from Japan. Her sister married the rector of a church in Brockton, Massachusetts, and he always teased her as being the "Rectorina" while he was the Rector. The high ground where their summer places had been built was a high-ish hill between two inlets of the ocean, where the wind never stopped blowing. Their hill had therefore been named Wynburg.

More of his farmland was lower, on a long peninsula that sloped gently down to a geological phenomenon known to Maine seafarers as "The Basin," a large, roundish body of water spacious enough to hold any number of large vessels, which often put in through the narrows to wait out a storm or to spend a night at anchor. That was where we were headed—to Brightwater. It was a long drive from New Haven to Maine, and Dr. Davis had at least one faithful listener. Next, he told me more about his connection with the missionary Berrys.

Dr. Berry's adult children and some friends built summer housing on the old farm, especially on the wooded peninsula just below. This was encircled by a rough stony roadway affectionately known as The Boulevard. A cooperative club was organized by the members whose log cabins were somewhat related to the Boulevard. The leader was Jerome Davis. They continued in adult years to gather together in the summer. When Jerome Davis heard that Dr. John Berry had returned to his family's old farmland, Jerome had a bright idea to establish a Cooperative named Brightwater. He made the legal arrangements, and about 15 "holdings" became available for $300 for a 99-year lease.

By the time he had explained about Brightwater and the people we would meet, we were already jumping over Stoney Brook Road, about to see Wynburg and the old farmhouse, and just beyond that, Brightwater's Boulevard. Shivers were going up and down my back and the children were beside themselves. One more corner off the bumpy boulevard and we were beside Mildred and Jerome's log cabin.

Journeys with a Real Jack in the Pulpit | 67

The silversmithing workshop in "St. Dunstan's" (the woodshed), with view of "St. Mary's" (a privy).

Judge Samuel Holten House, Danvers, Massachusetts

Drawing by Alfred Perkins, inspired by Helen's pirate story, which was published in "The Holten," Holten High School, Danvers, 1927

Franklin Porter.

Journeys with a Real Jack in the Pulpit | 69

Resurrection Communion Set by Franklin Porter, now in the National Cathedral, Washington, DC.

Helen Louise Porter in her Boston School of Occupational Therapy uniform

Chapter 7

Brightwater, My True Love

When one has a deep and overwhelming passion for a person or a place, words become thin and inadequate for any description. Brightwater is my true love. Partly it is the rocky Maine coast with its blue water (or its fog!) and the tall spruce trees, the blueberries, and the wild cranberries thriving on the top of a hill.

But deeper and wider than Nature are the people. The people who joined Jerome's cooperative at Brightwater were professional people. Educators, clergy, YMCA leaders, even one from the Brookings Institute. Between them they created a community, and Brightwater became, not a place, but a small assemblage of human people with all the graces and faults and foibles of real folks. Because they lived in log cabins only for the summer, they had other careers in scattered places. Everyone looked forward to the summer reunion, for heartwarming talks and lots of catching up.

Thoughts from Brightwater

> O Trees, who stand so tall
> And view the night in all
> Her purple majesty,
> O would that I might be
> As calm, at ease
> As you, O Trees,
> Who stand so tall.

I don't know when I wrote this poem but I clearly felt inspired by the beauty of the place.

First Summer at Brightwater—1936

That first summer I spent in Brightwater was so special it has never been surpassed in my memory. One day Jerome drove Patty, aged 10, and me over to Orr's Island to purchase a young goat. On our way home we stopped in Bath at Hallet's Drugstore. Patty went into the store and asked for a glass of water "to take out to my friend." The little goat was her friend who muzzled up the water.

We all took care of the milk goat, and played ball, and picked blueberries. I tried to teach Wilfred to knit, but he was left-handed and found it difficult. He preferred to throw stones. Living in the woods with candles and kerosene lamps and outdoor plumbing was a pleasant way to discover how our ancestors had really lived. The galvanized washtub and scrubbing board out in the clearing were new to me, and we loved the experience as long as summer lasted. The biggest thrill of the year was on the way home, when one turned on a water faucet in a wayside washroom, and hot water gushed out.

Sunday was a special day, and we worked all day Saturday getting ready for Sunday. Jerome pulled the rowboat close to land and helped us one by one to step aboard. "Mommy" Davis arranged Patty and Wilfy. I sat in my assigned place and Jerome plied the oars. It was not quite like being in church, but Mildred Davis had a very proper upbringing and her thoughts were spiritual. After all, it was Sunday morning. Her clear soprano rang out across the silent waters: "Safely through another week God has brought us on our way—Day of all the week the best, Emblem of eternal rest . . ."

We all sang. If there was a special holiday, like the Fourth of July, there would be an appropriate song. After that quite proper Sunday morning observance, the boat could be landed and we could explore favorite spots on the rockbound coast, with an occasional hiatus of sandy beach. It was so calm and so heartwarming, it was no wonder that I later wanted to plan our honeymoon for that spot.

Sunday Night Sing

But there was more to Sunday. There would be an invitation for everyone to come to sing at someone's cabin. Through the years the procedure was perfected and details ran smoothly. People brought their own chairs and the hostess prepared simple refreshments for later. Macy Whitehead shouldered the portable organ, and someone passed out the Gospel hymnals (the book with lively old songs). It was a community of professional people who loved nature and a very simple lifestyle, with none of our modern, so-called conveniences. In those halcyon days there were no delivery trucks ever driving into this woodsy refuge. No peddlers or agents or strangers. We lived in splendid rural isolation.

The sing would commence with hymn numbers chosen by each one present. As the years had passed on some friends had also passed away, and several hymns were memorials. That might seem a bit sentimental, but it bonded that group together. After a while we had covered the deeper feelings, and the mood would be changed by an elder's mellow voice singing authoritatively, to Macy's accompaniment:

> I ain't gonna grieve my Lord no more, no more

followed by

> You can't get to Heaven in Macy's car
> 'Cause the darned old thing
> Won't go that far

And the rest of the evening was just plain fun.

Dr. John Berry

We had to meet everyone. It was a busy summer. One day we went to meet Dr. John Berry, who in his old age was stone deaf but gentle and loving toward everyone. They told us he lived now in winter in Worcester, Massachusetts, where on one special day there was great and unusual excitement, and many shiny black automobiles arrived. Of course, the street became alive and people crowded around to see what was happening. Soon it was apparent that there were several Japanese people, whose attire indicated their position and their status and their mission.

They had come all the way from Japan to call on Dr. John Berry and to give high honors and citation for his work to a man who had devoted his life to minister to the Japanese as a medical doctor. Everyone was elated, and the citation was read by Dr. Berry's neighbor, Alan Forbes.

The day at Brightwater that Dr. John Berry was invited to come and bless a newly finished cabin, I almost fell asleep while he was blessing every board and every windowpane in the little home. After he passed away, the farmhouse became the choicest spot to rent for a delicious visit in a spectacular location, overlooking the Basin on the east. From the old farmhouse one could see the whole expanse of the great round basin.

Nearby was a dark woodsy road named Smuggler's Cove. Both must have been busy in the days of rum-running, which had been cleaned up many years before our sojourn in the area, but there was still a faint hint of the dark and spooky atmosphere of the old days. We occasionally saw a mysterious looking man whom no one knew. He trudged along the boulevard once in awhile. Someone found out that his name was Mister Thistle. One day he must have made a visit to our milk goats, Thisby and Phoebe. The only way we knew was that my father's brass scales vanished that day, and though we searched high and low, they were never seen again—nor was our mysterious but memorable visitor, Mr. Thistle.

Chapter 8

Partridge Manuscript

Yankee Magazine, December 1974
Yankee Publishing Incorporated
Dublin, NH 03444

[They published a second-hand version. The following is my almost on-the-spot version.]

John was in Episcopal Theological School, an old and enormously venerated seminary situated in Cambridge near all the other seriously respected educational institutions. One of his adventures there concerned the Partridge Manuscript.

While John lived in Cambridge, I lived at his family's house in Dorchester while working in Providence every day as an Occupational Therapist. By then, we had become engaged and discovered the luxury of the telephone to keep each other informed about daily happenings.

One evening John phoned. "We are in the middle of an exciting story over here," he said. "A couple of men in the seminary were listening to Dr. Nash in his class on the New Testament. They were studying Romans and he was lamenting the fact that no evidence had ever been found to establish certain facts of biblical importance. Two of the men in the class decided that if a manuscript was needed, they would produce one as a practical joke for the Professor." That was just a small part of his phone call and we went on to talk about other things.

Every evening his phone call would tell me a bit about the creation of the manuscript. They went to various stores until they found the right kind of parchment, which was a very fine leather they could write on. Then they thought it would look more authentic if they made it look old, so they boiled it in coffee grounds and tea for a while. That didn't age it very much so they were going to try a stronger treatment.

One evening John's phone call just happened to mention that the two men were still working on the practical joke and they had other work to do so they put the parchment under a mat where people would walk over it to make it look old.

He told me later that they were also working to get ink that would look ancient. They were just having fun trying to imagine how old manuscripts were made. Their names were Barrett Tyler and Reamer Kline, Class of 1936. Of course, other students were in on the joke, but everything was carefully kept secret from the faculty. Between them they playfully called it the "Kline-Tyler Codex," codex being an erudite name for biblical manuscripts. It was still a joke and a playful performance.

One of the men studied real ancient manuscripts and wrote the text that the Professor had said was needed in the style of ancient documents on lines drawn conspicuously across the parchment. At one line he made a mistake and had to scratch out and rewrite. No matter. That would just make it look more authentic. As John would fill me with these details day after day, it looked as though the men who were in on the joke were having a lot of fun.

Then they began to wonder how to present the manuscript to the authorities in the Seminary. Those in on the secret knew it would be embarrassing just to take it to the Seminary faculty. They tried to make a plan to make the whole thing look more real.

John's next phone call told of the plan. They—Tyler and Kline—knew that Howard Lowell, a 1935 graduate, was living in Egypt. They brewed up a plan to invent a Mr. Wilfred J. Partridge who had visited Howard Lowell in Cairo and had showed him the manuscript among a lot of other curios. Howard Lowell told him if he was ever near Boston he should visit ETS Episcopal Theological School and show the manuscript to the faculty there.

They had already a wide reputation for study and identification of ancient manuscripts.

When John told me this, he was obviously relating the sudden change of mood at the Seminary. What had started as a joke and was fun had unexpectedly become a serious hoax and the men could be in trouble. But, they went on with the plan and wrote a letter to introduce the Kline-Tyler Codex to "the dons of biblical scholarship." The letter was written on stationery from the Hotel Essex near the South Station in Boston. It was addressed to Dr. Nash:

April 27, 1936

Dear Professor Nash,

Enclosed you will find a manuscript which I bought during a recent trip in Egypt. I happened to be staying in Cairo and visited my friend Howard Lowell. While I was showing him various curios collected during the trip, he became particularly interested in this manuscript.

I called your house this morning but you were out. [Of course they called when they knew he would be out.] I am leaving for Portland on business but will stop on my way back. I would appreciate any information you could give me concerning this manuscript, as to whether it may be of value. Looking forward to meeting you, I remain very truly yours,

Wilfred J. Partridge
229 Greenwood Boulevard
Evanston, Illinois

John told me the men had phoned Dr. Nash's house when they knew he was busy elsewhere and now all they could do was to wait and see what would happen next. They had mailed the manuscript to Dr. Nash's house. It was only a little scrap of leather that would fit in a small envelope. Of course, I was following this story with great interest and feeling especially pleased to be in on the secret details as they developed, directly by telephone.

Everything was quiet for a few days. Then one evening John told me one of the men had heard, as two Professors met on the stairs, "Well, the letter was from the Hotel Essex so he probably didn't have a lot of money." That was all for a few more days.

Gradually, bit-by-bit, news began to circulate around the campus and John's phone reports kept me posted. The manuscript was taken to the Fogg Museum where the specialist in ancient manuscripts studied the details. They especially wanted to scrape off a fragment of ink to compare it with ancient samples with which they were familiar. But because the owner, Mr. Partridge, was still elsewhere, they could not get his permission. The scholars were investigating other aspects of the piece. Actually, the piece was small but it had a big reputation in those days and there were many authorities—both believers and skeptics.

One evening John's message was that Dr. Nash had received a postal card in the mail. The card, from *Alice in Wonderland*, read:

> "The time has come," the Walrus said,
> To talk of many things:
> Of manuscripts and sealing wax—
> And cabbages—and kings."

Mr. Partridge must have a sense of humor—but he still failed to show up.

The Fogg Museum sent word that the ink looked much like Dragons' Blood, the name of an ancient ink often found in manuscripts. They attributed authenticity to the erased spot where the writer had scraped and covered up his original mistake—which to the specialists made the manuscript a *Palimpsest,* from an ancient word meaning to scrape or erase. This added more authority to the reality of the manuscript and added terror to the perpetrators who now were afraid they might be forced to leave the Seminary.

Every one of the students by this time knew about the Codex and as the days passed and turned into weeks, everyone knew that the specialists in the Fogg Museum were by now debating pro and con and coming perilously near to declaring that it might be the real thing. The more the reports came from the Museum, the more the creators worried about the possible outcome. The time seemed interminable, especially when another card came with a rather blurred message from Alice. Everyone was waiting anxiously to hear more from the mysterious Mr. Partridge. John's telephone calls passed the mounting anxiety along to me and we all felt pretty edgy.

The fear was made greater by the fact that two Seminary professors of real stature as authorities were about to attend and present a paper on two other proven codices and one of them had promised to mention the "Codex Tyler and Kline." The site was to be the Annual Meeting of the Society of Biblical Literature and Exegesis being held at a college in New Hampshire. If the professors presented the manuscript to the assembled body and then found out it was a practical joke, they would be the laughing stock of the whole Society. The practical jokers decided they would have to face up to the truth.

The instigators of the fake Codex held council. They went to the Professor's house and confided in his wife. She received them graciously and quickly reached her husband on the telephone before he went down to the dinner. She only said, "It's a fake." He understood and passed it on to his venerable companion.

The two professors were about to go down to dinner. They sat together at the head table and the best part of the story is that they immediately recognized the humor in the enterprise. John told me—what he had heard from others at the dinner—that the two professors kept thinking how they had added their own ideas to make it more authentic. For instance, the scribe had copied something wrong because he himself didn't speak Aramaic. The two seminarians became famous instead of being expelled. They graduated with honors and everyone cherished the whole story.

But, this is not the end of the story. The years went by and everyone worked at his chosen assignments. Kline was President of Bard College and Barrett Tyler was a military chaplain killed during World War II.

In 1948, a magnificent stained glass window was dedicated at the Seminary in memory of Barrett Tyler. The window is circular, showing scenes of Pilgrim's Progress, Christian in the center. At his feet is a bird holding a string wrapped around a scroll.

The legend is that one of the Professors looked at the window and commented about the dove at Christian's feet. "That is an odd looking dove, and why is it there?" Whereupon the dean replied "The dove is really a Partridge".

The Partridge Manuscript appeared solitary in a special case in the school library with a small inscription: "The Partridge Manuscript—probably of the 20th Century."

Anti-climax: One day I met Reamer Kline and we exchanged a few words about the famous manuscript and Reamer grinned when he said to me, "If the authorities had only measured the lines with a ruler, they would have been surprised to learn that the metric system had been invented so early." The lines were each one centimeter apart.

The Partridge Manuscript will forever hold a place of honor at the Seminary in Cambridge.

Post Script to the Partridge Manuscript:

I can never tell this seemingly trivial adventure story without being deeply moved when I seriously realize the humanness of every detail of the events: first, the good humor of inventing the students' answer to their Professor's spoken need to find such a manuscript; second, the two students' creation of an impressively perfect imitation of an ancient piece; third, their skill in presenting the mysterious manuscript which was part of the fun and humor of the joke. But it was really too profound to stay as a joke. The emotional stresses were real and literally tried the souls of the scheming lads. They were deeply appalled at the thought of embarrassing their seriously studious elderly professors. They obviously were deeply pained—many of us would have run away or waved it aside or tried to pretend it wasn't very important. To hear the professor's wife making the phone call to say, "It's a fake," was probably the deepest real experience in their young lives.

But the crowning glory of the whole tale is the quick and sincere forgiveness of the two men who might have been embarrassed. They covered their own personal embarrassment by humorously sharing their own additions to the fake. They must have immediately experienced what we all mention when we say the Lord's Prayer: Forgive us our trespasses as we forgive those who trespass against us.

The whole experience makes a great story, and it deserves a moment of deep spiritual pondering. I must here add that few of us would ever rate a stained glass window to memorialize the forgiveness of our worldly mischief!

Chapter 9

Marriage and Groveland

As soon as John Philbrick finished his training at the Episcopal Theological School in Cambridge with the Class of 1936, he appeared in a new suit with a clerical collar. His trip by the T from Cambridge to Dorchester in his new suit was also his first experience wearing a clerical collar because the first drunk on the trolley car insisted on giving a handful of change to "the father," much to John's embarrassment—and, of course, amusement, although he had great sympathy for the poor fellow.

The wedding day was soon after. We had some trouble getting his sister Katharine, a bridesmaid, in from playing baseball in the street. The wedding was in St. Mark's Church, Dorchester. The bridesmaids wore pale green dresses. The bride wore a very simple white voile dress and carried a big armful of white daisies we had gathered from the fields around the house we would move to in Groveland, John's first parish. The bride was given away by her adopted brother. The organist played all the music planned for the occasion. Everyone was ready but nothing was happening. Our beloved Bill Bradner had not arrived to officiate. We had all enjoyed breakfast together that morning. Where could he be?

How long does one wait for a wedding? Twenty minutes? Thirty minutes? With the organist repeating the music for the third time, the regular Rector of St. Mark's came to the rescue and the holy knot was tied. The mystery has never been solved, although our beloved Bill came late and signed all the important papers. He never told us whether his car broke down or the drawbridge was up. Where was he during those harassing, mysterious minutes?

We journeyed to Rhode Island that evening to share a wedding meal with my mother, who was not well, but rejoiced in our happiness. My father had died suddenly on August 21, 1935, and my mother had since returned to Rhode Island. After a short visit with my mother, we went on to a popular church retreat in Swansea run by our friends, who obviously were ready for our arrival. It was late and the house was in darkness. Would they have left the door unlatched when they went to bed? We soon found out: when we opened the door, we were gently pelted with a flood of pink tissue paper rose petals!

Honeymoon

Of course we landed at Brightwater in 1937 to celebrate our honeymoon. After our wedding, we visited with friends there and eventually purchased the required 99-year lease and built a 10 by 15 foot "house." Macy, who was a Congregationalist, told me that the night we arrived there was a lot of noise and banging in our cabin, which was not too far from the Whiteheads's place. He said his mother, Aunt Miriam, had suggested that perhaps the bride was trying to get the groom's clerical collar off! That was one denomination poking innocent fun at another, especially aimed at a clerical collar (known in our ministry as "the dog collar"!).

Our Brightwater Haven

We owned our little cabin at Brightwater from roughly 1938 to 1943. On most Sunday mornings after the "Hymn Sing," we all returned to whatever was our choice or sometimes we chose to go out in the boat. One of the best features of the Maine woods is the feeling of freedom, independence to follow one's own leadership and to learn to think for oneself.

But when the so-called Boulevard was beginning to need pick and shovel work, all the men turned out to help. Howard Bowker was a neighbor who had lived on the road from Bath to

Brightwater for years. That road was so steep and so rocky that when John Morse, the lumberman from Bath, drove the Philbricks's lumber for their cabin, he told us that driving his loaded truck around the Boulevard "was just like driving down the front steps of the public library."

The gentlemen assembled with their instructor, Howard Bowker, ready to work to repair the road. He commenced the instruction with a respectful gesture and said, "Well, now gentlemen, if I was doing the job, I would do it this way." Of course he was "proud as punch" to be asked to direct such congenial men. Everyone went to work on his appointed task. It just happened that our best favorite, the deeply peaceful Quaker Tom Kelley, let a rock slip out of his fingers to land on his brother-in-law's head. There was no damage but Tom modestly explained as the stone was flying through the air, "I was remembering it does say in the Bible 'Let him who is without sin cast the first stone.'"

Carpenters Loose in the Woods

While John and I were trying to build our tiny house—10 feet x 15 feet—we had to work every minute to keep ahead of rain and all other distractions. We even had to beg our friends to help us by hauling heavy lumber down the path to our "holding" from the Boulevard. One Sunday morning we kept on building to be ready for the Sing that night. What we did not realize was that the noise our hammers were making was wafted across the peninsula and everyone could hear. They said, "That must be the Philbricks putting up the walls." We never thought anyone else could hear!

That night at the Sing the first announcement was: "We will sing Number 104 and dedicate it to the Philbricks." The words were:

>   Work for the night is coming
>   Work through the morning hours
>   Work while the dew is sparkling
>   Work mid springing flowers

Work when the day grows bright
Work in the glowing sun
Work for the night is coming
When man's work is done!

To bring all this up to the year 2002, when we had to leave Brightwater to work in Missouri, the family who took over our holding built their house onto ours and made ours into a small bedroom. We gave our 99-year holding to them and no money changed hands. They report a comfortable and well-built room on their pleasant, self-built house, and they have often thanked us.

Bayberry Candles

One summer at Brightwater was far advanced and the wild vegetation was beginning to produce a rich variety of fruits and nuts and wild grapes and berries. Every day we devoted our time to collecting cups and buckets and baskets of harvest. A favorite plant was the bayberry bush which always grew at the edges of the fields where the thick spruce forest began. Now, when a good cook builds a flavorsome stew, she always puts in one bay leaf, and before she serves the stew, she (obedient to instructions in her cookbook) removes that one bay leaf. (To tell the truth, to me at least it was never detectable if it was left in nor missed if it had never been in anyway.)

But to go on with the story. Some people buy their bay leaves from the grocery store, and they probably come from California. In the old days the early settlers used to use their own local bay leaves off the bushes on their own land. Well, anyway, we had found the bayberry bushes that season just loaded with bayberries and we had gathered about three large buckets of the fragrant berries covered with those tiny round pellets of gray wax. We planned to make bayberry candles. They always smelled so good as they burned.

Everyone had gone away, leaving Macy and me to decide how to spend the day. Now for the big industry. We knew to have boiling water in large quantities to melt the wax off the bayberries.

It took a long time to cool the skimmed off wax but eventually we were ready with pieces of string for wicks to dip into the cooling brew to make candles. The wax would stick to the string and each time we dipped, the candle would grow fatter—or so we thought.

The first dip with one string absorbed all the wax there was. There was only one bayberry candle—one piece of string with a slight coating of thin wax. Just another practical lesson in the real facts of an ancient art. Next time harvest a dozen buckets of bayberries—but be sure to save that one leaf to put in the stew.

Dr. Gordon Berry

I also remember Dr. Gordon Berry, an eye, ear, nose, and throat doctor, the son of Dr. John Berry. He vacationed at Brightwater and was one of our heroes because he had unusual ingenuity and skill. He lived in one of the houses owned by the Berry family, an old farmhouse that was beginning to show its age. Dr. Gordon Berry assembled his tools and went to work.

One of the first tasks was to remove the big old square cut nails that held the original boards in place. He studied the situation, aimed his claw hammer and gave the nail a mighty pull. The nail let go and the hammer came down and broke Dr. Gordon's nose. He knew exactly what to do, being an eye, ear, and nose specialist. He went to a mirror and with his own experience and skill set his own broken nose. That made him our favorite hero for that year.

Rufus Jones

One Sunday afternoon someone in Brightwater loaded her car with everyone who was interested in hearing a famous speaker. We were all eager to go. All we knew was that the speaker was to be Rufus Jones from Haverford, a Quaker school. Since Quakers never have titles, we had no way of knowing whether he was a reverend or a professor or what his subject would be.

When he appeared in the pulpit of a very small church in a Maine country town, one knew immediately that he was one of the great ones. He spoke with a strong positive voice and he plainly knew his subject. To this day—although I have forgotten most of his talk—I still remember my own amazement when he proclaimed the fact that he and his mother and his grandfather reached back over the years to the time of the Revolutionary War.

This simple fact made an indelible impression on my mind of the passage of years, when those years are related to history. We all span our own lifetime over years of history, with the old giving way to changes both good and bad!

John's ministry grew so busy in the summer that in 1942 our Brightwater friends had already gone home for their early fall school and business responsibilities by the time we could leave Duxbury to go to Maine. There were still traces of the war that we could hear. We heard ships somewhere in the distance shooting off bombs. We were close to the Bath Iron Works where American ships were built. Local people had stories about strange happenings. It was a spooky time to be living alone in our tiny cabin in Brightwater with the sounds and stories of war all around us.

One of the scariest was a huge ball moored in the ocean right in front of our cabin. We had to go out in a rowboat to sink the tin cans left over from our frugal kitchen. We rowed out, turned our backs on the scary mooring and sank the tin cans into the deep water—a practice that would never be permitted today. We asked everyone we saw if they knew what the big ball was. No one knew. It looked to be about 20 feet in diameter, went up with the high tide and down with the low. But it never moved away from its mooring. Perhaps it was moored there to scare enemy ships away from the basin. It was scary.

A place one loves because of its happy associations becomes desperately lonely when there are no people. There were plenty of memories, but there were too many mysteries—like the disembodied human hand that washed up on the shore. We used to break the monotony of the loneliness by visiting the Bowkers who lived on the road toward Phippsburg. Mr. Bowker had a wealth of good local tales, and Mrs. Bowker always invited us to have a cup of tea. Like many families of that time, they had their very own air conditioning. On a hot day they could sit in their chairs just inside the barn. With the barn doors open both front and back, the breeze would blow through, and everyone was cool.

Mr. Bowker loved to see us coming that early autumn. He especially liked to talk to our Labrador retriever, Judy, and tease her because she had "no cup of tea." Their telephone, the only one within miles, became a community utility. During the busy summer there were many occasions when visitors had to make calls for various reasons. There were also calls that came in to the Bowker phone. The route across to the house was rough and long over Stoney Brook Road. But from our road we could see across the valley to the Bowker clothesline. If there was a phone call for any of us in the Brightwater community, Mrs. Bowker simply hung out a sheet on the line.

That year in our somewhat saddened and lonely state we looked across and there was the sheet. It was sad news. John's father had passed away. We packed up and bid goodbye to the solitude and drove home to Duxbury.

The Thinnish Man

By 1943, we had given up our cabin at Brightwater and bought Faith Homestead in Duxbury. Before leaving my beloved Brightwater I want to write one more story about that magical place.

Before we were married, there was a family living in the old Wynburg farmhouse, summer visitors from around Boston. The father, Russell Gordon Carter, wrote books for children. His wife was friendly and so were the two daughters. We had many long talks about everything. When we were not chewing over the affairs of state, we often went swimming in the only cove where there was a spot of beach.

In Maine it is always understood that there is never such a miracle as warm water. We sometimes tried to convince ourselves that it was a little warmer than the air but it was in vain. One day the author presented me with an envelope handwritten, containing this:

Poem by the Thinnish Man
The Song of a Thin Man (after his first swim in Maine waters)

I love to swim in water that is cold,
    Where polar bears come gliding past upon a cake of ice,
        And baby seals disport
        And walruses report
That the way to be a hero is to do the crawl at zero;
I love to swim in water that is cold, cold, cold!

I love to swim in water that is cold,
    Where Eskimos stand shivering upon a snowy shore:
        On solitary nights
        Beneath the Northern Lights
Give me the kind of water that would freeze old Neptune's daughter,
For I love to swim in water that is cold, cold, cold!

I love to swim in water that—oh, hell!
    I cannot go on lying, there's no earthly use of trying:
        For I'm a thinnish man
        And I haven't any tan
I'm different from the ladies, I'd like to bathe in Hades—
Yes, I'd love to swim in water that's as hot—as—Hell!

Presented to Helen Louise Porter
From the thinnish man himself—
        Russell Gordon Carter
        Wynburg, Maine 28 August, 1934

Chapter 10

Over the Threshold

The next chapter in the plan was to be carried over the threshold of the Rectory in the tiny town of Groveland, Massachusetts. The house was loose and rambling, and smoke from the cellar furnace used to drift up through cracks in the floorboards upstairs.

The clergy salary at that lovely little church was all of $1,000 a year. The Occupational Therapist salary was also infinitesimal after the train rides between Haverhill and Boston every day.

The Reverend John's first ministerial encounter with livestock was about a week after we had moved in. Our neighbor in high anxiety accosted him and said "our cow is having a calf. What'll I do?," and John, totally ignorant of the intricacies involved, advised her ministerially, "leave her alone and see what happens." It came out all right.

That spring we trimmed the grape vines, and the neighbors told us we'd made a mistake. They put quart jars under every trimmed vine to catch the sap which would have nourished the grapes.

Our first parish was a good parish for very inexperienced people. The parishioners were gentle and forgiving.

Weymouth

John and I were in Groveland for only about a year. Before long there was a place open in Weymouth, Massachusetts, which needed a clergyman. This was a more complicated situation than our first parish but there was more salary, too. The first time the minister turned out the two electric lights over the altar to replace them with candles, "Tizzy" Bowles said, "I wouldn't want to be in your shoes." She was afraid we were going "high Church." The minister stood firm and the crisis passed.

There was a large group of young people eager for something to do. We suggested making a puppet show, Punch and Judy—an old "moralist play" which used to have great popularity. Mr. Punch was a wicked criminal who eventually got his just desserts. His mischievous acts were legion and the young folks were ready after they had made the puppet to act out the plot. One act involved Mr. Punch shooting a victim. The actor backstage was armed with a blown-up paper bag to burst for the shot. Somehow that actor was distracted and the shot was missing until "Tizzy" shouted, "Bang, bang, you're dead."

The Punch and Judy show became famous and traveled from one church to another. So much so that the Diocesan paper gave us honorable mention, both for the work of the young people, and for the traveling show which brought in some income.

Punch and Judy Make a Conquest

"What shall we have to amuse the children at the Parish Fair?"
"A Punch and Judy show!"
"Ye-es, that would be nice. But where would we get the puppets?"
"Make them."

This bit of conversation started lively activity at the Rectory in Weymouth, as the puppets were made by the young people with a few books and some friends to help.

The story used to be a favorite before TV. It was the history of the wicked Mr. Punch who was the villain, beating up folks and throwing his baby out the window. In the end the Devil came and carried Mr. Punch away on his pitchfork to the hangman (with a toothbrush moustache). The young folks made the puppets.

Mrs. Punch looks demure and sunny under her red cocked hat and her curls.

To tell the truth, the whole affair was a success because we had in the church the head artist employed by *Readers Digest* and his skillful little wife who was also a graduate of an art school. Their professional artistry gave the whole show a rosy glow and we all had fun.

from The Church Militant
By Helen Philbrick, February 1939

We had so much fun and such a financial success with Punch and Judy that the participants begged to work on another project. This time they chose to learn how to manipulate marionettes with a stage where they could stand higher and work the marionette strings from above.

They chose to work on stories about St. Francis. He came from a wealthy family who lived in luxury, which included a handsome house in Italy. After his conversion when he became a monk, he appeared in meager outdoor scenery in a simple robe. His story dealt with the people he met and with the Wolf of Gubbio, which he met and tamed.

Part of the charm of the marionette is that it is really a very small figure of a person. But surrounded by scenery to scale, he appears to be life-size. With marionettes it is traditional after the show to bring them all out so the audience can see how tiny they were. When our Wolf of Gubbio came out people always said, "That's not the wolf I saw. The wolf I saw was big. He was this big. I saw him myself." The Wolf of Gubbio marionette was really a four-inch piece of black sealskin, swiped off an old fur coat (when we used to have seal skins!) With a shaped head and tail and four legs this little figure looked big on the stage.

The show was a great success. It took 12 people to work it and we carried it to put on in several parishes and our loyal members again had great satisfaction. The production rated a write up by *The Spirit of Missions*, a national magazine published in New York.

Chapter 11

Weymouth to Duxbury

One day the archdeacon came to say there was an opening in Duxbury and also in Marshfield. In Duxbury, the Reverend Allen Jacobs had been minister to Saint John's Church for many years, and he and his lovely wife were ready for retirement. Mrs. Jacobs had founded the Junior Guild of young women. Their motto was "Do ye nextes thinges." They met around at each other's houses and enjoyed fabulous refreshments. They also worked hard whenever the church had a fair. The Senior Guild also contributed generously, more with work than with money, to support the church. However, in spite of all the work and enthusiasm of the members, it was impossible to raise the salary of a clergyman. Trinity Church in Marshfield had the same problem. A young man was needed to fill both places.

How to Call a Minister Without the Use of a Computer

Soon the archdeacon came to call at the rectory in Weymouth. He said, "Next Wednesday the Ladies Guilds from Duxbury and Marshfield are meeting together at Miss Margaret Nelson's house in Marshfield. You and Mrs. Philbrick and I will just happen to drop in." We dropped in, met the ladies, and drank a cup of tea. The Reverend John Philbrick showed early signs of a sense of humor, which proved a valuable tool of his ministry.

A lady studied him through her lorgnette—this is the honest truth—and said "Are you any relation to Ralph Philbrick?"

He replied, "Was he a horse thief?"

I was mortified that he should be so fresh, but it was his usual "Irish repartee" from his Dorchester neighbors. He outgrew it—but never lost his sense of humor.

The remaining conversation was conventional and not memorable. Within the month the Reverend John Philbrick was called to be Priest-in-Charge of St. John's Mission in Duxbury and at Trinity in Marshfield. Mr. Jacobs retired to Florida. So, there were two churches quite a few miles apart. (Today these matches are done by computers and take much matching and jockeying before the selection is completed.)

Busy Summer in Duxbury

As I've mentioned earlier, in 1942 we could not go to Brightwater during the height of the summer because Duxbury was a busy town full of visitors. The harbor was full of boats and the churches were also full (except when there was a Sunday morning high tide). Our best summer friends were here and the seacoast town frequently needed clergymen for church weddings and other glamorous occasions.

The yacht club quota was filled but graciously extended honorary membership to the local ministers. John was pleased and, of course, flattered and teasingly boasted that the yacht club had made him a member even though he owned no boat—only one pair of oarlocks, which he found in the back shed of the Cunningham House on Cedar Street when we moved in. (The Cunninghams always called the little building Cats' Hell. No one knew why, but the name was famous in this very small town.)

Now it was wartime and everyone was doing some kind of work to help the situation. When John's father died in 1942 we were able to buy an old house with five acres of land in Duxbury. War work was uppermost. Our neighbor, Dorothy, made bombs, the ladies under Gertrude Coffin and Florence Flannery made bandages in the Old Sailors' Home. We grew vegetables in our back yard garden and went to some conferences to learn more about gardening.

We needed eggs. Why not get some hens? Milk for a small family? Milk goats are easy to take care of. Gradually, we added some sheep and ducks and geese. All these creatures more or less took care of themselves, so there was time for parish work. The hens provided meat for parish suppers. Eventually, a pig or two gave bacon. We named the place Faith Homestead Economically, things were also happening in the community. Many old houses came on the market and quite a few were bought by our contemporaries who also had gardens and perhaps a milk goat or some sheep.

Marshfield

The Seaview-Humarock church was a reconditioned one-room schoolhouse, with simple facilities and parking space adequate for a good congregation and Sunday school. The early founders called it by an affectionately joking name: "Saint Giles in the Woods."

Two elderly sisters lived in a very old, very spacious farmhouse in Marshfield with a big barn. They had a couple who worked for them and they lived simply but rather elegantly, on what had been a very large farm, well-respected by friends and neighbors. Their father had been Rector of a large church in Geneva, New York and their older brother was Rector of a very thriving church in Cincinnati, Ohio. There was every reason for Miss Margaret to assume all the qualities which won her the respectful title of "a lay Pope."

She was organist in the little one-room schoolhouse church, skillfully pumping away every Sunday morning while the congregation rang out the hymns which she had chosen. We used to admire her arrival at the little church as she came early with a thermos bottle of cold water and a hassock to kneel on. She brought her handkerchief, her *Book of Common Prayer*, and her hymnal. There was a glass for her drink of water and a silver comb to separate and hold the hymnal pages apart. The organ bench had to be arranged at the right height and the numbers of the hymns were written on a list.

Many Sundays her brother George Nelson came from the Cathedral in Boston and it was his assignment to post the hymn numbers for the congregation. He would find the hymn and usually he knew each one by its number and we could hear him humming or whistling the tune as he fitted the cardboard numeral into its place on the hymn board.

Miss Margaret's only limitation was that she was a little hard of hearing, but not to worry: Miss Dorothea had very keen hearing, but her limitation was when it came to singing. She used to sit at the end of the front pew closest to the organ. She always stood with hymnal open to the right hymn. Although she did not sing, she always knew which would be the last stanza. For the organist's benefit at the end of the last stanza she used to clap the hymnal tight shut with a loud snap that told the organist that was the end. She also made the rule and always followed it that the offering hymn must be in the same key as the Doxology which followed the collecting of the offering by the ushers.

Although these two gentlewomen lived in a smallish town on a large and rather famous old farm, they both had a world-wide point of view and they had broad vision of how things should be done for the good of humanity. Miss Margaret used to send for the new minister and meet him at the front door with her list of the things she wanted him to do (not always the most tactful approach to a young trainee quite sure he knew all the latest administrative approaches).

But any over-zealousness on her part was forgiven when we were invited to the Nelsons's for Sunday dinner. Their hospitality was all encompassing. Brother George presided at the head of the table, proudly presenting the home-made wine he had made from local wild grapes he gathered in the woods every summer. It was excellent wine and he took great pride describing the adventures he had had harvesting grapes from tall trees in the family forest.

The conversation was serious and dignified, dealing with current events and no trivia. Mrs. Blaha waited on table, but she was also a good friend and a prolific knitter. She came from Germany and showed us a knitted sampler which was yards long, using dozens of different knitting stitches. The sampler, of course, was not part of the dinner. Mr. Blaha carried in the firewood, which was swept with a whisk broom before he put it into the wood box.

The grand finale of the dinner was Brother George's opportunity to shine again. We retired to the parlor. As he would raise the silver demi-tasse pot to pour into the demi-tasse cups, he would always ask, "Am I over it?" This was evidently a bit of Nelson Family Ritual that had to be observed—and answered with an indulgent snicker.

After dinner as we walked toward the chairs around the big fireplace, the two ladies, one or the other, would always point through the window to a little-used church on the hillside across the road. They always said the same theme, "And sometime we will own that." They were infallible. In due time the little church was for sale and the Episcopalians raised money to buy it. Eventually, they also moved the little old school house church up the hill to attach it to the church building, and now Marshfield rejoices in a thriving parish, thanks to all the generosity and good will of the people.

There was another funny little coincidence related to the Nelson family and John Philbrick. As a student he had attended Hobart College in Geneva, New York. The Nelson sisters' father was rector of the Episcopal church in Geneva, but many years ago the Reverend Mr. Nelson used to visit the old family farm in Marshfield, and he often brought "Little Meg" (Miss Margaret in her childhood) and her sister Dorothea. This annual trip from Geneva to Marshfield was always a special occasion, as we learned from what I am about to relate.

Change of location to the Marshfield Town Dump! One of the workmen was on his way home one night. He spotted a small book in the road and just put it in his pocket "to neaten up the road." He was on his way to play bridge in Duxbury with a woman who knew John. She borrowed the little book because it was a diary of an Episcopal rector from Geneva, NY. She showed it to John and we rejoiced to read about Miss Margaret's trips to Marshfield as a very little girl with her father. He even bought her a bracelet on one visit—"for little Meg."

The Nelson farm had just been sold and some contents, including the diary, had gone to the town dump. We all rejoiced at the coincidences and wanted to keep the diary but alas, it has been lost. May this be a gentle memorial of fine people who were all role models for ourselves. The twenty-first century Good News is that the Nelson Memorial Forest now belongs to the New England Forestry Foundation and is in the public domain for walks and passive recreation.

But now back to the church in Duxbury, where we moved into Emily Cunningham's. We liked having two churches. It was possible to work in each place while the other place did not quite know where we were. Unfortunately, that was wartime and gasoline was limited. There was also a problem with summer traffic when we had to drive from one church to the other in a limited time along a road filled with tourists.

For a young preacher, John had some unexpected receptions. He prepared one sermon and delivered it in each church. The Marshfield congregation praised him for his excellent Republican sermon—so of course the Duxbury congregation recognized it as an outstanding Democratic sermon. The real fun happened when the combined vestries of the two churches overlapped each other and somehow the telephone bill was overpaid by some thirty dollars. The telephone company called and asked John, as minister, to please do something about the overpayment. John explained that the telephone company only had to pay the churches the difference and the problem would be solved. The phone company told him they could not do that.

The next time the company called, John told them the same solution—for them to pay the difference. So the telephone company sent an officer with more "clout" and the answer was the same. John was enjoying the fun and shared the joke with his friends. The company phoned us regularly, as often as once every month. Finally, when we were about to move to Missouri, somehow the problem was settled and the telephone company could relax again!

Saint John's Mission in Duxbury

The following is my memory of events related to Saint John's Mission in Duxbury. In the 1930s, Bishop W. A. Lawrence was assisted by an archdeacon whose work was to visit all the churches and to know what was happening with the clergy. Progress in those days was very low key. Still paced by simpler, Victorian traditions, the Episcopal Church was frugal, practical, respectable and extremely conservative. Processes and decisions were simple and action was direct.

We moved into Emily Cunningham's house on Cedar Street. Mrs. Cunningham, widow of the former rector, lived in "the Dower house" behind us on the hill. Fisher Ames, the town librarian, lived in the big house on the right and Dr. Connie King in the house on the left. He was the only physician in town.

In those days none of the houses in town had numbers. Each one was called by the name of the family who lived there. Our house was called the Cunningham House, after the Cunningham family, who owned it. Sometimes this system of naming was not exactly a practical custom. When the minister was told that a child had been hurt by a car in the driveway of the Peterson house, John discovered there were sixteen Peterson houses in town. Fortunately, he chose the right house quickly to go and help the child.

There was no running water in the church. We walked over carrying jugs for the flowers. Once the gallon jug was too heavy for my fingers and I left it behind the fence which surrounded the Cable Office.

Our first official visitor came on moving day. Miss Annette DeCoursey, a most devout and devoted lady. She called through the pouring rain, "I have come to apologize for the weather." We ran to open the front door to let her in. It was a dutch door, open only at the top. The key was missing. She climbed over the lower door.

The church in winter was too large to be heated for the very small congregation who attended. Upstairs—yes, up those same stairs in present use (before builders followed the rule to make all stairs and risers of equal height)—was a chapel, small enough to accommodate the winter congregation. The pews were benches sawed in half with the arms forming an aisle down the center. The chapel was painted by a group of young Episcopalians visiting the Philbricks for one of many active weekends.

Along about April, Duxbury began to get ready for the summer people and Saint John's Church moved downstairs. The summer friends had been coming for many years and they rightly considered it their church. They were also generous in their support.

One has to be aware that everything was simpler and less sophisticated in those days. People lived in the same houses for generations and everyone knew everyone else. Every summer it was not unusual for Mrs. Cunningham and Mrs. Soule to walk from house to house requesting financial help "so the little church can stay open all winter." Mrs. Cunningham gave a Silver Tea to raise money for the church. No one could miss her printed sign "Nickels are NOT silver." Mrs. Soule's neighbor was high on a ladder in the hot sun repairing his house on Sunday afternoon. He called down "What can I do for you, Mrs. Soule?"

She spoke firmly: "If you'll go in the house and put on some clothes, I'll talk to you." He gave generously to the church.

Wednesday was the day the Senior Guild met at Mrs. Maude Bigelow's house at the corner of Washington Street and Winsor Lane (now Winsor Street). Her house had been a tavern often visited by Daniel Webster who named it "Cracker Tavern," and her hospitality was all-embracing. Her big oval dining room table seated at least a dozen people, and a smaller table by the settee in front of the fireplace accommodated six or seven others.

Mrs. Bigelow, whose marriage to a clergyman was terminated by his untimely death after three years, was a distinguished and courtly lady. She used to say, "Every meeting of the Guild is always a lovely party." John Philbrick's strong conviction was that the way to insure the parties would always be lovely and peaceable was for him to be right there to keep the peace. The very first meeting made an unforgettable impression on me. The early formalities having been completed, the details of old business were coming up. Suddenly Mrs. Cunningham, at the other end of the table arranging her veil below her hat said loudly, "This meeting is getting boring. I'm going home," and she got up and stomped out, brandishing her cane. (The same lady, our Mrs. Cunningham, even made *The New Yorker* witticism contest one summer in a report of the Ladies' food table which read: Mrs. Cunningham presided over the table full of jams and jellies.")

The ladies must have given freely to every missionary appeal. They, of course, helped supply the needs of the church and the altar guild. For several years, Miss Frances Howland was on the Diocesan Board for the Women's Church Service League, as it was called in those days.

A Junior Guild assembled by Mrs. Jacobs met around at each other's houses. They, too, worked faithfully for the good of the church. This special help was most welcome at the time of the Fair.

The Saint John's Fair followed the timeless pattern of all church fairs—some potholders, a table full of cakes and jellies, perhaps a few plants. There might even be a poster or two advertising "From 10 to 2." Around one thirty no new customers were appearing and it was quick work to gather up everything to be ready to leave at two o'clock.

The site in the 1930s-1960s was old Sprague Hall, now the Queenies's dwelling house. It stood squarely in the middle of what is now Beaver Brook Lane. The "hall" historically was part of Seth Sprague's shipyard and was built for a sail loft and "head" for his working crew who were building ships. It had been used as an Odd Fellows Hall but in 1895 when the Odd Fellows built Mattakeeset Hall, it was given to St. John's Church and was named Sprague Hall.

As a parish hall it had some memorable features. First and foremost the toilet. The seat raised at a 45° angle. When the seat was pressed level, a valve was opened in the water pipe below the frost level. While one sat on the seat the water rushed up and filled the tank, which then flushed by itself. No danger of frozen water pipes in that lavatory! But the shock of the rushing water was *memorable*.

The next most memorable feature for a public building was the window structure. They were very tall, divided horizontally by the second floor. This created a space beside each window which acted as a sound tunnel. Anything said downstairs could be heard upstairs. Gossip aired upstairs was heard downstairs. Anyone involved in parish work does well to learn discretion and the value of holding one's tongue.

Those same windows were unscreened. The church members who gathered one July evening for the Saint John's Annual Meeting, chaired by Archdeacon Bartow, could hardly hear the items of business above the din of members slapping mosquitoes.

With a young clergyman and a loyal parish, the work began to grow. It was not always easy to make changes. When an improvement was suggested, the customary answer was inevitably: "No, not this time."

We were going to have a parish fair at a handsome house on Washington Street. It seemed only hospitable to suggest sandwiches for the workers, but the suggestion had received the routine NO. This was my idea: as minister's wife I could make a lot of sandwiches and just sneak them in anonymously with the White Elephants. In those days one put a sandwich in an envelope called glassine, neat and clean and made of waxed paper—before plastic. The boxful of sandwiches was on the back seat of the car when the door was opened, and somehow the box tipped over and strewed the slippery glassine sandwiches halfway across the lawn. No more disguise, no more anonymity!

Like many of life's apparent calamities, that was the beginning of a new development: church fairs with plenty of food. The ladies did the luncheons with exquisite attention to details. The men got together for fifteen minutes and executed the details for a fried chicken supper—outdoors, informal. It was fun. We had auctions. We brought in unheard of amounts of money.

The fried chicken for the men's supper at the Fair came from Faith Homestead. We also raised and packed and delivered cratefuls of fresh laid eggs for Saint Margaret's Convent in Boston during those war years. We had the Convent's summer camp spend a week doing their "war work" at the Homestead.

1942-43: As I've mentioned, World War II was uppermost in everyone's mind. From this clergyman's point of view, the appropriate work was to grow as much food as possible. With an inheritance, we bought the house on West Street, named it Faith Homestead, and proceeded to produce milk goats, sheep, hens, pigs, angora rabbits, vegetables and fruits, thus becoming pioneers in the Homestead movement, teaching some ancient arts which needed to be restored to backyards all over America. The movement which started way back then is still strong, and a great many lives were changed by the influence of a couple of crazy pioneers (who were sometimes observed with slightly raised eyebrows by the conservative part of the church). Enough of that!

Chapter 12

Stone Bridge/ Faith Homestead/ Peterson House

When John's father died, we were already established in our favorite town, Duxbury, and it suddenly became possible to think about buying a house. In those years there were only two real estate gentlemen in town. One was Jo Lund who sometimes went to Boston, and the other was Mr. Percy Walker, who took care of real estate matters for local people year-round and especially cared for the needs of the summer people who came faithfully to enjoy the charm of seashore living.

Mr. Walker came to talk about available houses in Duxbury. He came in and John invited him into his office. Mr. Walker sat down behind John's desk and proceeded to describe all the houses that were for sale. During the interview, Mr. Walker asked John, "Did you ever know Captain Jonathan Appleby?" When John expressed regret that he had never known him, Mr. Walker said, "Well now, there was a character." Our town had many memorable "characters" in those days. And John recognized that Mr. Walker was also a "character" whom we all loved and respected.

But to get back to Mr. Walker and the possibility of buying a house. It was past the middle of September and all the summer people had gone home for the beginning of the school year. Mr. Walker drove us to the nearest house that was now empty. There were no secrets. He led us into every room downstairs and upstairs

103

of every house in sight. Sometimes he even showed us the well-packed attic of an available home. When I look back, I have a feeling of familiarity for at least a dozen houses which he showed us. Finally we found the right house and the negotiations commenced.

Using that word reminds me of a tradition we had heard about Mr. Walker's repartee when he answered the phone in the early days of the telephone. We were told that when the phone rang, Mr. Walker would lift the receiver and say, "commence the conversation." Anyway, we moved into this house, built in 1772, which has sheltered us well for about 60 years. We named it Faith Homestead to keep company with Douglas and Dorothy Pease's house which they named Hope Hollow.

Twenty more years passed before the houses in this little old farming town were identified by street numbers. Cove Street did have numbers, perhaps to identify the houses with bad reputations. Otherwise, every house bore the name of its inhabitants. It was sometime many years later that the town officially required numbers on every house. During the years we were in Missouri we rented Faith Homestead to Mr. and Mrs. Benjamin Alden, who had a grown-up son, Willard, who taught school. The Year of the House Numbers we received a letter from Willard telling us that he had followed the instructions from the town regarding house numbers. He was informing us that our house was now number 165 West Street. He had undertaken the small task of numbering both the house and the mailbox on the street. What he waited for us to find out when we came to visit our tenants was that he had also put a number on the old cobbler shop in the back yard. But on said cobbler shop, the number was in Roman Numerals: CLXV.

The house we bought with the cooperation of the bank had belonged to the Peterson family for about four generations. It had undergone a few changes, but the original house is still extant and very habitable. The original house, which had been built in 1772, was purchased by Thaddeus Peterson when he was preparing to be married. He bought it from Judah Delano and here follows the proof of purchase from the Plymouth County Registry of Deeds.

Book 120, Page 50, recorded December 5, 1805
(Book 57, Page 184 Plymouth County Registry of Deeds.
Copied 1976
Judah Delano to Seth Sprague, 20 November 1793

Know ALL MEN BY THESE PRESENTS that I, *Judah Delano* of Duxborough in the County of Plymouth in New England, *yeoman* for and in Consideration of the Sum of one hundred Spanish milled dollars to me paid by Seth Sprague of Duxburough,—yeoman—a certain piece of Cedar swamp lying on the town of Duxborough at a place called *North Hill* and is bounded as follows viz, beginning at a sts in *the Range of Thaddeus Peterson's land* at a place called the *Stone Bridge* right against a *point of upland* that makes a narrow place in my swamp where we cart accrost the swamp, thence running west in the range of said Peterson's land to the brook called *North Hill Brook* to a tree marked running upstream by the brook to a sts standing in the range of Thomas Weston's swamp line, thence running easterly in the range or line of Thomas Weston to a sts standing at the stone bridge or cart way across the swamp near the point of upland. Thence running *northerly* by the *stone bridge* or path across. The swamp to the first mentioned bound in the range of *Thaddeus Peterson's land* about three acres more or less. To have and to hold all the above piece of cedar swamp as above described with all the profits, privileges, and appurtenances thereunto belonging with the *privilege of a cartway, not* thru Peterson's land, to and from said swamp through my land where it shall be most convenient to said Sprague and lease prejudicial to said Judah Delano and I the said Judah Delano do promise to warrant and defend the above bargained premises against all the legal claims of all persons whomsoever—and Lydia Delano, wife of

Judah Delano, doth by these presents give up all her right of dower or power of shares on or unto the above bargained premises. In witness and confirmation hereof we the above said Judah Delano and Lydia Delano his wife have hereunto set our hand and seal this 20th day of November, 1783 signed sealed and delivered in presence of

Charles Thomas   Judah Delano
Philip Delano   Lydia Delano

Plymouth, December 3, 1805 Then Judah Delano acknowledged the above by him subscribed to be his act and deed before me
Judah Alden, Justice of the Peace

Received March 25, 1813 and recorded

We have been told on good authority that in the above thirteen pounds, six shillings & eight pence quotation the six shillings and eight pence really meant one-third of a pound.

Another observation: in many such documents one often finds frequent reference to finding "sts on the southerly side of said way . . ." That was just their shorthand treatment of "stake and stones," which was literally a pile of stones surrounding a piece of wood to verify the accuracy of that spot.

After we became owners, we evaluated our five acres, which revealed evidences of an old farmstead. There was an old hen house we could use for the hens to produce eggs. Gradually, we added one item after another when it became evident that we should be raising food because of the wartime stringencies.

The white pine woods were a special joy to walk and find the old woods roads. One day John Merry, the youngest son of Hortense E. Merry, a venerable dairy farmer who lived on North Hill, came out of "our woods" and told us he had a right of way over our place. It was true. The Right of Way was a continuation of the Old Stone Bridge and it led through our east field and out to the road. We later found evidence of the old road when the grain we sowed in that field grew with a barren streak which marked the trail they had trampled down when they hauled things from North Hill farm out to the road.

    St. John's in those years consisted of a very small number of people, mostly older women, who were very faithful but who were quite willing to let a couple of youthful enthusiasts undertake the active work around the Church. There was no Altar Guild to decorate the Church for that critical midnight service. John did tell the Senior Warden that there would be a service with candles. The Warden did not forbid him. He only said "You'll burn the church down."

    John developed the War Chapel in the little upstairs room, where everyone could worship and ponder the spiritual questions raised by the war or pray for the soldiers. It was open all week. There were services on Wednesdays and there were intercessions and a special ministry for everyone. A candle always burned. They were special long burning candles in Pyrex glass. For one midnight service, John and I actually climbed out on the rood screen, one on each side, to place the special candles for the service.

    There was no invasion. Although there never was barbed wire on Duxbury Beach, it was steadily patrolled by both soldiers and local civilians. The latter were most conscientious and vigilant to keep Duxbury in the dark. Everyone had to paint their headlights with black paint, and someone even scolded me for cheating by opening the refrigerator door to get some light one evening.

    It was wartime and everyone gave whatever he or she had to give for the "War Effort." Some of us made bandages in the Old Sailors' Home, now torn down. Every part of our lives was devoted day and night to our knowledge and consciousness of the terrible war in Europe.

    At night we were still made conscious of the war because the Civil Patrol was trained to see that no lights were visible in case Hitler's armies might be trying to land from ships off Duxbury Bay. When the Roman Catholic Church sent out an order to all the RC churches that there was to be no midnight mass on

Christmas Eve in case there might be an invasion, John's response was: "What could be a better place to be than in a church?" We had the service and that was the occasion when John and I had earlier prepared the church by climbing out over the Rood Screen to place candles.

Faith Homestead

Because we had just bought a house with some land, we felt we must also add our effort to the war work by raising food. We decided the most immediate food production would be a flock of laying hens. There was already a large henhouse in the back field. Hens were easy to acquire and the daily eggs were practical to gather and give away if there was need. It wasn't long before we were also adding chicken to the family menu.

Next were two milk goats, which we named Aggie and Lizzie for the sisters of a former rector of the church we had just left in Weymouth. They were famous for hauling milk along the sidewalk in a small cart to deliver to needy parishioners. Some things were still rather primitive in the 1930s, even in Weymouth!

Lizzie and Aggie were delightful pets, full of mischief but also producers of good rich milk. And we learned reams of information. In the first place, only a buck goat smells. The does have no more smell than a cat. We proved it every day when we went into the new barn we had built—which is still standing (now as an office). Either John or I would do the milking two times a day, preferably about twelve hours apart.

We would go into the milk room and call out "First Goat" and Lizzie would jump up on the milking bench. We would put the stainless steel milk pail with the removable cover on the bench below her and proceed to milk her. If she lifted a hind hoof it was still small enough to control with one hand to prevent the abhorred hoof in the bucket that is one peril in milking a cow. The secret of good tasting goat milk is to chill it immediately, and then it tastes like cow's milk. Over the years, we had several good milkers and we were proud to purchase—for about thirty dollars apiece— two more milk goats with titles and pedigrees from the mythically famous Ingersoll herd in Bourne. Mrs. Ingersoll had given them the names of Leiden Lassie and Leiden Lantern Light from the Ingersoll Leiden herd.

Leiden Lassie was a Toggenberg with a special interest in cloth. I recall her always nipping at whatever skirt I was wearing. Of course, milk goats, like cows, have no upper teeth, only a soft warm pad in the top of the mouth (like the baby calf you remember sucking your hand). No teeth, but she still could gobble down a five-dollar rose bush in a twinkling. She never looked at a two-dollar rose bush.

In spring there was a surplus of milk and we learned to make wheels of cheese in the round flat tins coffee came in. A one-pound tin made a two-or-three-pound wheel of cheese like cheddar, which we dipped in paraffin just like the big cheeses professionally made in the dairy. Of course the milk goats had to be bred so they would have kids to continue the production of milk. We used to take the back seat out of our automobile and put Lizzie or Aggie into the space while we drove her over to Brockton to a large milk goat dairy to meet a buck.

Now we can talk about the smell of a goat. When the buck is ready to inseminate the does, he takes on a rather musty indescribable smell which only exists during what one might call his rutting season. The people who talk loudest about how obnoxious goats are, are always the neat people who never even looked at a milk goat, and they have missed a lot of fun.

It was true even back in the 1940s that people who could not tolerate cow's milk could easily digest goat's milk, which is now available canned in many grocery stores. There was even back then one dairy that specialized in goat ice cream. The milk goats in our small dairy were proud to hear about it.

I have to admit that I just couldn't resist the temptation to try to squirt milk into the cat's mouth when she happened to stray into the milk room. It wasn't long before the cat was right on hand beside Lizzie with her mouth ready to open. The first drops of warm milk made her open wide. The milk tasted so good, she would come closer and closer with mouth open to catch every drop. The length of the stream of milk got shorter and shorter until she was right underneath the patient Lizzie—and I was somewhat penitent for wasting the good milk.

Another of the minister's errands was to ferry Miss Alice Henderson's milk goat to the Brockton goat dairy to have her bred. Miss Alice and her sister had another sister who for years had been confined to her bed and who required special invalid's food. Their milk goat named Pansy Petunia lived in their barn. It had been an ancient school house, with plastered walls.

The usual rule in the milk goat world is always to have two does together because one alone will pine and bleat constantly. Miss Alice worked in Boston, taking the train from the Duxbury station every day. When she retired she would prepare Pansy Petunia's salad. When she took it out, she always took along her knitting and sat down so Pansy Petunia would have some company.

As economics evolved in those post-war days, many new families were moving into Duxbury. Old houses were coming on the market and young couples were remodeling old houses. These younger people were finding themselves at home at Saint John's Church. The Church was growing. The couples wanted to get together to talk about their interests, perhaps to help each other with their building. By the time they met, there were about 30 couples. They wanted to meet but not to organize. They didn't even want a name. The group became a congenial assembly who liked to see each other formally, but mostly informally. They decided to call themselves the Nameless Group. When a notice on the front page of *The Duxbury Clipper* quoted the Nameless title, Jimmie Ingalls, organist of the Unitarian Church, murmured "The poor bastards." His quotation traveled from his house to Paul Peterson's drug store, a local rendezvous in those days. When the Reverend John walked into the drug store one day, Mr. Peterson told him what Jimmie Ingalls had said. John shot right back, "Paul, from now on they will be known as Father John's children." The members of the Nameless Group were always coming to ask questions about breeds and how to shear sheep, all the practical arts of the small farm.

On summer Sundays we always looked for Bishop Frederick Lawrence who lived in an ancient Winslow house in Marshfield. He would come with his lovely wife Katharine and a group of smaller Lawrences of assorted sizes. They filled a couple of pews of the summer congregations. Across from them would be the Sister of Saint Margaret from the convent in South Duxbury, which originally was called St. Margaret's Hospital, their Boston name and vocation. With these special friends and the summer regulars and all the new Duxbury residents, John used to remark that he hardly knew what to preach about.

Anyway, they came often to Faith Homestead to see the milk goats or to learn how to build a hen house. By this time we had added three sheep. Hort Merry had walked them down from North Hill to our shed for ten dollars apiece. We named them Nancy, Susie, and Emma. Emma was probably a Hampshire, but Nancy and Susie were both Corriedales.

By this time, Winthrop and Jane Coffin, who lived in the big white house on Washington Street, had decided they really should no longer keep two geese in their yard. "Would we like to have the two geese?" Would we ever! When they came we named them Cabot and Lowell from the Old Bostonian rhyme:

> Here's to good old Boston
> The home of the bean and the cod
> Where the Cabots speak only to Lowells
> And the Lowells speak only to God.

"Cabot" and "Lowell" were excellent watchdogs. They helped our dog Samson—a cross between German shepherd and Labrador.

"Woody" was the name we all loved, as we loved Woody himself and his wife Barbara. His proper name was Barclay Jeffries Woodward. He had retired from the military and was active in the Nameless Group. His family, like several other Duxbury families, had milk goats and rejoiced in the home grown fresh milk. Woody stopped in one day to ask if we would like to add three re-deployed carrier pigeons to our small farm. Of course we would. With the help of others of "Father John's children," we built a large kind of rookery for the three pigeons, who came and flew around and multiplied until we had a flock of 80 or more. It used to be part of the ceremony of greeting a new day when the great flock of pigeons wheeled up out of their house and traveled off into the sky on their various missions. We gave many away and probably many came back. We had intended to use them as squab but never really wanted to kill any of them.

Pioneers Unaware

When the *Boston Sunday Globe* was delivered to us on Sunday morning, April 7th in the year 1946, the first shoe dropped! I read the headline and hid the whole paper. My fear was that if our parishioners read those headlines, St. John's Church might just fire their new minister. The pictures were too good (by Earl Banner) and I expected trouble if the parishioners saw Father John in his cassock feeding the hens. The headlines read: "Rev. and Mrs. John Philbrick Have Almost Every Young Couple in Town Farming." My fears were calmed when the young people in the Nameless Group rejoiced to see their minister feeding his hens just as they had to feed theirs. That was the first shoe.

We had no intention of big time farming, but we observed that the church was thriving with the advent of young families who welcomed some casual introduction to growing their own vegetable gardens without the poisonous sprays that had already appeared.

Little did anyone realize, the Philbricks included, that we were pioneers in a new effort to produce food. Shortly after that date, when Scot and Helen Nearing became famous producers, it became evident there was a movement afoot. All of us organic gardeners were becoming members. Our very local practice was so new and so small we never realized we were pioneers of what is now so strong and so much more developed that whole farms across the country are changing to organic and our stores sell organically grown food every day. The other shoes have never stopped dropping!

Angora Rabbits

When our soldiers came back into their former world here in America, many of them were in search of new jobs. Sometimes they came to talk with the minister about work. We saw this new development as an opportunity to try everything ourselves as a possible example to someone who might be searching.

A new cottage industry had recently sprung into being: Angora rabbits. There were fabulous stories about their silky white wool, which would sell for fifteen dollars for a large grocery bag filled full of long staple, white wool, plucked from the rabbits. Our rabbits lived in the old Cobbler Shop, each rabbit in its own wire cage. They had feed and water at the same time each day. They lived calm peaceful lives, producing valuable white Angora wool.

We kept careful records of all the vital statistics. Every day, people visited to see the rabbits or to help shear the sheep in season. Parents brought their children and their neighbors' children to romp with the milk goats or to learn how geese can work as watchdogs. With so many visitors coming to inspect Faith Homestead, sometimes we never had time for a meal all day. Sundays we were usually fairly proper and attended church services several times a day. But for the rest of the week, this small farm was a center of information and encouragement to anyone who came to learn.

Chapter 13

Biodynamic Gardening

Soon after we moved into the house in Duxbury, we learned about a conference for backyard gardeners and set off for Spring Valley, about thirty miles from New York City. There were about 25 people at this new kind of conference, called Biodynamics, derived from two German words that meant "the dynamic activity inherent in living plants." It was strong in European countries, having been taught by the philosopher Rudolf Steiner. Biodynamics was based on Steiner's philosophy of anthroposophy. Michael Dobson and Christopher Bamford wrote in a 1991 letter from the Anthroposophic Press that "Anthroposophy is a spiritual movement reuniting what is spiritual in the universe. Its strength and purpose depend upon our courageously working together and becoming alive inwardly, so that spiritual beings who care for the earth and humanity can work together with us for the sake of the whole."

John and I were glad to learn how to manage a garden, large or small, without using the new chemical fertilizers that were just then being advertised. We learned to make good compost, and we learned that Biodynamics produced food of excellent quality by following rather simple practices. We also were impressed with the friends who helped us to learn.

From its start in Germany in the 1800s, it is now in almost every country we could name around the globe. Very exact in some ways, it is lenient in others. There are more and more large conferences all over the U.S. It is perhaps a bit more mystical than Organic, paying more attention to the Elementals, which are the influences we live with: the soil, the rain, heat and cold, and the strongest intention is to help our agriculture to heal our earth. There are regular publications with volumes of information, and it appears currently that Biodynamics is growing everywhere, in many countries.

We had to learn first in order to teach and studied under a scientist who also was an agriculturist, Dr. Ehrenfried Pfeiffer. He had arrived in America just ahead of the second World War and his knowledge was tremendous. New at gardening, we were eager to learn a new system.

Dr. Pfeiffer called it in German Biologisch Dynamische. In English that meant to watch for the dynamic happenings going on in the biology of the garden. We learned to make good compost to nourish the vegetables growing in the gardens. We learned how to make valuable compost using the droppings of all the Homestead animals. Our gardens flourished and we taught anyone who wanted to learn the secrets of Biodynamic gardening. We spent every vacation we could get away learning more at Spring Valley. Then we would rush home and dig up another garden.

Perhaps the most important lesson was close observation of whatever is happening in the world of nature. In the course of our studies we also learned that Biodynamic vegetables and fruits were carefully tended not with chemicals, but with homegrown natural materials that helped the earth itself to retain and develop its fertility—and all the time these Biodynamic gardeners were carefully observing everything. The purpose of Biodynamics is to heal the earth.

Biodynamics has become the technique for growing nourishing and profuse crops. (Biodynamic crops that meet the strictest standards are certified by Demeter, an organization that has taken the name of the ancient Greek goddess of agriculture and of the fruitfulness of mankind and guardian of marriage.) More than that, the use of Biodynamic preparations is helping the surface of our planet in every country.

The demands of Biodynamics took up half of our Duxbury summers and the demands of St. John's active summer parishioners took up more than their share. The result was that we had to give up our ninety-nine year lease on our holding at Brightwater. The buyers were friends and they built a modest summer cottage against our whole one-room house, ten by fifteen feet square, making our former house one bedroom of the larger house. It was a practical solution that everyone endorsed. But we were sad to give up our one-room castle in the woods and, worse than that, to leave our beloved friends.

> A salutation goes to one whose expert garden toil
> Results in first prize crops of all that's nourished by the soil;
> Of all his splendid produce he is not an advertiser,
> Except that even stones grow best with Natural Fertilizer.
> —Source unknown (probably a friend or neighbor)

School Teacher

Shortly after we bought this house, which cemented us here as Duxbury citizens, there was an opening for a teacher in a private school a few miles from home. It was a small school with perhaps two or three dozen students of various ages. When the owner, superintendent, head teacher, and boss—all the same person—tried to hire me, I denied ever having any training or experience related to teaching. He waved me down and said, "But you have a bright look and that will be sufficient." He assigned me to teach third and fourth grades, which consisted of about eight children.

Since several of the children in the school lived in Duxbury, our ever-challenging head of the school—his first name was Nathan—coaxed John to be the chauffeur who delivered all the Duxbury children and the teacher every day. There were five or six other faculty members who welcomed the Duxbury group with great enthusiasm and school opened.

The classrooms were located in several small buildings at odd places on the farm. Some classrooms and a room known as "the Great Study" were in the big old farmhouse. There was an active barnyard and barn. Chickens and other poultry supplied eggs and meat. There were several cows for a milk supply. The oldest of the students tended the cows and brought in the milk. It all appeared to be an ideal arrangement for a small rural school. There was never any mention of salary.

Soon the school program began to function. Everyone knew where to go, and the day's program was working smoothly. Nathan made an effort to bring the entire faculty together often, and he would lecture to us, dynamically pointing out all the unusual privileges and specialties of the whole school. His long teachers' meetings were well lubricated by wine, strong coffee, and his increasingly intense proclamations.

After a while it became apparent that any child who was delinquent in his learning was spanked. Some of us thought this was not a very good practice, but the teachers who had been there awhile explained that at that time there were no laws regulating private schools. We teachers had no recourse. There was nothing we could do. As the year went on, things became stranger and stranger. My third and fourth grades were given the assignment to straighten out a huge woodpile of big boards and scrap lumber.

In the classroom one day we were having a spelling class. The next word in the list was "penguin." On the blackboard I had written: pen—when the door blew open and Nathan burst in and said, "Pick up all your books and papers and chairs, and take them all up to the Great Study. That will be your classroom from now on. This room will be the boys' dormitory because the present boys' dormitory will be the new kitchen." On the blackboard of the Great Study I finished "penguin." Nathan's dynamic personality worked on all of us to the extent that we went through the whole year switching from one program to another almost literally at the drop of a hat.

One day he proclaimed there would be a cold cellar built right here under our feet, and the boys' mathematics class would begin immediately to figure the dimensions. He also admired our house here a few miles from the school and tried to convince us we should make some classrooms in the house to facilitate the changes he had planned for the school over there. He wanted to annex this house to enlarge the school.

His schemes went beyond even this area. He and his long-suffering wife used to go to two favorite cities: New York City and Cincinnati, Ohio. They would hire rooms in a hotel where they would interview parents who had children they wanted to send away to school—with the stipulation that the parents would not be coming to visit the school. Then he would present them with a handsome school catalog showing the school family having a meal at a big table on the terrace overlooking the farm pond in the near distance. He never explained to the prospective parents that on this side of the terrace was the big open pit that would sometime be finished as the storage cellar for the garden vegetables.

School had finished in the spring. One day Nathan's wife called on the phone. Her message was that "money is very tight this spring. We're sorry but there will not be any salary." It was no surprise. By then, I had experienced enough of his terrible rules and mercurial behavior. Other teachers from other years, we learned, all had the same message. We also learned later that the boy who could not learn to read was dyslexic and was seriously affected by all the spankings administered by the headmaster.

Fortunately, now there are enough laws to prevent such treatment in a private school.

A year or so later—c.1944

There was need of a teacher for the "Opportunity Class" in the Duxbury school system—eight boys with learning disabilities. Because of my degree as an Occupational Therapist, I could be hired to keep order in the little class held in what is now named the Setter Room of the Duxbury Library.

The boys were fairly cooperative, but still a little mischievous. When I provided them with toothbrushes and tooth powder (because I knew what could be done with toothpaste), they sprinkled tooth powder up the long stairway to the Boys' Room—and the Custodian came and scolded me.

One lad really was a problem. One morning our School Superintendent, who was very thoughtful and kind, stopped to tell me that he had just learned a new way to help control an overactive child. He said, "If your lad gets unruly today, please call me and I will come to help." The latter part of the morning the unruly boy began to act out, and I sent out a request for help from the Superintendent. He came and gently took the boy away. The class quieted down and all was peaceful in the classroom.

The Superintendent's office was upstairs in a nearby house with an empty room adjoining. His strategy to help quiet the child was to wrap him in a blanket and lay him down on the floor in the empty room where it was so quiet that he might go to sleep. It all went well except that a PTA meeting was scheduled for that evening. An active mother needed to see the Superintendent. She happened to come upstairs by the back door so she had to walk through the room with the child wrapped in a blanket. She exploded. Such cruelty—and on and on. When the Superintendent explained, she understood and peace returned.

But the saddest part of the story was still to be revealed: during recess the boy had bought two Eskimo Pies—there had been one in each pocket while he was wrapped up in the cozy warm blanket. At that point, I decided to end my career as a teacher.

Herman Smith

We had lived at Faith Homestead for several years when Carl de Suze phoned us that Duxbury was soon to be honored by a spectacular personage named Herman Smith. Carl explained that Herman had owned and run a very exclusive restaurant in northern Connecticut where one had to have made reservations to be admitted. His reputation had spread all over the most sophisticated dietary world and his creations were without peer. Carl, by way of introducing us to each other, had prophesied with Carl's usual word skill that I would probably weave Mr. Smith a delicious salad while he might cook me a beautiful dress. (Carl specialized in twisting facts!)

As this story developed we learned that Mr. Smith was a close friend of the Weber-Fulops who lived in the house once owned by Ezra Weston, the shipmaster who had a worldwide reputation as the owner of ships in the 1770s and early 1800s. (The Duxbury Rural and Historical Society later purchased this building, which is now known as the King Caesar House.) With Carl's introduction, Herman Smith and his man Charlie Mullen became our friends. They lived in the cottage connected with the big house.

Herman Smith had a slight infirmity, which made him dependent on "Mullen" to help him with entertaining. Instead of a dining table, he had a long and wide marble slab where a dinner would be laid out and guests were free to help themselves. Friends were introduced to other friends and soon Carl de Suze came and introduced us all to Marjorie Mills, a radio personality who broadcast a program over WBZ every noon. She had what she called her "mouse's nest" of little papers to advertise a tremendous variety of food products. "Confidentially," she said one day, "I am just another Feed Bag Fanny."

Her program every day was a hodge-podge of advertisements and recipes and philosophical thoughts, and always bits of humor. There was usually a deep expression of the happy relationship between Marge and Carl. And their audience was eager to share in the serious and in the humorous. For instance, one day Carl said to Marge "You know, Marge, that after one is forty she has the face she deserves. But I think you have a much better face than—Oh no, that's not what I meant to say. I really meant to tell you that you deserve a much better—Oh dear, I'd better change the subject." They both laughed and some of us have never forgotten what a memorable pair they were back in the old days of radio—before television had been invented.

In reality, Marge was a wise and compassionate woman with a steady sense of humor, and Carl de Suze was her "straight man." Of course our old childhood friend introduced Herman Smith and Marjorie Mills to the Philbricks, and Herman appeared every Thursday on "the daily chat." It wasn't long before Faith Homestead in Duxbury was part of the WBZ noontime "Soap Opera." Carl would start the program by telling Marge that Faith Homestead has three newborn lambs. He would mention in passing that the Homestead produced the eggs that Herman Smith used when he made the soufflé. Or "the latest event at the Homestead this week is the addition of a pair of Toulouse Geese."

When the school superintendent brought three baby pigs to be raised at the Homestead, the word went out that they were named Faith, Hope, and Charity. This was a neat touch for the Soap Opera—and we listened to hear Marge speculate on the ensuing bacon as she enumerated, "Now I must have Faith that I will be remembered when the bacon is passed around. I certainly Hope so. And that would certainly be an act of Charity."

Even today if I mention WBZ and the Marjorie Mills show, or the name Carl de Suze, people often recall that they used to listen to that noontime program. Carl wrote to us his tribute to Marge telling how they had gone to visit on Nantucket. There had been a death in a friend's family. Carl's poem seemed to write itself as he revealed Marge's compassion for the needy family having to cope with a sad situation.

The free-form poem Carl sent to me is one of his most tender in observing and telling what had happened, with a very soft touch of humor, gentle, not mean, touching upon the shine of the minister's old best suit and quoting the minister's actual subtle quotation: "They almost didn't ask me to come."

The background of the story was that Carl and Marjorie Mills were at her house in Nantucket, where she had lived for many years. They went to a grocery store to buy food, but also for Marge to "puff" (obviously a food promoter's term) some items for the store.

In the store they met an old friend of Marge's who told her about the recent death of a mutual friend who lived with her husband Norman and her sister. They had had hard times and it was all very sad. Then she asked if Marge would drop in just to see the bereaved husband and the helpless sister.

Marge was immediately touched, and she and Carl bought flowers and other items to make the dreary funeral a little more bearable.

Carl told us that the whole episode was so intimate, and Marge's kindness made such a quiet change, that he was suddenly moved to write it all down, and here it is—a kind of word picture that does take a little quiet study.

"Good God," a voice named Harvey grumbled.
Who brought all this?"
We had been led to a porch entrance
Hesitant shapes reflected in the door's beveled glass.
Two rocking chairs, sagged and silent,
In not too friendly union, stood watch with rusted glider
Among the Autumn-leaved neglect.
We'd been asked to come, Marge added,
Because a neighbor spotted us at the supermarket
Where we had gone to puff some product or local opening.
(Part of our pledge to radio sponsors of the Daily Chat.)
And the half-apologetic minister, flock-worn, bent,
The late sun burnishing the shine
From his worn black double-breasted, said,
"Well, I'm surprised they even asked me!" He felt
He was an after-thought like most religion,
Dropped in because a kin had reasoned, "now really—
It would be proper. No clergy? What would people say?"
Hurled rectitude from a sister the loved one never liked.
Forlorn herself, and cornered for once by cares other
    than her own,
Impatient with empty duties for this one fled from
    loneliness
Lying unknown among strangers, children, friends gone
As spent days leave home, by puzzled hour forgotten
    rooms—
"We need some flowers," Marge said, quickly taking charge.
I was dispatched—the market was still open—to claim
    those bargain blooms
Flaming with one last burst of color before the weekend
    fodder.
Marge broke up the groups of aimless,
Pointing everyone to tasks—even the minister.
Two orderlies from the house had brought the coffin.
"Everything prepaid," they noted cheerfully,

Hustling about, two high-schoolers, I guessed,
Needing a little money before college.
They made room for the drop-leaf table and its burden
In the parlor meant for formal teas and less than joyful calls.
Surroundings were mute with absence, grayed drapes,
A carpet drained of life, the plump stove resigned as
    folded hands
To these last changes. They set her out with space enough
For viewing, like the oblong copper boiler
Enthroned on the kitchen Greenwood
An eastern potentate of Lamdry awaiting obsequies
The minister prepared his smile, throats cleared,
Stillness invited wonders of end and beginnings
Impossible to link together. The stairway creaked
With heavy steps, and then the voice
"Good God—who brought all this?"
Startled, a woman answered, "Harvey, we thought that
    you were dead!"
"Not quite," he wheezed, "I spose I'm on Louisa's list—
Long lost brother and all that." "Well somebody had to do
    for"—
The hanging sentence dripped guilt and blame
Falling on silence, vexed healer of old discomforts.
The minister began his comforting drone, antique truths
In which we lost ourselves, Marge and I,
Strangers among strangers, yet more familiar to them
Than they were to each other, reminded us all, I think,
Of our inevitable sameness in things that matter.
Harry stared past Louise,
Past their playgrounds, past their battles,
Past hurt and shame and waste and longing.
In those few moments of shared togetherness
Marge's encompassing kindliness flowed life into graying
    elders
Even as her flowers warmed the dimmed memories of the
    room
The Reverend closed his book and we spilled out.
Divergent streams, separate again beyond each secret door.

Not Cost Effective

The most damning statement one can make at the present time is to call something "not cost effective." This has the effect of short-circuiting whatever is thus maligned, with the end result that the activity, whatever it is, must cease.

There is another dimension to be defended. For instance, the backyard garden never pays for itself in dollars and cents. What is the monetary value of a display of pure spring bulbs at the end of a long dark winter? The value is in the message that we have survived the cold and the dark and the uphill experience of winter. The warmth of the sunshine has returned, and our spirits are refreshed and reassured. Is there a dollar value for that experience?

Anyone who works fingers to the bone in a garden, or in any other cost-*in*effective but favorite occupation knows the intangible satisfaction of creating some kind of order out of chaos, a process. The process itself is the important part. The substance created may or may not be important.

The process of gardening seems have an inexplicable effect on many of us gardeners. We work so hard, we nearly exhaust ourselves and yet we keep on working. There is something about contact with earth and water, with exposure to sun and air (there are the classic four elements). Would we work half as hard inside the house?

In ancient times, human beings felt that everything had a spirit within. Animals, of course, had their own spirits—and still do—but plants and rocks and mountains and rivers all were imbued with their own spirits. Perhaps it is association with these strong but invisible and intangible qualities that endear nature to people.

Many wise people have studied hard and have created important theories to name and explain how a person "ticks," but after spending quite a few years in the process of creating a non-profit garden, just for love of the process, I am willing to grant that the substance of the garden is not my highest priority. For me the highest value is my love of the process itself.

Duxbury Beach

Duxbury was originally a very small area—not even a town until the County of Plymouth became organized after the well-known Landing of the Pilgrims. After a few years the space in Plymouth was not enough for the families and their fields. Families moved to farms and shore lots in Duxbury. Some paths had already been carved out of the wilderness and other pathways went from farm to farm or to the shore lots, which accounts for Duxbury's criss-cross roads today.

For many years as the town grew larger and the population increased, there was a small ship called the Packet, which came regularly across the inner bay to deliver goods and stock at Bourne's Wharf on the very edge of Marshfield. Goods were then delivered to Ford's Store on Tremont Street, claimed to be America's original "department store." As the town became better known and had summer visitors, Duxbury Beach became a popular destination, but as a barrier beach it was hard to get to from the mainland. So the town built Long Bridge to connect the beach with the mainland.

The Long Bridge prevented the Packet from reaching Bourne's Wharf and perhaps signaled the end of Ford's Store. But the Long Bridge inaugurated a different kind of activity in Duxbury. At last the beach was accessible to everyone. The evolution of the automobile was timely. There is a photograph of the bridge carrying a long procession of automobiles—every one of which was a Ford, all the same model.

Rules at first were casual. Anyone could drive to the beach and park anywhere. There was erosion and the sand dunes were being diminished by the cars.

The town built a spacious parking lot where one's car would not get stuck in the sand. But there were still hordes of people wanting to go to the beach. Parking permits were the only solution, controllable by their cost. A big sign at the land end of the Long Bridge displayed the rules in large and very legible letters.

John, the minister during those war days, was also filling in as a substitute teacher in the High School. The sign on the land end of the Long Bridge tickled his sense of humor. During recess he told the English teacher about the sign. She enjoyed the joke too. The next day when he walked past the English classroom, he saw the text of the Long Bridge sign written out on the blackboard. Obviously there had been a lesson on how to rearrange the existing words. The sign was as follows:

Parking RESTRICTED to residents with a sticker at the other end of the bridge.

The Gypsies

It was wartime and John had been teaching chemistry at the high school, where students baked bread and learned about good citizenship. One day, we were enjoying a rather humid afternoon up in the pinewoods where I was writing a letter. When I finished the letter, I walked down to the mailbox to mail it. There was an automobile in the driveway. As I came closer, I saw a live hen tied with a rope to the car. Up jumped two young men who were sitting on the ground watching a small fire they had built in the driveway. They were cooking something in a pan over the fire.

They were pleasant and laughing as they said, "We are Gypsies! And we asked at the drug store where was the nearest Protestant Minister. We are really ministers and were trained in the same seminary in Saloniki." I couldn't believe my ears. Saloniki is a Biblical name, familiar to all students. John came down from the woods and we invited them into the house. Each had a story to tell.

Willie Kahlert had worked in Germany for a court-type position where he was in charge of all social programs. This was only the beginning of the War and we knew very little yet about the Nazis. Willie had come to America on the great ship *Bremen*. As soon as the ship landed, it "disappeared"—that is, it was taken into custody for war work somewhere. Therefore, Willie could not return to Germany. The other clergyman was from Greece and his name was Focas Stavrianos, which he later translated and was known as Paul Cross.

We were very happy to "entertain Angels unaware." They were insistent that they wanted to sleep in their automobile, and they would like to drive into the woods to park. They said, "If we

can visit with you, mornings we work, afternoons we play."
Apparently in Europe people walk everywhere. As we listened to
war news, these two men could show us on the map exactly where
the action was. Willie even lived in a stone house which was a
thousand years old. He had family and friends over there and he
spent hours packing boxes of food to send across to those in
need.

They did work every morning after a big breakfast of hot
cereal, which they insisted on cooking for themselves. They
rearranged the east garden, changing its direction to east-west
where it had been north-south. They renamed what we had always
known as the Cobbler Shop. Inside were my Angora rabbits so
they named it "Rabbit Castle." In front and around Rabbit Castle,
they landscaped the little hill so it became a replica of Switzerland
containing the three highest of the Alps in each of the three
countries: France: Mont Blanc, Germany: Grosseglockner, and
Switzerland: die Jungfrau.

At night, they armed themselves with glass jars and flashlights
to go fishing off Long Bridge. Daytimes we included them in our
work and found them delightful companions. They dug a
barbeque pit in the backyard, and somewhere they bought a
large rabbit, so we all enjoyed barbequed rabbit, which I tactfully
skirted around after finding the rabbit's head in the oven in the
kitchen.

Willie became pastor of a fairly large church in Union, New
Jersey. Focas had a church in Woburn and we saw them both for
many years. We were invited to Focas's wedding at a big church
in Brookline. It was an arranged marriage but it was a happy
one, as we learned forty-eight years later when mutual friends in
South Yarmouth arranged for us all to meet after all those years.
Focas and Willie, our beloved "gypsies," have both gone on to
their next adventures.

Duxbury People and Places
Ray Taylor

One of Duxbury's favorites—I mean well-accepted and, in a
way, beloved—was Ray Taylor. We used to see him often walking

the different lanes and streets, carrying a burlap bag. He was gentle and friendly, often asking for some money. Sometimes he would work with the men who were mowing and loading hay on the wagons. Apparently he had a surprising talent for music. The story is told that he would sing at mid-week the hymn that had been sung in the First Church the Sunday before. He also could play the piano.

One early evening he came to our house. He said, "Mr. Philbrick, have you got some money for me?" John gave him a dime and he continued to walk down the road. Two ladies lived in the next house. It was getting dark and we knew someone from the police station would give Ray a ride past the ladies' house. The policeman knew Ray and he picked him up. Ray got in the car and grinned. "Mr. Philbrick's a nice man," he said. "He gave me a dime. But nothing is open."

A Small Summer Crisis—St. John's Church

There had been a strange smell in St. John's Church that no one could locate or identify. One Saturday afternoon John Philbrick asked the Warden, Donald Walker, to come to the church to remove the big pot-bellied stove that had heated the church for many years. Inside they found fourteen dead flickers which had come down the chimney and the long stove pipe and could not fly back. They had solved the long-standing mystery.

The next day was Sunday and Mrs. Addie Soule, the summer organist, arrived to play for the service. Mrs. Soule was an expert organist and she always chose the hymns. The service progressed well with hymns out of the old hymnal:

> "Pleasant are thy courts above
> In the land of light and love . . ."

The second stanza continued:

> "Happy birds that sing and fly
> Round thine altars, O most High!
> Happier souls that find a rest
> In the Heavenly Father's breast

> Like the wandering doves
> That found no repose on earth around
> They must to their ark repair
> And enjoy it ever there."

Those of us who knew about St. John's dead flickers were convulsed with laughter.

A Duxbury Tradition—Bishop Oliver Loring

When the Reverend Oliver Loring, who had grown up in Duxbury and was Rector of a large church in New Bedford, came back to Duxbury for a brief visit, he had been greatly honored by being elected to become the next Bishop of the Diocese of Maine. He stepped into Paul Peterson's Drug Store and was affably greeted by Mr. Peterson himself, who said, "Well, Oliver, here are my congratulations, and I want to ask you how it feels to be Bishop-Elect of Maine?"

Mr. Loring smiled. "Well, you know, Paul, what I have always said is 'the bigger the woodpile, the longer I sit and look at it.'"

Malcolm Brock

Duxbury was a very small town when we came here to live in 1939-40. The winter population was around 2500 and there was some increase in the summer, mostly old families who had been coming here for years. Town Meeting was in the early spring before the summer people came.

Once in awhile a new family would buy a house and move into town. When Mr. and Mrs. Malcolm Brock came to town they were popular people and were welcomed by all of us. At Town Meeting the next spring, Mr. Brock was impatient to see affairs move a little faster. We heard him say, "You people in Duxbury don't know how to run a Town Meeting. Now in Nutley, New Jersey, we would do it this way . . ."

About five years later, we heard him speak again but this time he said, "All these people are moving in from other places and they are spoiling our little old town." During those few years the town had won over one newcomer, Mr. Brock! Now, in the year 2005, we are becoming aware that the little old town is being swallowed up by all the newcomers and it has become a different kind of town. Not to be judgmental. This is just how it is! Some things are much better than they ever were before. But the little old coastal town of farmers, shipbuilders, and ship captains is in real danger of losing its simple historic picturesqueness, which was the way it really was in those days.

Beulah and Jack Kent

After retiring, we came back to Duxbury several days before Anne Kent's wedding, because John Philbrick was to tie the knot. Anne's friends came and had a wonderful time folk dancing and practicing music for the wedding ceremony. The plan was to have two recorder players, one on each side of the balcony. They were practicing their duet along with the dancers down at Netty Eddy's house. Jack Kent seemed to be everywhere, and his friendly disposition made everyone feel skilled and wanted for the festivities. At one point, Jack came back to the house where his wife Beulah was hand sewing some of the wedding finery. Jack burst into the house and reported, "They're all down there dancing all around the driveway and playing on their Terwiligers." From that moment on Terwiliger became the familiar name of the recorder.

That night, long after everyone had been bedded down, Beulah was still sewing on the wedding dress. The hours wore on, and the hem seemed to grow longer and longer. The first early rays of dawn began to glow in the eastern sky and Beulah went to the window to raise the shade. As she stood there looking out on Washington Street, a vehicle pulled up and stopped in front of the Kent residence. It was a hearse.

The word was heard later around the neighborhood that the neighbor next door was also looking out her window and when she saw the hearse, she sighed and said, "Poor Mrs. Kent." But it was not poor Mrs. Kent at all. It was the bridegroom arriving with his skiing equipment packed away in the hearse, which was his mobile home.

While everyone was exhilarated in anticipation of the wedding, the Kent household underwent the usual painting and polishing and preparing to entertain many people. One Sunday Jack and Beulah were exhausted with all the extra work. They decided to spend Sunday afternoon doing nothing. It was a pleasant day with the sun shining and a gentle breeze blowing. The trees spread welcome shade over the back yard where they sat, completely relaxed. The phone rang. It was the bridegroom's mother and father in Boston, planning to drive to Duxbury. They agreed it would take an hour or so to arrive. The Kents had never met them. Jack and Beulah relaxed again in the comfortable shade. The minutes flew by unnoticed. Suddenly Beulah rushed upstairs to put on the new dress she had planned for the occasion. The guests were arriving. Buttoning the front of the new dress while she was rushing down the front stairs, she was having trouble with the buttons. The greetings were effusive and cordial and suddenly Beulah gasped, "No wonder this dress feels different than when I bought it. I put it on backwards!"

It was late afternoon when Jack Kent left his store and stopped at Wint Coffin's to deliver an order. He visited briefly with Wint, who gave him a drink, which he noticed was a bit strong. At his house supper was not ready and he had to hurry to get to a Vestry meeting at St. John's.

Because of the strong drink he resolved to keep quiet and not to speak during the Vestry meeting. The Vestry members were discussing the various pieces of ecclesiastical furniture, all made of dark oak. They were so heavy and so dark in color that they looked a little dismal, even the Eagle Lectern from which the lessons are always read. The Vestry decided it would brighten the chancel if all the pieces were to be painted white, even the eagle.

Jack sat there silently listening to everyone else. All of a sudden he heard his own voice saying, "If you paint the Eagle white, you'll have a Seagle." Nothing was painted!

Summer or Winter Measure

Every town up and down the Atlantic coast and in other places where people come to enjoy the summer says the same thing about its summer visitors: "We love to see them come and we love to see them go." This does not necessarily mean that towns do not like summer people. It is just a simple statement of fact.

Different temperaments handle the summer-winter situation in different ways. Some people complain. Our friend Jack Kent, who had a marine store, revealed a whimsical sense of reality when John went into his store to buy two yards of plastic tubing of a certain size.

Jack said, "Do you want it by summer measure or winter measure?"

"What's the difference?" John asked.

Jack demonstrated with the end of the tube in one hand and the other hand at his nose: "This is summer measure." Then he turned his head so his nose was a few inches further away and said, "This is winter measure." To which John, a year-round local resident, said: "I'll take winter measure and thanks to you, Jack."

Another Duxbury Celebrity!

One of Duxbury's ladies was a faithful visitor at one of the churches in Boston. She was responsible for the condition and the appearance of the interior of the church. Late in the afternoon one dusky day, she stopped in at the church to make sure everything was in order. As she walked forward, she almost tripped over a prostrate figure up near the chancel. In her surprise she blurted out: "My goodness, Susie, is that you? You ought to have a tail light!" The event would never have been recorded had it not been for someone else sitting in the back in the shadows, enjoying the peace and quiet of the almost empty sanctuary. He saw and heard and told us.

Another Classic Duxbury Story Too Good to Be Forgotten! (Back when we had a railroad)

In the early days of the railroad, one morning on the first day of the month the regular ticket agent was away and a new man was taking his place. Because it was the beginning of the month, the passengers had to purchase their new tickets. The railroad carried passengers on a daily schedule into Boston. Everything was running smoothly. There were four men who took the train every day.

The first man came up to the window and the new agent asked him his name to identify his new monthly pass.

"John Alden."

The second man approached the window. When the agent asked his name, he said, "Myles Standish."

When the ticket agent asked for the third man's name, he was beginning to suspect something but the third man answered his question politely.

"My name is Faniel Adams."

This really began to look like a practical joke. The agent was beginning to warm up to the idea, so he said, in all seriousness, to the fourth man:

"Now I suppose you will tell me you are Christopher Columbus."

Whereupon the fourth man said, "No, I am Leif Erickson."

Alden Recipe Book

When we were faced with the prospect of a challenging assignment working for the National Council of the Episcopal Church in Missouri, we had to rent Faith Homestead in Duxbury. Mr. Percy Walker, a keen and conscientious real estate gentleman, found exactly the right family to live in this ancient house, built in 1772. Mr. Benjamin Alden was a direct descendent of John and Priscilla whose house is still not far from Faith Homestead. Mrs. Susie Alden, who came from Nova Scotia, was Ben's faithful and competent wife even though she must have been descended from the Tories who fled north from the Revolution.

Benjamin Alden's grandfather, Mr. Thomas Alden, lived a mile or two west of this house but when he walked to meetings at the Cornerstone Masonic Temple he used to stop to visit with Susie and Ben Alden. He was the one who told them that the two smoke bushes on the front lawn were one hundred years old. He also told the Aldens about the cattle grazing on Simmons property across the road from this house. In those early days there were grass-covered fields where now we have houses and scattered trees.

Mr. Alden had in his possession a handwritten document which bore the title *Miscellaneous*, compiled by Thomas Alden, born 1827, died 1916 at 89 years, 8th generation descendant from John and Priscilla along the David Alden line. He is listed on page 142 of *Historic Duxbury* by Laurence Bradford as having served in the Civil War. He seems to have written the book in 1870 when he was 43 years old.

While Susie and Benjamin Alden were living in this house we used to come to visit them to make sure everything was in good condition. They presented us with a *Book of Recipe Articles*, handwritten by Ben's grandfather. When Thomas Alden found an interesting recipe, he would add it to his collection. Here are some of his best suggestions, according to the practices of his times.

P. 7. Washing fluid: A Gill Alcohol to 1 qt soft soap and mix intimately. Apply the soap in the usual way to the clothes and let them soak in the suds some hours, then rinse them out with a very little rubbing.

P. 8. Cough: as soon as the first symptoms appear get the child's feet into warm water, and as soon as possible administer a dose of something nauseating, say a grain or two of Ipecac, antinomie, wine, or Cox's hive syrup, then oil a cloth with goose oil, pig's foot oil, skunk's oil, or any other soft animal oil. Then sprinkle Scotch snuff on the cloth until it is pretty well browned and apply from the chin to the middle of the chest, and repeat in two hours if necessary.

P. 75. Horse Power: The power exerted by a horse is taken to be equal to a pull of 33,000 pounds at the rate of one foot forward.

P. 76. Cheap Barometer; to make. Take a cheap bottle and put in a small quantity of finely pulverized alum. Then fill the bottle with Spirit Wine. The Alum will be absorbed by the alcohol and in clear weather the liquid will be as transparent as water. On the approach of rain or cloudy weather the Alum will be visible in a flaky spiral cloud in the center of the fluid reaching from the bottom to the surface.

P. 89. To Prevent Horses from Jumping: Make a hole through each ear of a Horse disposed to jump and tye the two Ears together.

P. 92. To give stiffening to Collars: A little gum Arabic and common soda added to the starch gives extreme stiffening and class to collars.

P. 92. Cure for ivy poison: Hold the part affected in hot water as hot as can be borne.

P. 98. To destroy borers in Fruit Trees. Bore the tree about 1 inch in depth with a gimlet or small auger; fill the hole thus made with Sulphur, then secure with clay or shoe wax. If the tree is large more Sulphur will be required, and a large hole perhaps an inch larger.

P. 10. Events—Sundries.
1854 17th November commenced digging parsnips
21 November finished digging parsnips
1854 21 November Two pigs said of Columbus County breed
114 + 135 = 249 @ 6 1/2c = 1618.50 _ G. Bradford.
1854 Nov 22 Geese migrating south
1855 June 1 Geese migrating north some few
1856 April 6th Frogs and turtles

P. 11. *Life Its Constituent Principles*
A little Carbonic Acid water and Ammonia contain the support of animal and vegetable life. The same substances are the ultimate products of the chemical process of decay and putrefaction. All the innumerable products of vitality resume after Death the Original Form from which they sprung. And thus Death a complete dissolution of an existing generation becomes the source of Life a new one.

P. 13. Diamond: The great Kohi-noor. It weighed 186 1/16 carats prior to cutting; after cutting it weighed 102 12/16 carats. To arrive at the value of a Large

> Diamond square the weight of it and multiply the square by 8 which give in _s.
>
> P. 23. Insects to destroy: It is said the Spirit Turpentine is a deadly enemy to all the insect tribe.

All my life I have caught veiled hints from people who handled figures that there was something useful about the figure 9. No one ever explained what they meant and it seemed to be a mystery.

Right here in this all-embracing Alden Recipe I have located the story about number 9. They originally called it by the title of Mathematical Curiosity.

> "The properties of the figure 9 are peculiarly curious and capable of being used in a variety of tricks not to mention the fundamental facts of arithmetic are proved by the nine. There are, among others, the following curiosities connected with this figure.
>
> Add together as many nines as you please and the figures indicating the amount when added together will always be 9 or 9 refracted. Example $2 \times 9 = 18$ and $8 + 1 = 9$; $3 \times 9 = 27$ and $2 + 7 = 9$; $4 \times 9 = 36$ and $3 + 6 = 9$, and so on until we come to $11 \times 9 = 99$. Here we have two nines or 18 but $8 + 1 = 9$. $12 \times 9 = 108$ and $1 + 8 = 9$.
>
> Another curiosity in these different products of the 9 is that when the 9 is multiplied by the digits 2, 3, 4, and 5 as follows the products are 18, 27, 36, 45, etc. Reverse these products and we have 54, 63, 72 and 81. Again 123456789, the 9 digits added together = 45 or 9 x 5 but instead of adding multiply the middle figure 5 by the last 9 and the amount will be the mysterious nines or 45 and $4 = 5 = 9$.
>
> One of these properties is of importance to bookkeepers and accountants. It will be of essential service in settling complicated accounts. In this the difference between any transposed number is always a multiple of nine. For instance, if an accountant cannot prove or balance his account because of a difference

between debits and credits, and after careful and repeated addings the difference can be divided by nine without a remainder, that indicates that somewhere figures were transposed: 92 for 29 or 83 for 38. The difference of any such transpositions is always a multiple of 9.

Obviously this document was drawn up before the invention of the calculator! But even a calculator cannot change nine and its factual mysteries!

Chapter 14

Roanridge 1949-1957

Moving to Roanridge (after a Surprisingly Short Adventure in Orleans)

We had been very contented living in the generally quiet little country town of Duxbury with its kindly people and its Pilgrim background. The gardens and the small farm animals kept us busy at Faith Homestead. John's musical abilities were appreciated, and the Bell Ringers Beta Quartet traveled extensively to present various communities with vocal music originating in Plymouth, which had always had a fine record for musical groups. (This was before anyone ever dreamed of television.) The region was conservative and mirrored all the old familiar New England traits and conventions. No one ever suspected there was anything else. But after a long stay in Duxbury, we felt it was time to move on, perhaps to Orleans.

Orleans

We had met the Rev. Richard Kimball and his wife Florence on visits to Orleans. Enthusiastic neighbors had helped build a new church building on the Kimballs's land. Their own house was part of a shipwrecked vessel, small but charming. A gift shop brought in capital and the church became a spectacular and popular center for a large summer group of admirers.

Florence had milk goats and sheep, and John and I enjoyed our new friendship. After a few years the Kimballs began to talk of retirement. When they talked to us, we listened eagerly. They planned a gradual retirement and suggested that we might take over eventually, so we moved to Orleans, bringing our own milk goats and our three sheep.

When we moved to the Church of the Holy Spirit in Orleans on Cape Cod, we intended to continue the same peaceful, contemplative life we had lived for eight or nine years in Duxbury.

With a new younger minister, the congregation increased. But before long both Florence and Dickie realized that they could not play the roles of retired pastor and wife or turn that establishment over to anyone else. Quite contrary to the usual orderly conduct of clergy affairs, Florence fired us on the spot. We had kind friends who had known all along that this would happen. They came to our rescue, adopted our animals, and gave us safe lodging. At breakfast the next morning, George Canham handed John a fifty-dollar bill, which he said someone had just given to him.

The whole impossibly romantic performance was quick and decisive. What was a recently fired clergyman in the Diocese of Massachusetts to do next? Suddenly, we were free to go to New York to national headquarters to see what was happening elsewhere.

The center covered all the churches, both in America and the foreign missions. When we arrived at the headquarters of the Episcopal Church, a big office building in New York City, we were announced at the Church Missions House. There was no red carpet, but a secretary in the Home Department, Marie, had been one of our young people in the old days in Duxbury. It was a joy to find an old friend in that formal atmosphere. When her director, the Reverend Clifford L. Samuelson, arrived it was another reunion because he and John had gone to the same seminary.

Dr. Samuelson, Secretary of the Division of Town and Country, had been wrestling with what to do with a 400-acre farm in Missouri, which had been given to the national church by Mr. Wilbur Cochel, a professor of agriculture in Kansas and Missouri, and his wife. Cochel believed that the churches should support the farms which supplied food to all people. (Perhaps he inspired the bumper sticker we see now: "NO FARMS, NO FOOD." Mr. Cochel had named the farm "Roanridge," but the national leaders of the denomination could not find a purpose or use for the big farm. They could not manage it, nor could they sell it. The big question was what to do with it?

At the same time they realized that there were a great many very small churches in country towns that needed help and encouragement and leadership from clergy trained for rural work. After several years of negotiations and discussion and endless planning, it had been decided that the big farm should become a training center for rural clergy, starting with young men still in the seminaries who were ready to work with rural clergy to complete their degrees. The rural clergy, who were also to be trained at Roanridge, then became supervisors of the younger men. And right there in that office was John Philbrick, who had just doubled the activity of a rural church, asking for more work. Wheels began to turn instantly. John had come from a rural church where people had small backyard farms and raised their own vegetables. We knew about the local affairs of churches but the national organization of a very large body was a new experience. With a much broader vision than ours, they described Mr. Cochel's gift and the mission that had been created for the farm he had given to the Episcopal Church.

It looked as though the minister's need for a job fitted neatly into the huge church farm's need for a director. Marie, the secretary, knew that Dr. Samuelson was a very exclusive and demanding man. She helped John to get the job by assuring her director that John was much too "homespun" to fit the position. She knew that John's down-to-earth, practical, "homespun" quality would fascinate Dr. Samuelson and lead him to approve him for the job, if she only took an opposing view. And so, after a long conference, John Philbrick was deemed by Dr. Samuelson to be the ideal clergyman to combine his ministry with the rural demands of 400 acres of fertile farmland—not to do the farming himself but to be responsible for a training center to prepare young clergymen how to lead country churches.

As we journeyed back to Massachusetts, we wondered what we were getting into. Back home, we traveled to a tiny country town to ask the Presiding Bishop, Henry Knox Sherrill, if he would approve of the new job and recommend John to take it. The Bishop could be fierce and had once told John, "You should be shot," because he had not studied Latin and Greek in the seminary. Fortunately, we found Bishop Sherrill weeding his onion patch. Over the relaxed atmosphere of summer and the vegetable garden, formidable Episcopalian formalities were relaxed and the Bishop was friendly. The two reverend gentlemen settled the matter in the garden, while Mrs. Sherrill and I drank tea in the kitchen.

The Missouri farm project was reputable, Bishop Sherrill agreed. There was money in the budget to promote what was conceived as a large country training center to encourage and teach clergymen who were struggling to maintain small rural churches all over America. The dream was beginning to take shape and John was soon to become a member of the team of leaders of the Roanridge Rural Training Center.

Big enterprises gather momentum slowly. A rural training center made sense to us, but we had no vision of Roanridge. As we prepared to leave our cozy New England habitat for Missouri, one summer resident of Duxbury said to me: "Oh, I don't believe there's anything very interesting west of the Hudson River." Meanwhile, Dr. Samuelson had written to let us know, "I covet your arrival."

In 1949, there were very few major, modernized roads. We drove from town to town with only the Pennsylvania Turnpike to speed the trip along. As we left Indiana and passed into Illinois, we passed through Vandalia, a large town where we fully expected to see American Native tribes. To us New Englanders, it felt so very far west! Even after East St. Louis, Missouri, we were still miles and miles from our destination. At last, after driving up a hill and around a curve, we arrived. We were a bit terrified to be so far from home, but we were surrounded by friends, headed by Dr. Samuelson and Mr. and Mrs. Cochel, the donors.

Our homesickness turned to amazement at everything around us. The sky was so much higher and wider, the sunshine seemed brighter and hotter, the wind blew incessantly, and the people were so friendly, I can think of no word to adequately describe them. Roanridge itself was located on one of many ridges along the great Missouri River. As we looked around we saw a hundred head of purebred shorthorn cattle. Some were white and some were dark red and some were mixed, the type called "roan."

A Whirlwind View of the West

We didn't have long to settle into our new surroundings. The day we arrived, almost before the car engine had cooled, Dr. Samuelson said, "You effete easterners! You think you have driven to the other side of the world but the day after tomorrow we leave at the crack of dawn to drive west until we reach the Pacific Ocean and your eyes will be opened even more." He had come from Longview, Washington, and spoke to us shrinking little New Englanders with his western breadth and his natural magnanimity. He had now become our teacher.

At five o'clock on the morning of the appointed day, we drove over the nearby Kansas line on a fairly good highway that was absolutely straight for as far as the eye could see. There were seven of us in the station wagon—Dr. Samuelson and his fiancée, Elizabeth; Justin and Tamar, his adopted children; their aunt; and John and I. We were taking the station wagon to be wintered in Seattle, Washington. For some reason, it could not be stored in Missouri. Along the way, Tamar read the historical signboards out loud, perhaps for our benefit. When we stopped that evening at a motel, we were still in Kansas.

From the first mile it became evident that this was a voyage of discovery. We never took well-known routes, and we explored unmarked roads. On the second day, for our instruction in geographical wonders, we skittered up the mountain to the top of Pike's Peak on that Sunday afternoon, where our new teacher made John and me throw snowballs at each other, while he took motion pictures to record the presence of snow in mid-July. That was our lesson about Pike's Peak.

Instead of heading for Denver, the usual route, we traveled toward Leadville, where the next morning we had breakfast in a local joint with people Dr. Samuelson knew at the Colorado School of Mines. Then, back on the road again, we streaked through Wyoming to Jackson Hole for more education of us inexperienced easterners. Our leader led us to the biggest gambling joint and supplied us with quarters to try our luck. The one-armed bandits looked mild enough for a timid customer to try. The quarter he had given me slipped into the slot, just as it would have in a gas meter back home. Justin's aunt sputtered about the sin of teaching those two children to gamble, and, ironically, Justin's quarter brought down the whole jackpot and auntie was for the moment silenced.

Somewhere in the middle of our peregrinations, Dr. Samuelson took us to Yellowstone National Park, where we watched bears and the geyser and all the other sights beloved by tourists. A small brook thereabouts was pointed out as part of the source of the Missouri River.

We zigzagged from state to state and through the Grand Tetons. This was plainly our new teacher's method of proving to us that there is a great world outside New England. In Montana, we visited at a small church whose rector was a mutual friend and whose view out the sanctuary window was breathtaking. There I recall noticing that our flamboyant and spectacular friend and his fiancée signed the guest book simply with their names, no impressive titles.

Bozeman, Montana was next. Auntie and Justin had a plane to catch there. When their plane landed at the airport, the pilot turned off only one of its two motors. When the last passenger had descended the gangplank, Dr. Samuelson jumped to attention and commanded John and me to run up that ramp into the plane, then turn around and walk down as though we were just arriving at Bozeman. His everlasting motion picture equipment was already in gear.

I had never been on any plane, nor had John, let alone a plane with one motor still running. We were still tenderfoots and were scared beyond speech. Was he teasing us or trying to see how obedient we would be under orders? There wasn't time to ask, so we walked down the steps expecting the motor to turn inside out and come to bite us. Justin and Auntie climbed up. The plane flew away and we all went to breakfast. Whenever on the highway we came to an historical marker, Tamar was instructed to stand by it and read "in a loud clear voice" so that we could learn of the early settlement of the western wilderness of America. John and I learned by seeing the actual places—and our intense eastern loyalty was beginning to be stretched just a bit more with each history lesson by Tamar.

There was still the trip across Idaho, where we drove many extra miles to stay at the Samuelson Hotel in a very small town. There was no family connection, but obviously our Dr. Samuelson was well known there from former visits. By now, the days were flying past. John had an engagement to preach back in Missouri the next Sunday. It was already Thursday. As we speeded across Idaho through the Bitteroots, Dr. Samuelson recommended that John go back to Missouri and give lectures on "Our Trip through the Bitteroots at Eighty Miles an Hour."

We whizzed into the railroad station in Seattle. The train was on the track. We jumped on. No books, not even a magazine, miles and miles through the Dakotas and the Badlands and with no one to give the historical events! After a long slow ride south along the Mississippi River, we arrived back in Kansas City.

One of the best lessons taught by our indomitable teacher was to observe the differences in people from different sections of the country. He supplied us with Edna Ferber's books, including *So Big*, about Missouri country folk. Later, we often heard mothers and grandmothers use just that expression when speaking to a little child. Dr. Samuelson also recommended that we read all of Willa Cather's books about the mid-west. These were tremendous and valuable lessons for narrow-minded New Englanders to absorb. There were no illuminated diplomas but we took in one heck of an education.

Before the necessary buildings had been built at Roanridge, the seminary students began to arrive in Parkville, Missouri, for their training for rural ministry. Fortunately, there was a missionary college in the town which was congenial and even eager to help the people who were trying to invent the new and evolving

Roanridge Rural Training Foundation. President Zwingle of Park College welcomed all of us tenderfoots working on the creation of a somewhat similar type of missionary enterprise.

Dr. Zwingle agreed, yes, the college could offer dormitory space during the summer, but he also offered to introduce us to someone he thought could be even more helpful. When he presented Miss Constance Vulliamy, we knew we were in good hands. She located an available office on the college grounds. She arranged for us to use Chestnut Dormitory. She arranged for dining room facilities. But best of all, she arranged for the right people to meet other appropriate specialists, and the work began to grow.

As the Roanridge project developed, it grew closer to Park College in an academic way. A college professor was forced to leave because of ill health. A Roanridge clergyman had adequate training and skill to take the professor's place. In fact, Roanridge had enough ministers to fill in several vacancies at Park College, including the Reverend Bill Spofford, father of triplets. When someone else took on a class in child care, there was a chuckle about "Those who can, *do*. Those who can't, *teach*."

Connie Vulliamy was a staunch ally whatever the course. Before her death at 100 in 2004, she wrote to me regularly on her typewriter. The little chapel from Roanridge, which became the Church of the Redeemer in Parkville, has now been expanded with three new building projects, and Connie used to keep me up-to-date on the details.

Dizz Viggers of Park College was my lanky sophomore friend who was supposed to help me count the dormitory linens. During relaxation time he had draped himself sideways across a big rocking chair and said, as he chewed on his pipe, "Yep, sometime I hope to know as much about somep'n as I know now about everythin'." He is now, some fifty years later, an ordained clergyman.

Settling in at Roanridge

At Roanridge and in Kansas City, we had to learn local customs that seemed at first strange to us. For example, locals did not refer to "Kansas City," because there are two Kansas Cities. They called one K.C. Mo and the other K.C. Ka. The boundary between the two is the Missouri River, which makes a right angle turn between the two cities—or two halves of the same city. When we arrived there in 1949, the Kansas Cities were about ready to celebrate their 100th birthday, but more of that later.

Sometimes we were cheered by coincidences. One day we stopped the car in Kansas City for a streetcar. A man ran past us to get to the streetcar, shouting, "What part of Massachusetts do you come from? I have a sister who lives in New Bedford." At other times, we learned many new things.

It was quite a few years ago that we all saw the show *Oklahoma!* and came away from the theatre humming "Everything's up to date in Kansas City. They've gone about as far as they can go." Roanridge was so close to Kansas City, Missouri, that we often drove the twelve miles over the S-shaped bridge over the Missouri River to get into the city. We frugal New Englanders were shocked to see a huge bronze plaque on one of the financial institutions advertising "Assets $9,000,000." How loud could they brag?

We knew about a lot of things in the city that were not at all up to date but we still spent time there in spite of Missouri's devastating and intolerable heat. Local people had told us of various practices to escape some of the heat, like soaking your bed sheets in ice water before you went to bed or sleeping outdoors in a breezy spot, none of which helped much.

Then someone told us they had invented a new system called air conditioning and we could learn about it if we would go to the evening movie at a certain theatre in Kansas City. That was the beginning of our acquaintance with what everyone has now, even in their automobiles, so common we call it "A.C." Many people now have it in their houses, their cars, their stores, etc. etc. etc.

John and I used to sneak away from Roanridge on a special evening to sit and shiver in the one theatre that had A.C. while we happily watched all of Alec Guinness's films, commencing with "The Lavender Hill Mob."

A New Plant—Marijuana

One day I read in the *Kansas City Star* a new word and puzzled over it as I tried to pronounce it. The article was about a foreign plant we had never heard of—marijuana. That was only the beginning of our acquaintance with the plant. It was soon evident from observation that the plant grew thick and as universal as grass grows elsewhere. Marijuana was common all around us. Along every roadside it covered every inch of space and grew six to eight feet tall, the remains of the old crops of hemp. We learned that it was familiarly known as "pot" and had become popular among students. In Missouri, it was a remnant of the manufacture of hemp rope, which had been a big industry in early days. It also had medicinal uses. Now it is famous!

Perhaps I had better not tell how one fine summer's day a number of clergy were taking a walk on the Roanridge farm. Our ever-present photographer swooped in and snapped the whole group, up to their necks in marijuana! Where are those pictures now? On another day, the farm superintendent, Arlo Cottrell, who really ran all the details of the cattle farm, brought a county agent to visit the Demonstration Homestead that we ran. Out in the vegetable garden there was a large plot of seedlings too young to have identifiable leaves.

Arlo asked the county agent to identify the plants. The county agent bent down and studied the patch. He shook his head and said, "I don't recognize them."

Arlo grinned and announced, "It's marijuana."

"Well," the county agent said rather fiercely. "It's illegal but we have no way to control it."

Our real purpose in growing it was to make a patch of shade in the garden. The plant grew eight feet tall and made a welcome spot of shade.

Chapter 15

The National Town-Country Church Institute (NTCCI) and the Roanridge Demonstration Homestead

It took a long time to create the organization that was to carry the title of the National Town-Country Church Institute (NTCCI), which was also a section of the Roanridge Rural Training Foundation. It seemed as though only our national government could invent more colorful titles than the Episcopal Church.

Whatever the titles were, we were getting organized. The Roanridge Demonstration Homestead was our responsibility. We lived in the old farmer's house on about one acre on the top of the ridge, with a small barn and several beehives. The honeybees were fascinating to study, and everyone welcomed honey on their pancakes. In the barn we had a couple of milk goats, a sheep or two, hens for eggs, and some bantams for fun. It was easier to explain about animal care and animal breeds on this small scale than to demonstrate on the hundred head of shorthorn cattle in the Roanridge pastures.

The Donors and the Superintendent

A mile away, Mr. and Mrs. Wilbur Cochel, the donors, lived in their large new house. They were surrounded by their farm, which was managed by the very competent farm superintendent, Arlo Cottrell, and his wife. He tended the hundred head of pedigreed shorthorn cattle that roamed the pastures every day, and trained the mules. Mr. Cochel said that no Missouri farm was complete without its mules. There were also any number of hens, ducks, and geese.

Arlo knew all about the current practices of fertilizing the fields of grains, wheat, barley, millet, and clover, and the pasture lands had been thoroughly studied and planned to be an example of the best management of water. Missouri was famous for horrendous thundershowers which would ruin the terrain if it was not protected. The local name for a big shower was "a gulley buster." To prevent that kind of damage, the 400 acres had been grassed over with various methods. There were "grassed waterways" and terraces, which were narrow slopes to carry the water, slowed by the grass, into a low pond known as the Morning Glory structure. The cattle were free to graze on the grass, and the wild rainstorms were somewhat controlled by all manner of controls built into the fields. They used to say that there were 100 miles of grassed waterways on that farm.

Because the total Mississippi Valley of America was eons ago created by wind—blown soil, called Loess Soil (Greek origin), there was never even a small stone anywhere. The soil went down 40 feet, as we could see when they excavated to build the Institute building. When Loess soil gets wet, it becomes mud (locally pronounced "merd") and every activity becomes dependent on the condition of the soil—or where your car was stuck.

Mr. Cochel had great pride in his accomplishments. He was editor of an agricultural paper, and we never heard the end of his good works. He was also a character to deal with. Very taciturn, no conversationalist. I was his secretary. Trying to make him talk one day, I said, "Isn't five thousand dollars a pretty large sum for St. Luke's Hospital to raise?"

"They'll make it," he said. End of conversation.

He smoked a cigarette that drooped from one side of his mouth, and ash fell everywhere. Among us workers it became a legend that no paper with his signature was complete without a burned spot.

The Training Programs Begin

Very soon, the training programs were up and running at Roanridge. When the first planeload of seminary students arrived at the Kansas City Airport around June 1949, it was our assignment to meet them and bring them back to Park College in Parkville, Missouri, just a few miles from Kansas City, where they were housed until we finished building a headquarters for the National Town-Country Church Institute. Students came from all over America, from seminaries mostly in cities. Every summer there were 40 to 50 students there for a session before they went off to their summer jobs working for clergy in rural areas. Every winter those clergy came to live in the same Institute building to learn about training the students.

Our overall special responsibility was to teach city-born seminarians to get along with the farmer types. They were trained to work in small country churches out in the "boondocks," among farmers and orchardists, where they would meet a surprising mixture of ignorance and lack of schooling combined with a shrewd and surprising amount of skill in country living. Both the men and the women who lived the rural life knew how to make the most out of their country resources and events. The students might have to learn a lot of new rural words, and that was part of our work.

There were so many new and puzzling names commonly used by people in the country that John and I compiled a dictionary of rural terms and made mimeographed copies. John's favorite trick question was: "What is the difference between a castrated bull and a steer?" (They are the same: two names for one condition.) Once, when a local housewife said to a group of students, "My cow is fresh," one student said, "Do you have to tie her up?" With a shocked expression on her face, the woman explained. "The cow has just had her calf and she now gives us a milk supply." The student learned that the birth of a calf creates the fresh milk supply, and he should have congratulated the farmer's wife on the improvement in her lifestyle.

The farmer's wife wears an apron, but the apron of the barn is the big cement slab that slopes up to the barn door. And a machinist who works with metals may speak of an apron, which for him is a steel rod. An important fact for the city slickers was knowing that if you open a gate to walk through it, you must not fail to close that gate or you may let a whole pastureful of cattle into another farmer's field. The students were cooperative after a few boo boos.

Over our time at Roanridge, we learned that students excel at impersonating their professors. One evening all the faculty were "honored." The lad who impersonated the Reverend John Philbrick appeared wearing John's bee veil and bee suit. In his right hand he carried a bee smoker, smoking gently. In his left, he carried a tall plant of marijuana and proclaimed, "Put this plant in your bee smoker and you will really have a religious experience." Our reaction was, "How keen these students are!" That was before we learned about "pot" and its effect on people, both good and questionable.

The Reverend Norman L. Foote Arrives

In due time, we had a director of the NTCCI named the Reverend Norman Foote, a tall, thin, taciturn man, who taught us to work independently without bothering him with details. His was the simple, direct, practical approach. If one asked him how he wanted one to do a task, he would say, "I don't care how you do it. Just get it done."

His best-loved pet was the raven he bought from a liquor store where it had advertised Old Crow Whiskey for many years. The raven learned quickly and was even obedient. "Pick up the bottle cap" was one of his talents. He even learned without lessons, especially to copy sounds. He could mimic the sound of the litter of puppies raised nearby.

When John Philbrick was speaking with Mr. Foote on the phone, he could hear the raven saying, in Mr. Foote's voice, "Margaret, get off the phone."

Any group of people living and working together develop a family kind of relationship in which each one develops his own personal pattern and everyone else understands and respects everyone else. That is the ideal. Our years at Roanridge had the usual ups and downs common to most groups. As one of the few survivors, I would like to make it known that we all were hard-working, peace-loving, cooperative, ecumenical co-workers. Looking back, I recognize a happy spirit that existed among us, and it is my purpose to witness, in spite of the "ups and downs," that Roanridge and our work there was a source of happiness in intentional Christian behavior. Our Director lived with his family and dog in a new house near the Roanridge Demonstration Homestead.

It was Norman Foote who supervised the construction of the Institute building. When a building is going up, there are always people who want to watch it grow. They want to know about the foundation and all the pertinent details. One day Mr. Foote learned we were to be visited by Mr. J. C. Penney (yes, the REAL J. C. Penney, founder of the famous stores), who had a farm nearby in Missouri. We were most happy to know he was coming and, of course, we hoped he would help with the construction expenses.

Mr. Penney Pays a Visit

Mr. Foote met Mr. Penney and led the way to the new structure, which was still a foundation surrounded by walls. They stood discussing the ultimate shape of the building when Mr. Foote's dog Penny whizzed in with a stick in his mouth, ready to fetch if Mr. Foote would throw. Mr. Foote was busy talking with Mr. Penney. The dog pawed him. Mr. Foote was talking funds and paid no attention. The dog pawed again and Mr. Foote's patience reached its end. He thundered at the dog, "Penny leave me alone— Penny stop—Penny you get out." There never was a gift of any funds.

It was a sad day for the staff when our teacher became the Bishop Elect of Idaho and departed after all the bishops in the country had voted their approval, taking his raven along—after it had questioned John Philbrick many times in Norm's voice: "Hello, boy, what's the matter?"

A Grand Celebration

When the Institute building was finally finished, it was time to celebrate. The Presiding Bishop Henry Knox Sherrill would be coming from New York with several other important leaders of the national church. We assembled the usual details to maximize the occasion: a portable organ, bleachers to hold 100 people, folding chairs, several choirs in colorful robes from local churches. The procession assembled in the big barn and gradually formed in line with the processional cross, the choirs and finally the reverend dignitaries in the usual reverse order of their importance—with the Presiding Bishop at the end. John had been delegated to help wherever help was needed.

It was very quiet. The procession emerged singing from the barn at the top of the hill and processed in a great sweep around the hill and down to the bleachers. The service began with expressions of gratitude for the completion of the Institute Building. Bishop Sherrill climbed to the pulpit to deliver his message. With his usual ecclesiastical dignity, he opened his address by saying, "Today a new Rubric has been added to the Episcopal Prayer Book. John Philbrick announced 'start singing when you pass the chicken house.'"

Now that the Institute Building was finished, the dormitory held about 40 students and the dining room and kitchen were presided over by the Frazier family. Because they were local people they sometimes brought unexpected ideas like the cook's panic when she, being pregnant, cracked open a double-yolked egg. That was supposed to be a sign she was going to have twins, and she just couldn't work in the kitchen anymore that day.

Of course, the Christian Education women who came from New York shuddered at the idea of drinking goat's milk. John invented a contest with a prize for the one who could tell goat's milk from cow's milk. If the goat's milk was chilled immediately, few people could ever tell the difference. And most students enjoyed the playful nature of well-bred milk goats and their kids.

Up on the big farm where Mr. and Mrs. Cochel lived, the farm superintendent, Arlo Cottrell had studied to manage every detail of a farm with skill and precision. Early in Arlo's employment with Mr. Cochel he had taken on an unusual job. He earned the admiring title of "Cow Boy" when he accompanied ten Holstein dairy heifers and one bull on a ship from New York to Istanbul, Turkey. Cottrell's trip of a lifetime was highlighted when through all the storms at sea and many frustrations with dock officials, he was able to deliver not eleven but twelve head of cattle. During the trip a calf was born amidst the excitement and delight of the crew. This was done through the Episcopal Church as a part of its contribution to Heifers for Relief, which currently is known as *Heifer Project International*.

Compost and The Minister's Vegetable Garden

We wrote two small books on gardening while at Roanridge, *Compost* and *The Minister's Vegetable Garden*, which were published by the National Town-Country Church Institute, Parkville, Missouri. Our Director, The Reverend Norman L. Foote, wrote in the Foreword . . .

> The reader is asked to bear in mind the limitations of this kind of pamphlet. The material is based on one particular kind of gardening procedure, which the authors have found practical, efficient, and economical. This in no way implies that everyone should follow this system, nor does it indicate that this method has ecclesiastical blessing not given to any other method. The Roanridge homestead is surrounded by Roanridge Farm, four hundred acres of land cultivated by the latest methods and using modern farm equipment. The farm represents another method of agriculture using machines, chemical fertilizers, and highly organized methods. The Farm and Homestead get on well together. There is mutual respect and exchange of ideas. Here students and visitors can compare close together two agricultural methods.
>
> You may wish to use other methods in your garden. Some gardeners use chemicals, some use compost, some may even use hydroponics. Some may use something from each of the three ways of growing crops. At the Homestead library there are books and pamphlets on all three methods. In this pamphlet, however, the attempt is to tell what the authors have used and experienced. They started out to produce food to supplement a marginal income, using as little cash as possible and making use of the materials at

hand. As a clergyman and his wife this was also of necessity a spare time activity. The method used was limited to these conditions and organic gardening seemed to come closest to these limitations. It is the authors' hope that other clergymen in similar situations may find what they have learned useful. It is not their purpose nor intention, in any sense, to evaluate the different methods, nor to pass judgment on varying procedures.

After Mr. Foote's rather dry presentation, I have to quote the following from our pamphlet:

> Make Plans on Paper. Year after year we make our garden too large. The joke is old and threadbare but still worth keeping in mind. *Never plow up more space than your wife can take care of.* It is said that the " . . . English clergy gardening the glebe lands around their churches run into the dilemma of having a large tract which they cannot cultivate and being called poor managers, or of cultivating a small piece well and being accused of wasting the land."

The pamphlet ends with advice about calling for help from your County Agent or if he fails, calling the Home Demonstration Agent, both State employees. This is followed by a long, long list of agricultural books now probably too old to be available in this new century.

Philharmonic Music Society

The Philharmonic Music Society gave regular concerts every year in the elegant Kansas City Music Hall with the orange plush seats. It was announced that there were to be performances of grand opera and volunteers were needed. We could not volunteer fast enough! The principal parts were played by Metropolitan Opera stars. The manager had announced that "We can do grand opera just as good as the Metropolitan in New York."

John was chosen to play the part of the bishop in *Tosca*. I was always hidden in the choruses. After *Tosca* we sang in Gounod's

Faust and, of course, *Carmen*. Working on the stage side of the orchestra one could see things one never dreamed of from the audience side. For instance, the tool box full of tools beside the kettle drums, or the paperback books some musicians pulled out to read while their instrument was not sounding. How could a violinist possibly chew gum in synch with his music? They really did!

Backstage we could talk with the Met singers, depending on their degree of friendliness, and their free time during a performance. They were the very same artists we used to listen to on the Saturday afternoon radio broadcasts of the Metropolitan Opera Company in New York City. When it came time to dress for the performance of Tosca, John was handed his wardrobe, provided by the Chicago Grand Opera Company. Everything was there in fairly good shape, a trifle worn but in general acceptable. The final item was the bishop's red gloves. They fitted well and they were brilliant red, but they were both for the left hand.

June Bug and the Buick

There was a kind of dumbed-down feeling in the National Town-Country Church Institute kitchen one day as the staff jumped in to make meals for the forty or more Seminary students, in the absence of our cook. The small panic was caused by Mrs. Frazier's little grandson, "June Bug," who had discovered at four years of age how to start the family car—a big second-hand Buick exactly like Mr. Cochel's. After he got it started, he fiddled with various things he could reach, with the result that the car wandered slowly around the backyard until it was interrupted in its route by the family chicken house. That stopped the car and alerted the family. No work at the Institute for them that day. June Bug was unscathed, but a little wiser.

Really, we didn't miss Mr. Frazier too much. He used to sit on an upside down bucket just outside the kitchen door with a fly swatter, swatting the flies before they could come in the door. He did keep the Chapel dusted by carefully dusting the chairs on one side of the aisle and then carefully dusting the chairs on the other side of the aisle. Then he stepped into the aisle and gave his dust cloth a good shaking.

The Cottonwood Tree and the 4-H Workout

The phone rang early one morning and it was John Marion Reineke calling to tell John that he was going to cut down that cottonwood tree by the Institute building today. John had a very even temperament and he never used a swear word, but that morning I heard him say "John Marion, it takes a hell of a long time to grow a tree that tall and I hope you will let it alone."

John Marion must have been convinced to let it grow, but the incident made us notice how few trees were just left standing. And that particular tree was our only shade on a hot summer's day. That was where the Sunday school children played their games and where we met our friends who came to visit. The tree survived.

Soon after the tree episode, the extensive lawn was all in the shade on a summer day. The county summer 4-H Club was having its seasonal workout under a huge four-pole tent. Wind whistled through the tent and we all enjoyed the breeze. Parenthetically, we learned by observation that if you had a big family and it was a hot day, you prepared for the day by getting one white facecloth good and wet in your cold cold well water at home. You carried the wet face cloth with you to the "doins." If one (or all) of the children fretted because of the heat, you just handed him the face cloth and it was passed around, wetting down everybody's face. Eventually, it turned into a hot wet rag—not much comfort.

The 4-H exhibits were excellent and we all rejoiced that there was such an excellent organization to help educate the children in rural areas. All the Platte County officials and the State Representatives attended. There were contests for the best care and grooming of sheep. There were calves and chickens and rabbits and pigs. Sometimes there would be a cow almost ready to "drop her calf." That the birth would happen right there at the show was part of everyday life for the 4-H Club members, but a big event for visitors to the show.

The 4-H members who brought their animals stayed with their own to feed and clean them. Of course, the owner never led his animal because that would reveal ownership. In the ring, one couldn't even speak the animal's name, and there was a penalty for any infringement of the rules. We were greatly impressed with the courtesy and good manners of these young people because of the good training they get in the 4-H Club.

When our Executive Secretary came to visit from New York City, he looked with amused tolerance at what he considered the simplicity of the country folk. In time he learned to respect and admire their wisdom, their skills and their ingenuity. Of course, this was before the advent of television and the world of computers, which now has changed our whole culture in America.

And while we are thinking about the big 4-H contest, there is a slightly different story about a fall contest and Agricultural Fair up at Platte City, the County Seat. Our students wanted to participate in the county fair. They prepared jams and jellies and candied grapefruit peel in their spare time, some of the goodies one always sees at country fairs. We assured them there would be ribbons for the winners, sometimes even a dollar or two, but always ribbons.

The date for entering the items was advertised for a week in the local newspaper. No entries after the closing date. We helped the students pack up their entries and we all drove up to Platte City. When we reached the place of the little fair, they met us with a sad look; we were too late. They decided there would be no more entries, so they had closed the contest already and we were just out.

That was such a blow. We had to do something to salve the hurt feelings, so the NTCCI put on its own Fair. Someone whizzed into Kansas City and bought ribbon enough to decorate every entry and we celebrated the spectacular achievements of the students in the culinary arts! Everyone legitimately won a special rating for her entry and had a ribbon to prove her achievement and the men applauded.

A Christmas Poem

In 1953, mid-way through our tenure at Roanridge, I wrote a poem for John as a Christmas present. This could be sung, if anyone wanted to:

> I heard the bells on Christmas Day
> Their old familiar carol play
> Of What-on-Earth or Heaven-Above
> Can I give you to express my love?

So first, t' express Infinity
This little black book you will see,
To measure days of sweet content
And all that kind of sentiment.

Here, to prove that Spring is near
Three fat Gloxinia Bulbs appear:
Their culture, like the Violet:
"Keep not too dry nor yet too wet."

The Herbs may smell like bitter gall
To you and me and moth and all.
Here's hoping we're no more molested,
Nor longer by the clothesmoth pestered.

The check enclosed will help to pay
For records bought the other day,
With some additional for pictures
And books and other Homestead fixtures.

And next to tell my Passion Sweet
Are several favorite things to eat,
Like hot fresh bread and chocolate cake
Which I have made or soon shall make.

Last, lest you think I'm growing old
And really getting rather bold
I'd like to say, however gray,
Is all my love this Christmas Day.

—1953

Chapter 16

The Three Churches

After the students were prepared in all subjects, they went to their designated parishes all over America and some in Canada. Several stayed near Roanridge and helped with the local parishes. Because the members of the staff at Roanridge were all ordained clergymen, it was considered important for each man to continue to minister to a congregation. There were many small churches in the area surrounding Roanridge, and when it was known that there were eligible trained clergy who could minister to them, three church groups asked for help.

Each of the three little churches was administered by a caring adult member of the Roanridge staff, and the three Sunday Schools had the best and newest training techniques from Tish Croom, the Director of Christian Education. At the same time, the students participated long enough to observe and learn the techniques one has to know to succeed in country living:

1) Smile and say hello to everyone.
2) Don't be afraid to shake hands.
3) Remember—a stranger is a friend you haven't met yet.

The closest was Union Chapel. It was a pretty little church building distinguished by theatre seats screwed to the floor. The total congregation was not more than forty at the most, but there was an active though small church school with lively young people. The adults were friendly country folk. One of them, Mrs. Brink, was always vocal about her problem. She had "a dreadful fixination about wasps" for which she always kept a small bottle of whiskey in her handbag. One of the students asked which side her father had been on in the Civil War. Her answer was, "Oh I don't know. They would just come through and pick him up one night on one side and the next night they'd be on the other side."

The students worked with the members and through the years they had many "occasions" to celebrate. One detail the students tried to emphasize was the importance of making the church warm and welcoming to everyone. They even painted the church door red, and explained that it was a custom to welcome people by a red door. That was fine for teaching but it was not long before the door was painted white again, and one little boy knew where the bucket and paintbrush were in his family attic.

Another small church was in a community named Tiffany Springs. In much earlier days it had been a place where people went to bathe in the waters. Somehow the waters had changed and were no longer considered therapeutic. Or, perhaps, Tiffany Springs had been eclipsed by Excelsior Springs, which had elaborate facilities only a few miles away.

Anyway, there was an exceptionally active congregation in that tiny church building. Letty Baldwin was a lively leader, and she was always ready to follow the plan for new activities. There is a picture of the Tiffany Springs church on the cover of *Vision Fulfilling*, by Leo Maxwell Brown, William Davidson, and Allen Brown. *Vision Fulfilling,* published in 1998, describes all the work done in those years to stimulate the growth of churches in small communities. The picture includes Dr. Clifford L. Samuelson, our Executive Director and also Roanridge Director, Letitia Croom, teacher of Christian Education, the previously mentioned Letty Baldwin, and nine or ten children all playing a game in front of the church building. Connie Vulliamy was a local neighbor who helped the Institute with every detail.

The people, like most Missourians, were quick to be friendly and loyal in their friendships. No one had any money to speak of and their tastes were uncomplicated, but their loyalty is a reality not to be forgotten. Only one feature of the place is to be deplored: whenever there was a dust storm, there used to be an inch of fine loess soil over the whole floor of the church building.

The third church was in the town of Farley. "Population 98, Water Supply Approved" it said on the sign as you went past the grain elevators near the Platte River. The town is too small to show on the atlas map but most of the people lived on big acreages in the bottomlands of the Platte River. In the early years of farming, the soil was fertile and the farmers did well. As the years went on, the soil became depleted and the householders suffered severely.

There was a warning in spring that the melting snows north of us were filling all the waterways. There would be a huge flood. We drove over to Farley to see if we could help. The people had already taken everything movable out of their houses and had moved cattle, pigs, hens and mules to higher land—usually to a neighbor's safer place, or to a relative's land.

An official in a uniform who was trained to be present during a flood was with us as we stood where we all could see the wall of water in the riverbed coming closer and closer. Trust John the joker to watch the sight with a touch of humor. "Back where I lived the tide in the Atlantic Ocean came along this way every day," he said. I knew what he was talking about, but the Platte River dwellers hardly believed him.

Eventually, that part of the flood raced on down the river bed, but the agent who was watching with us said, "You have no idea how many tons of water are still thawing out up there. And it will all flow down here."

Some people prepared for the flood by putting everything, including the refrigerator, on the second floor. Our students went as a team into North Kansas City to help people prepare for the flood where the Platte River would flow into the already flooded Missouri at a great right angle curve (which, of course, was why Kansas City was built right there by the early pioneers who had not yet experienced the spring floods).

The Farley Church was John's responsibility. We had a warm and friendly group of friends there. This was the largest of the three little churches and there were enough ladies in the congregation to have a Women's Group, which had meetings on regular days and a program for every meeting and, of course, refreshments. That group was a miniature of all the larger women's church groups everywhere. Tish Croom organized the study program and John and I were always present to give support.

Every group of adults, whatever their persuasion, will inevitably have some dissenters. There was one evening meeting in the little church when the discussion indicated there were two (or more) sides. The peacemakers who were leading the discussion were clearly not winning the peace and suddenly someone slipped out and slammed the door. If you had looked quickly enough, you would have seen a man's hand and arm slip in through a crack in the door to retrieve his hat from the back pew.

The Big Fish Fry

It was in the Farley parish that they had the big Fish Fry every summer down in Bill Cannon's grove. Walter Humphrey had a springhouse with a tank of spring water deep enough to hold any number of catfish to freshen them in the clear water to take away the taste of the Missouri mud. Someone prepared the catfish and Bill Cannon hauled down the great big iron "Hog Kittle" to hold the lard to fry the fish. The fire was fed with plenty of wood. When the coals were red hot and the lard was melted, Bill laid a flat strip of hen wire cut to fit down into the kettle with slices of fish arranged to be fried.

While the fish was frying, the women were making the hush puppies, which were like corn meal muffins laced with chopped onion rolled into a ball the size of a baseball. When the fish were lifted out of the kettle, the hush puppies went in to fry in the bubbling fat. They sank for a minute and then bobbed up to be poked a bit until crisp and browned. The name, they told us, came from the custom of quieting the hungry dogs by tossing them a hush puppy. They are no relation to our modern shoes!

On a long table set out under the trees, the ladies had laid out salads and desserts and cakes of all kinds. Every year the display included a bright green cake which elicited the annual joke from one of the farmers that "that must be frosted with 'Paris Green,' the stuff we use to 'pizen the pertaters.'" He really meant to take care of the potato bugs, not the potatoes themselves. There was much friendly chatter as we enjoyed the feast.

Bill Cannon

As we walked with Bill Cannon back from the fish fry to his house, Bill said to John Philbrick, "I just wish I knew as much as you know." John was astonished and I heard his reply. "Why Bill, you know twice as much as any of us. You can live so close to the earth and you live with Nature and don't ever have to study out of books." We could see by Bill's grin that he was pleased.

Bill's small farm was always welcoming on any occasion. He was generous with information about everything around him. One day he took several of us, with his wife, Opal, on a walk through the woods. It was late summer and he led us to the paw-paw patch. The children had been singing, "Where, oh where, oh where is Susie?" and Bill responded, "Way down yonder in the paw-paw patch." Paw-paws, he said had to be real ripe, almost rotten, before they were edible. "We'll see if they are ripe. Some people call them custard apples but we've always called 'em paw paws." They were dead ripe, richly sweet and juicy, as Bill pulled them from the trees.

As we walked back to his house, we could see his simple farm implements scattered here and there where he had dropped them after the job was finished. He said with a twinkle, "My implement shed leaks." In other words, he had no implement shed. John praised him for his wonderful knowledge of his surroundings and he received the praise with simple joy and pride.

The students who were with us asked why when farmers did have implement sheds, they didn't ever spruce them up and paint them? The answer was that even just paint enough for a barn would cost maybe six hundred dollars and probably that farmer never handled six hundred in a whole year, but even so he and his family managed to survive. We hoped the students would be aware how important farmers are for our foods. They still need all the help we can give them.

Even country-living farm people sometimes have troubles. One of the men in that particular church went off his rocker, with some amazing results. He purchased a huge bundle of American flags from a railroad shop that sold goods undeliverable by the railroad for some reason, such as no address. He decorated his whole house and barn and all the little farm buildings with these flags. The neighborhood was alerted and the sixteen-party telephone line was busy all the time. As soon as one party was called, the next party listened in to hear the latest [this was before television!]. The first party asked the second party if anything was happening. The second party reported that there was more traffic than usual down Road C where Mr. H. lived. The third party had been listening and she reported that sometimes a car would drive slowly past the house as if it was studying, or perhaps, counting all the flags. By the time the fourth party called in to listen, someone was telling that sometimes a car would whiz past as though they feared an evil spirit was in that house. Anyone on a sixteen-party line is aware you can tell whenever a new listener picks up her phone because the power is stretched and the sound weakens. The telephone wires were draped between trees along the country roads.

According to the telephone reports, the gentleman in the story had ridden roughshod through several pastures and left gates unlocked all over several towns. He was finally captured and tried and ultimately found himself in the county jailhouse, which was in the center of the county seat next to the courthouse, facing toward the sidewalk. He then expressed his feelings by opening the window so he could throw a basin of cold water over anyone who walked by on the sidewalk. He was finally helped by a psychiatrist.

Two-Legged Visitors

One of the best features of Roanridge was its position in the world assembly of Episcopalian, Anglican, Australian, Indian, and Canadian churches. There was a steady stream of top flight leaders from all those countries coming to visit as the Roanridge Rural Training Foundation became more famous, and visitors came to observe our training systems and perhaps to install teaching programs of their own back home. We never knew who might be coming. John and I were especially glad to welcome the visitors from other countries, where agriculture was practiced on a different scale.

The first visitors came from India—a young clergyman, Inaiyat Massih, which means "long-awaited messiah" in Hindi, and his wife, who wanted to learn three things especially: how to hive a swarm of bees, how to can garden vegetables in glass jars, and how to make soap. At the Homestead we had the canning equipment and while we were canning, there was a telephone call telling about a bee colony that was beginning to swarm. We took the young man out to show him how to hive the swarm.

Early in the summer, the honeybees are likely to swarm when the hive has added too many bees and the old queen takes half of the bees to make a new hive. The neighbor's swarm had followed the scout bees to their chosen spot on the lower limb of a tree. When the bees leave to swarm, they first take a long drink of honey (just as we would grab our pocketbooks before going out), and there is little danger of being stung. That day, Inaiyat Massih and his wife learned the well-worn technique of spreading a white sheet on the ground with the hive in the middle with the cover off. The bee man's job is to prepare everything and then to shake the limb with a great shake, which everyone hopes will drop the queen into the hive.

He was successful. Immediately, every one of the ten thousand bees turned to the hive and hurried to get inside with the queen. It was like looking at streams of water to behold every bee moving so quickly into the hive to begin making honey again.

Soap was an easy assignment because we always had a surplus of bacon fat after feeding breakfast to about 40 students from neighboring Park College every Sunday morning. Back then in the good old days before the discovery of cholesterol, we often cooked three pounds of bacon on Sunday morning. It was easy to make laundry soap to use up all the grease, if one was careful. A can of lye from the grocery store poured very carefully into the grease would set up and turn the grease into a solid. Pour it while warm—from the potash—into a flat shallow cardboard box. You could cut the soap into cakes with a knife before it hardened.

I can't resist a 21st century interpolation here. Some modern, up-to-date people have just rediscovered how practical it is to make your own soap. It is also interesting and fun to use colors and flavors made from herbs. At Christmas-time, every street corner seems to have a pretty young lady selling homemade soap to an admiring public. So we became Foreign Missionaries long enough to teach the leaders how to teach their followers how to make handmade soap, which was desperately needed in every household.

One of our favorites visitors was from India. His name was Bishop Philoxynos Anastagoras, which we shortened to "Anastagoras," but his rose-colored robe won him the affectionate name of "the Pink Bishop." While he was visiting, our beloved cook Mrs. Fraiser came down with a "run around"—also called a "felon," a common usage in England—on her finger. A doctor probably would have called it a paronychia (around a nail) and prescribed a medication. Mrs. Fraiser had her own ideas, traditional for generations for that ailment. She cut a lemon in half and stuck her ailing finger into the center of one half of the lemon. Of course, we all noticed her attacking her work with a half of a lemon on her hand. The Pink Bishop spoke with her and then told us all that in India everyone would use that identical treatment. He also agreed with her plan for after the infection was better. At first she would wrap her finger with the thin white tissue from the inside of an eggshell. He then said that people in India would use the same medical treatment.

Our next visitor was a geographer named Dr. Kuleratnam, who was from a large island off the tip of the Indian subcontinent named Ceylon. It is now known as Sri Lanka. He impressed us with his great wisdom and his concern about the orientation of our cots on the lawn behind the Homestead, where we were sleeping on the desperately hot nights. Were we located north and south or east and west? As a geographer he knew about vibrations from outer space.

When Anglican Bishop Lewes came from England to visit Roanridge, we were all on our best behavior. He was a delightful visitor who entered into all our activities and made memorable assessments of some of our staff members: viz. the one who spoke little but said a lot and another who talked all the time but really didn't say much! He explained the British custom of a bishop using the name of his Diocese instead of his personal name. This prepared us for the next two visitors.

One day the Philbricks received notice to meet a train at the Kansas City railroad station at seven in the morning to welcome Bishop Rockhampton and Bishop Kalgourlie, who were arriving from Australia by way of New Orleans. We could hardly wait to meet them because we had learned how people bring their own country's traits along with them, and we wanted enjoy new insights into Australia.

They were delightful men who went by the names of two geographic precincts for which their dioceses were named. Bishop Rockhampton told us he used his own name so seldom he had to think to recall it. We took them out to breakfast that morning. Bishop Rockhampton tried to get the plastic wrapper off a pack of cigarettes with a nail file.

"Let me show you," John said, and showed Rockhampton how to remove the plastic cover by pulling off the red strip around the top.

The bishops told us that they were personally considering a big problem for Australia. Should the country allow television to be introduced? They rehearsed its good points and considered the bad things they had heard about the medium. We told them that the little we knew about television in America had come just that week from Mrs. Foote, the Director's wife. She came to our house and said, "The most awful thing has just come into our house—a television! But we had to get it because our 12-year-old daughter was watching a television in the nearest joint down town." This was in the mid-1950s and none of us had ever seen or wanted a television.

It was always fun to pilot visitors around Missouri—after we had learned to understand the Missouri accent. Kalgourlie's southwestern Australian accent was a cryptic variation of English. We took him to the Red X, a grocery store. He wanted to buy beer. He said, "Do you have any be-ah he-ah?" and the clerk said, "Huh?"

Kalgourlie repeated, "Do you have any be-ah?" He stopped and pointed. "Oh, the-ahs the be-ah, the-ah."

Another visitor was from New York but his clergy son and his daughter-in-law were ministering to a parish within the Arctic Circle. In those days all their food was delivered monthly by ship. Was there any way they could grow some food during the brief warmer weather, our visitor asked? We worked hard over that question, with not much success. We corresponded with *Mother Earth News* in England because they had experience with the Arctic Circle. They could raise radishes but the rest of their food would continue to be delivered monthly.

Fortunately, not all the visitors came at the same time. The next one, the Honorable Mr. Cisneros Falconi, was the Minister of Agriculture in Ecuador in South America. He came to Roanridge as an observer, on a tour to see American farms and learn various methods of farm management. Mr. Cochel was pleased beyond measure to have such an important statesman coming to visit Roanridge.

Everything was prepared. The grassed waterways were mowed and the bushes around the Morning Glory Pond structure were trimmed. The handsome Red, White and Roan shorthorns were groomed with little waves in their fur instead of their usual straight look. Arlo, the Farm Superintendent, was almost beside himself rushing to get everything shipshape for the Minister of Agriculture from a foreign country. Of course, the excitement filtered down to us in the Homestead, but we did not expect to be involved in the big farm show, except perhaps as spectators. But we were there ready anyway.

At the appointed time the black limousines arrived and out poured all the dignitaries. There was representation from our State Department from Washington, several very official gentlemen. Then there was an interpreter ready to make sense between two languages. There were several gentlemen of various persuasions to accompany the Minister, and finally the Minister himself came forward and everyone shook hands. Mr. Cochel came forward and the introductions were profuse even though the speeches were unintelligible!

We were swept up by the exuberance of the occasion and Mr. Cisneros Falconi, Minister of Agriculture in Ecuador, began to ask questions about everything he was seeing. We went into the barn where Mr. Cochel's prize shorthorns were standing ready to be admired. For some reason, Mr. Cochel asked John to explain some of the details of the farm but as soon as John spoke, the interpreter began to interpret. John had been trained not to speak while someone was speaking so he would stop. The interpreter must have met that situation often. They finally set their mutual rhythms and the Minister of Agriculture must have enjoyed his visit to Roanridge, judging by the flowery things he said.

This kind of language repartee went back and forth while the group walked around the farm studying the flood control elements and inquiring about the fields full of small grains. As the morning wore on and we all got a little more used to each other, I began to notice that when the interpreter spoke to Mr. Falconi in answer to many questions about the planted crops, he often used the word in Spanish "legumbre." I knew no Spanish, but I did hear that word so often I knew it must be Spanish for vegetable. We certainly didn't have that many legumes growing in all the fields at Roanridge.

It took some courage, but I actually got up nerve enough to tell the interpreter that legume is our American word for only one special kind of plant, like peas or beans or clover, which have nitrogen nodules on their roots. He understood immediately and explained the difference to the assembly. It was an exciting morning, and the Minister of Agriculture must have taken much wisdom back to Ecuador. We assumed that Dr. Falconi had been directed to Roanridge by the State Department. That made us swell with pride!

Another Guest

A young woman from India asked to be allowed to work in a kitchen. At home in India, there were servants who worked in the kitchen where she was not allowed. She chose to make chapatis, and I was eager to share my kitchen with her.

She gave the directions. I rolled out the circles of wheat flour and water dough. We let the dough rest a few minutes to prevent it from shrinking. Then each circle was cooked in an iron skillet until it puffed up. We ate them with plenty of butter and strawberry jam and never went to the dining room for lunch!

Displaced Persons

At the end of the Second World War, there were displaced persons living all over Europe in refugee camps and minimal living situations. The Presiding Bishop of the Episcopal Church gathered together people who would willingly take on the care of a family in need.

The first news we heard at Roanridge was that the Episcopal Church had agreed to take on twenty-five families from Europe. Mr. Cochel was delighted and asked for three or four carpenters because he could supply work for as many men as he could get. He would also welcome them if they had families. There would surely be room enough for them at Roanridge.

The members of the staff were taken by surprise at these sudden developments, but, with our usual good nature and inventive skills, we laid plans to house the new people, and brushed up on our German and French. We knew we would have some language problems to overcome.

Afanazi and Anastasia Abramoglu from Germany, who had been in a concentration camp, were the first to arrive. Afanazi had signed on as a carpenter. In fact, most of the displaced men came as carpenters. Mr. Cochel welcomed him because he hoped to construct a new building to house all the Roanridge staff. We all greeted them and found living quarters for them. Anastasia settled comfortably into the Cochel's living quarters and everything seemed well.

The language barrier proved to be hard for Afanazi to overcome. He appeared, someone said, to be speaking Turkish. So we didn't have much conversation. He loved to drive Mr. Cochel's big Buick. One morning he took me on an errand and spoke what I imagine was his longest speech in English. It went like this. "Maama Bee—very smart—sunny day she say—Go to work." He was an accomplished beekeeper.

When "Afanas" learned that Mr. Cochel needed a trash container, he made one out of very fine lumber that would fit under Mr. Cochel's desk. He could easily drop papers into it without moving from his desk chair. When the "basket" was full it was almost impossible to pry it out from under the desk.

During one summer night, there was a total eclipse of the moon and Afanas collected several pots and pans which he shook and rattled and pounded during the eclipse to drive away the evil spirits.

Anastasia did well. She quickly learned to speak English. She helped with housekeeping for the Cochels and eventually found a job at Bellas Hess, a pre-cut dress factory, in Kansas City. She became a forelady in the factory where they put together dresses that were half finished. In those days, one could buy a dress ready to complete oneself—long before our present system of pre-fab garments.

Once during her stay at Roanridge, she was confined for a short time at St. Luke's Hospital in Kansas City. When Mr. Samuelson opened the bill, he laughed and said, "I knew what was going to happen. The bill is made out to Mrs. Anesthesia instead of Anastasia Abramoglu."

The next couple, Mr. Alex Filinos and Mrs. Filinova, also came from a concentration camp after the war. The husband signed up as a carpenter but he really was more familiar with masonry and soon found a job with a decent salary. They had a little girl and among them they knew no English words at all. There was a big argument over whether her name should be Filinov or Filinova. Male names end in "os" and female names in "ova." What would the daughter's name be?

Every day I gave the wife an English lesson while the little girl was in public school. The mother was a delightful person and we had lots of laughs and good humor over the words. Sometimes I learned more German than she learned English. She had difficulty with pronouns: which was you and which was the I-me combination. We enjoyed a big laugh the day I met her walking from her trailer toward the Cochel house, carrying a bath towel, face cloth, and soap in her hand and obviously ready to take a bath. "You have to take a bath," she said. The little girl grew up and eventually entered a college in Oregon, helped financially by John Philbrick's New Hampshire cousin, and she graduated with honors.

In all, there were twenty-five displaced persons who came to Roanridge. Several women traveled to the stores together to help each other with the language. It was from one of their shopping trips that I first learned the meaning of the little dancer's name: Petrushka or Parsley, remembered from all those years ago in Middleton.

Let me digress for one more Middleton story. A gentleman who had emigrated from Hungary smiled with rows of stainless steel teeth. He had once had a position in Middleton as a police officer, and he could not understand why America made any distinction at all between black and white people. One day he showed me a snapshot of the very "gypsy" we had entertained in Duxbury. They had been together in a school in Greece long before the war. Willie Kahlert, the "gypsy," had gone into the ministry while his friend had chosen the police force.

A Visit from the Illustrious Dr. Albrecht

To our surprise, Dr. William A. Albrecht, Professor Emeritus of Soils, visited from the College of Agriculture at the University of Missouri. He wanted first to see Mr. Cochel's big farm, which was famous for its modern machinery and its well-respected methods. But after his visit to Mr. Cochel, he and his wife came over to the Homestead to see what we were doing.

We were using only primitive hand tools and natural fertilizers, but we had also learned much from the big farm. Apparently Dr. Albrecht had read my book entitled *Companion Plants* and had found an angle on insect control in the backyard garden that was not being taught yet in the College of Agriculture. We rejoiced that these simple, old-fashioned practices had been rediscovered. And in 2005 they are becoming more and more acceptable as an alternative to the commercial agricultural insecticides.

The Albrechts were delightful guests, and we felt honored that they were willing to stay all night at our house—after our lively evening discussion about the work of the Homestead. In August 1962, when we were in the vicarage at Ashfield, he wrote us a long and breezy letter from his home in Columbia, Missouri:

> Dear Friends:
>
> We appreciated the copy of "A Closer Look At Your Garden" as put up by Free Deeds, Volume 2, No. 1 in March, 1962. Do you have anyone print your sermons?
>
> Enclosed herewith is a paper (and a poem) which I wish you would read as if you were an Editor, and your paper anticipates readers with a College or Baccalaureate degree.
>
> The subject, as listed in the paper, will be discussed (without manuscript, but with slides) at Montclair, New Jersey, September 8th evening at the Natural Foods Associates. meetings of New Jersey (statewide, I believe). Mr. F.E. Sadowski, Valley Brook Road, Long Valley, New Jersey, is chairman.
>
> I am trying to make a case for plants using organic compounds from the soil as nutrition. If you will read the paper, criticize, etc. it will be appreciated. Places lacking clarity will be especially appreciated since in the habit of more technical thinking, we take too much for granted.
>
> Your citation of what might be called "compatibility or incompatibility" of plants, like strawberries and beans, reminds me to inquire how extensive a list of those you have, including protective effects against insects, e.g. clove of garlic with bean planting to prohibit bean beetles, attacking chrysanthemums as well as beans. I am hoping to make an extended collection and theorize as to organic compounds (chemical) possibly responsible. Recently a new insecticide has been found in turnips that does not affect man, but is effective against house flies, aphids, beetles, cockroaches and mites. The compound is thio phenyliso thio cyanate, or we might say phenyl mustard oil, or thio carbonil, C_6H_5 N:C:S:
>
> I am anxious to use all the empiricism, folklore, etc., to move along, but why not add the science to the

folklore? Nature has always been wiser than we are, but we don't believe it until we make a *saleable* compound which nature used during the ages. We now know that the emanation from horseradish will destroy many bacteria in laboratory test, note, just the volatilization. Spring doses of horseradish were great medicine, in my youth.

We are in the midst of temperatures at 100 and no significant rainfall since the first of August. We are in a "disaster" area.

With kind regards and appreciation of any editorial help you will suggest, I am

Sincerely yours,

William A. Albrecht
Professor Emeritus of Soils

The Piglet

One bright morning, Arlo Cottrell phoned us to say that the Farm's Mother Pig had just had a large litter of piglets. The runt of the litter was in a weakened condition, because his mother had stepped on him and injured his eye. Would we like to try to raise him?

Of course we said yes, and we prepared for his reception at our house down in the valley, which had once been occupied by the tenant farmer. Because it was still winter, we arranged a space in the kitchen where the little piglet would be warm and where his needs would be taken care of in detail.

The first demand was to find him a name. Every shorthorn in the Cochel herd was given a long name which condensed all the detailed identification. First the name of the herd or the owner, then the site he occupied, his home. Next came the beast's name and, finally, any qualifying word that would identify him. As we worked out the details, the name gradually stretched out almost as long as the little pig himself. His name was Roanridge Demonstration Homestead Stuffy the First.

We were very proud of the title and happy to welcome Stuffy into our kitchen. The weekly church bulletin was in preparation, and we naturally wrote up Stuffy's story. Every week a copy of the weekly bulletin was mailed to the Home Department at the New York office, where Dr. Samuelson, the Executive Secretary, was in charge. The letter that came back from the New York office had so much dynamite in it that it hardly needed any postage! "What do you think you are doing with a pig in your kitchen? Are you trying to look like Greenwich Village? What will people think of you and what kind of a reputation will you get for such foolishness? You will be the laughing stock of Platte County." The paper sizzled and crackled, and we wondered if we had made a big mistake, but of course we were still caring for Stuffy and watching him settle into the family.

The next Sunday, John had the service over at Farley. After the service, while everyone was enjoying refreshments, John said to one of the farmers, "Wyman, did you ever have a pig in your kitchen in the early spring?"

Wyman Croskey grinned at his wife. "I've got two pigs in my kitchen right now," he said. "I've had pigs and rabbits and chickens and ducklings but, Mr. Philbrick, a calf in the kitchen is the damnedest thing."

The following summer when the students were assembled with Dr. Samuelson present, John told the story of Demonstration Homestead Stuffy the First, and the Executive Secretary graciously admitted that he had written the blistering letter but might now sing a new tune.

His Passion for Perfection

Anyone who knew Dr. Samuelson will recall his passion for perfection. The buildings must be absolutely perfect and maintenance was to be immaculate. Dealing as we did with rural people who had their own standards, we often failed to reach the heights of excellence demanded of us. Then there would be tempers and recriminations and long sessions of long words—at the end of which Dr. Foote would disentangle his long legs and drawl, "Come on now, it really isn't worth getting emotionally upset about it." The sun would shine again, and we all would rejoice in the passing of one more storm.

The press camera accomplished wonders and was always ready to roll. The motion picture camera was even more in constant demand. Ceremonial occasions were given full treatment, but seemingly inconsequential events also received special attention, like the day we cleaned the barn and baby mice were photographed peeking out of Letitia Croom's shirt pocket.

That same shirt, after many years of wear. was finally reduced to the status of a duster. The kind gentleman who kept the chapel in good shape was often seen dusting the chapel with Tish's old shirt.

But, as you must realize, my point of view was not as high or as broad as the vision of the clergy and the field workers, who were establishing policy and conducting conferences to blend experience and expertise.

Chapter 17

Duxbury Madras

Every summer we used to drive from Missouri east to spend some weeks at the old Faith Homestead in Duxbury. One friend we always went to see was Mrs. Elinor Lord, who lived in one of the houses that had been made out of the old Standish Hotel. Mrs. Lord explained to us that she had had the big house placed in such a way that the sun would shine into every window during the course of the year.

We asked her to tell us about her trip to India, when she was privileged to have a visit with Gandhi. She had been much impressed and, of course, was happy to tell us all about it. One summer when we called, she told us another story. She was a great swimmer and swam off Standish Shore every day. Her friend, a woman named Hilda Ives, who was a minister and lived in Maine, was also an enthusiastic swimmer.

One day Hilda Ives phoned Elinor to tell her that she, Hilda, had been invited to attend a convention in Madras, India. Would Elinor like to go? Elinor's smiling reply was that she would very much like to go to Madras. The two old friends chatted for a bit and the trip was planned.

Their itinerary led them to the Dardanelles and they held a conference there with each other. They said Lord Byron was said to have swum the Hellespont. Shouldn't two old ladies also swim the Hellespont? They agreed and together swam across. After that, they continued on their trip to India to attend an international conference intended to improve the conditions of humanity. We enjoyed hearing Mrs. Lord tell about those two old women emulating Lord Byron, who was really a rakish character! He is reported to have been trying to emulate Leander, who swam across to visit Hero every night and eventually drowned, as the legend tells it.

The Episcopal Triennial Convention of 1952

By a happy coincidence, the Episcopal Triennial Convention of 1952 was to be held in Boston, while we were still on the Roanridge staff. It was very exciting to prepare our exhibition from the Roanridge Rural Training Foundation to show to our friends in Boston—as well as to thousands of other people who would attend the convention.

Months before the official dates, we planned the exhibit to represent each facet of the Homestead: from the hens, a dozen eggs; from the milk goats, a quart of milk (obviously!); from the garden, dried herbs and teas elegantly wrapped, vegetables, of course, and some fruit. But the honeybees were the best advertisers. They provided us with literally thousands of cubes of pure beeswax (made in ice cube trays) for waxing one's sewing thread. We were happy to come back to Boston, where we knew polite Bostonian ladies still waxed their hand-sewing threads with pure beeswax. The preparation of the wax cubes took many hours of work, as each one was wrapped with a label stating the source of the beeswax to advertise Roanridge.

The exhibit was located on the third floor of Symphony Hall just beyond the head of the left hand staircase. There were so many visitors we never could count them all. Of course, we were all very proud to be included in the Convention. Symphony Hall was for the Convention House of Deputies, while across the street Horticultural Hall was for the House of Bishops. The convention is always bi-cameral, because the early founders were the same dignitaries who originally invented our government's Congress of Senate and House of Representatives. Every three years, we Episcopalians faithfully explain this piece of historical information.

The Convention was assembled in Symphony Hall for the opening speeches. The first speaker was our dearly beloved Dean Sprouse, the Dean of the Kansas City Cathedral. We knew him well and were rejoiced that he was to speak. As he neared the end of his speech, he said, "It is our hope that what we do in this convention may affect the peace of the world."

He stopped speaking and eased down to the floor. From our viewpoint on the third floor we could tell by the activity of the people surrounding him that he had passed away. He was surrounded by all his best friends: his wife and his doctor and many others who were there to help. This was an unexpectedly spectacular opening for a Triennial General Convention.

Although the Roanridge Demonstration Homestead got good publicity, and was always mentioned as a valuable presentation of good techniques to be used in rural areas, publicity still seemed to miss the real heart of the demonstration. The need for personal commitment to rural life was never really emphasized. We tried hard to practice and teach how important it was to be wholly committed, to love the earth, to weave together the sun and the rain and the gardens and the livestock. The best newspapers failed to proclaim deeply enough that one's devotion must be absolute.

This lack of positive conviction was revealed at General Convention in Boston in 1952 when the Roanridge Demonstration Homestead presented a display of home-grown products: a dozen eggs, a loaf of bread, a small wheel of homemade cheese, and, of course, a jar of honey from the Homestead's bees. The whole display was never officially photographed, although it attracted streams of people who recognized familiar rural skills and searched for techniques to upgrade their own lives. The nitty gritty of successful rural living seemed always to be officially kept at a distance. We as a nation do love our comforts and our mechanical conveniences.

The Cattle Auction

There was to be a cattle auction on the 400-acre farm. The big tent was erected, and chairs enough for two or three hundred cattlemen were set out. The Auction Block was the bed of a wagon and the space in front below was the area for displaying the Red and Roan and White Purebred Cattle of the Rosewood type, belonging to Mr. Wilbur Cochel. The hay was deep to emphasize that shorthorns have short legs!

The sun shone on the occasion, and we all were eager to watch the proceedings. To my surprise, the auctioneer asked if I would be clerk of the auction. Of course I would—little knowing what the job involved.

This was probably the only Missouri cattle auction that season that was opened with prayer—a long and all-inclusive prayer, which detailed many intimacies of cattle breeding. Finally, "Amen," and the auctioneer burst forth with his version of the auctioneer's chant, which split the silence and sent chills up and down my back. How could I be clerk when I couldn't understand a word? Not to worry. They gave me the cattle lot book and a small address book. When a shorthorn was bought, the auctioneer would look at me and say the lot number and the name of the buyer. The price went on the page with the name of the buyer. At the end of the day it all balanced.

Then the clerk's work really began. The cattle buyers came to the tailboard of the wagon with their stubby pencils and checkbooks. "You make out the check, please ma'am" for nineteen thousand dollars or for forty thousand. One by one, they handed their checkbooks and their pencils up to me and I had to make out amounts larger than anything I had ever dreamed would be the value of a Shorthorn bull.

The sun set that day on proud farmers with beautiful dark red and roan shorthorns traveling in every direction to many Midwest states. The auction finances balanced to a penny, but the ladies in the tent with the popcorn and soft drinks were still agonizing to make the petty cash balance.

Kansas City Centennial Celebration

While we concentrated on our local work, trying to keep up with the accomplishments that the New York Home Department expected of us, the years had passed by, and Kansas City was about to celebrate its one hundredth anniversary around 1955.

There was a great pageant that described everything about the early pioneers who first explored the territory around the Missouri River. The Lewis and Clark expedition was a beginning. The pageant followed history through early beginnings and the Civil War until the proud growth of the modern city.

One special feature was the personal life of the outlaw Jesse James, who had fought well for the South in the Civil War. Later, he had become an outlaw and a robber of vicious reputation. In the pageant, Jesse James held up a real streetcar, right there on stage. After that he robbed the bank on the corner.

What really took our breaths away was that Mr. Cochel had actually known Jesse James. Not only had he known the outlaw, he had also known Thomas Hart Benton, a famous artist, and Kit Carson, a typical frontier hero and Indian fighter. He didn't care if T.H. Benson was a great artist. He had known him as a politician.

When we asked him if he had known any of these famous early figures, he would say, briefly, "Oh, yes," but never told us any of the gossip. It was fun to see the sophisticated seminarians light up when we would say, "Mr. Cochel actually knew the outlaw Jesse James."

Sometimes our New York associates and directors would come to the wilds of Missouri. One gentleman noticed an auto license plate ready to be put on a car. He looked closer and noticed that little Platte County was specially indicated in dark red. His New York sense of superiority led him to label that "a desperate effort at self-realization." Sometimes it was not easy to explain the virtues of the simple lifestyle to smart people from higher places.

Leaving Roanridge to Drive to Massachusetts

After six or seven years, it was time to return home. The departure happened on a Sunday morning, and there was the regular church service at the Chapel. John preached with an attempt to balance the pain of leaving with the anticipation of going home. The little congregation felt their sorrow about losing us, balanced by anticipation of welcoming a new minister.

The joys and sorrows telescoped into a most generous farewell gift of several pieces of handsome new luggage, which we accepted with warmest appreciation and affectionate thank yous to all our good friends. It was deep and moving and was sealed by many warm hugs. The last one we saw as we drove away was Tish, our staff associate, standing alone by the back door and waving slowly, sadly.

We left the chapel that morning—after the gift of the luggage—with slightly guilty consciences. All our goods and chattels were already packed in our own luggage, tightly jammed into the back of the automobile. We couldn't have unpacked all those containers and repacked them while the congregation watched.

Gradually, as so often happens when a problem comes up, the sense of humor comes to help. The result was that before we entered the first motel to spend the night, we made a joke out of the event and carried in the new empty cases, pretending they were full, and then the old laden cases, pretending they were empty. John shaved off his moustache.

Roanridge Postscript 2002—Great good news!

When the old Roanridge suffered change and, finally, its end in the 1960s, the organization called the Rural Workers' Fellowship also suffered and faded. The good news is that in 2002, it began to be resurrected and will include clergy in small country churches in rural places, both in the U.S.A. and in Canada. There is a prayer list in the publication and every member will have his day. Several former members were present at the historic meeting that is bringing this work back to new life.

Chapter 18

Ashfield—1957-1962

A Beloved Voice Near the Massachusetts Border

Traveling east was always a joy. It took several days but at last we were in New York State, close to the Massachusetts line. At the border, we switched on the radio, tuned to WBZ—an act of sentimental loyalty, tinged with exuberant joy to be back. It was noontime, and we heard the voice of our beloved Carl de Suze. He was as usual introducing the Marjorie Mills program. We heard him say "You people who look as though you are wealthy had better go home and put on some decent clothes." Music to our ears. Back in those years—the 1950s—as for many, many years before, eastern customs were more subdued than customs in Kansas City, where, for example, if one had money he or she dressed up to display it. Now, in 2005, extravagant display seems still more insidious!

Ashfield, Pop. 1,000

We were headed for the town of Ashfield in western Massachusetts, population 1000, to a small church, with a loyal congregation and an unusual arrangement. The Congregational Church in town was much larger than the Episcopal, but neither church could afford to pay a living wage for a minister. For eighteen years, the two churches had worked separately but together in everything under a wise and competent clergyman named Phil Steinmetz. It was he who recognized that the two churches could not unite and become one church, but they could occasionally share a Sunday together, and in all the big occasions they could unite to work as one. It was a famous experiment and had a good reputation in church circles.

John was to be the vicar of St. John's Episcopal Church. (Vicar means one who acts in place of the Bishop.) He was also the Pastor of the Congregational Church. All inter-parish affairs were held at the Congregational Church in Friendship Hall. My assignment as clergy wife was to be on hand whenever I was needed and to entertain the combined church boards at the house we lived in, which belonged to the Congregationalists but was called the Vicarage. It was so cold that one lady wrapped herself in a portiere curtain during meetings.

The house was very large, with ceilings so high they seemed to be in heaven. The minister's study was half a day's walk from the kitchen—so far, I used to phone him when lunch was served. Our dining table could seat 18, and one guest asked, "Have you had this surveyed lately?"

It had been the custom to use the Vicarage for Smith College students, who came from Northampton to stay two or three days for a retreat. The carloads of girls were arriving. One of the girls said to John," Mr. Philbrick, do you remember me?"

John looked at her and replied, "No, I really don't recognize you."

"I'm the one that ran away when you were baptizing all my brothers and sisters," she said. "I ran to the end of the driveway! I was four years old!"

"Yes," said John, "even though I hardly recognize you after all these years, I certainly do remember you running all the length of the church driveway!"

This was in 1957 and the thwarted baptism had occurred back in Duxbury in the 1940s.

My favorite memory of that house is the glassed-in sun porch where I watched the work of a huge wasp's nest being built against a pane. The wasps were all outside and I was inside. There was no danger of being stung. I watched each wasp through a magnifying glass as each in turn built a tiny edge of paper on the paper of the nest already built. The papery fibers, chewed off old wood somewhere, would show along the edge because it was wet with the wasp's saliva. Even after the big paper nest was finished, I could still see the tiny little strips of paper of varying colors, which had been built up one millimeter at a time. This was an example of the origin of paper, invented by wasps.

John was not a pompous clergyman. He was expert in winning friends and making himself a member of the community, as the following anecdote illustrates. Not far from our house was a big house on a high hill named Mizzenmast. It had been built by Admiral Farragut (1801-1870), who had done distinguished work during the Civil War. The house stood as a monument to architecture in his day. One day the lady of the house asked John to come to see her. He put on his clerical collar, pocketed a Prayer Book, and drove up to the house. She met him at the door, invited him in, and explained that her cat had just had six kittens and she wanted to know which were boys and which were girls. They were in a closet under the stairs and she led him into the space. John had had plenty of experience, and he gave her his census report on the kittens—three females and three males. Then he said, "I notice that my ministry often leads me into the danged-est places!"

Of course we had a garden on a fine piece of land, level, plenty of sunshine and rain enough to keep everything growing. One day, my neighbor, one of the Selectmen, was out in his garden. Suddenly, I heard two shots and saw him pick up something from the ground. I immediately felt furious and walked over to him. Equally quickly, I pushed the fury down and became on the surface "all sweetness and light." I greeted him cordially and gently and we talked about our gardens, and I complimented him on his fine grass.

Then I asked him, still sweetly, "Did you catch something?" He answered with venom, "Yes, those darned tree swallows drive my blue birds away. You know, I kind of hoped nobody would see what I did." My violent rebuke to a respected Selectman had been accomplished, and he had delivered his own reprimand.

We grew to love Ashfield. The people were very friendly and we had many good times. Almost everyone, it seemed, would ask us if we had met Mr. Bullitt yet. He was a summer visitor, and we had to wait for him to come.

The school superintendent was interested in learning to cane a chair. Whenever there was a free evening, we stopped at the house where he lived with his wife and ten children, to work on caning chairs. He even acquired a big loom and wove some fine tweeds—friendly competition with his teachers.

The town of Ashfield was happily energized by a visit from the Pilgrim Bell Ringers from Plymouth—instigated, of course, by the Reverend John, who had once been one of the bell ringers when we lived in Duxbury. According to Ashfield legend, certain pieces of land had been given to early settlers of Ashfield, who had helped early settlers in Plymouth. The Ashfield locals were interested to hear some Plymouth ringers, and to learn what they could say about the land.

The twelve Bell Ringers donned their robes and processed from the Vicarage up "the street" to Friendship Hall. The concert was, as always, a rewarding experience. On their way home, the Bell Ringers reassembled at the famous Sweetheart Tea Room on the Mohawk Trail to have dinner and to sing Grace before the meal.

There were other visitors to the Vicarage. My colleague in Occupational Therapy, Grace Tinkham, came to spend a few days in early summer when our beehives were beginning to be active. We had ordered a container full of honeybees to enlarge one hive and, as it always happens, the bees in the box pick up any stray bees en route and the Post Office is not happy when they arrive. They called on the telephone to ask if we would please come get the bees right now. John was away. I took the wheelbarrow and trudged up "the street" to the Post Office.

Beginners sometimes have to learn the hard way. In my haste to get the box out of the Post Office, I failed to notice the safe way to pick up the box. Instead, I placed one finger too close to the screen and was stung. I had heard that the juice from chewing tobacco was helpful on a bee sting. In our garage, I was shaking out all the crumbs from a dozen tobacco cans when a car drove into the yard. It was our dear friend Richard Gregg, a long-time associate of Gandhi in India, and co-author of several books. He quickly noticed the swelling finger and spoke quietly—he was a Quaker—and said, "I think I have something that will help."

From his car, he pulled a small case of homeopathic remedies. With a small whittled bone spoon, he took out a bit of white powder and put it in the palm of my hand and told me to lick it up, which I did. "I believe that will take down the swelling," he said, which it did. His quiet modesty was also part of the cure. His book, *The Power of Non-Violence*, was well known in the days that Gandhi lived and demonstrated the strength that non-violence has against demonstrations of violence. I presented my copy of *The Power of Non-Violence* to the Ashfield library, where there is a collection of his books. He also wrote a book about spinning. Richard and I later collaborated on my book, *Companion Plants and How to Use Them*. It was a joy to visit with him again.

The Grange

Back in the days before automobiles and electronic devices captured and remodeled our culture, small towns and large ones, too, had their own local organizations, which enriched their total environment and significantly influenced their calendars. The Grange was greatly respected and warmly received in farming communities. Everyone was a member. It was recognized by the state colleges, and the Extension offices generously distributed excellent information on the household arts. Farmers belonged to the Grange and joined in its rituals, which were related to other secret organizations like the Masons, the Odd Fellows, and the Improved Order of Red Men. These social organizations also offered insurance to help members with an emergency or funeral expenses.

Our Grange chapter in Ashfield must have been a ghost of its glorious past but still it carried on faithfully and with a sort of stubborn determination to "hold the fort." It was continued partly for the benefit of one lady member who lived close to the Grange Hall and took some responsibility for its care. When the small remaining group was almost ready to vote to disband, they frankly said, no, we will keep the trust as long as Amy needs us. So the Grange calendar evolved, and we all attended faithfully because our friendship went deep.

In the ritual there was a reference to "our glorious cause," which originally referred to farming. By the 1960s, local agriculture was really a thing of the past, either because the farmers were too old to work or because our culture had begun to consider agriculture as an industry and was using the attitudes and practices of the industrial world. It was a little sad, but like all change it seemed inevitable.

The Grange calendar had always scheduled a "Literary Night" for the March meeting and had always invited the members of the Hatfield Grange down in the Connecticut River Valley. After the formalities, the meeting adjourned to the basement where the long table was set for "Sugar on Snow." In the kitchen, the two men who knew how to do it were cooking the maple syrup down to that exact instant when it will become like wax when poured on snow.

The round tin plates—like cake pans—had been stored after a big clean snowstorm in someone's deep freeze and each place at the table had a dish of sparkling pure snow. The hot syrup came in big pitchers which would pour a fine stream and we watched one of the elderly experts pour a small spiral of maple syrup. He would then wind the chilled syrup like wax around his fork and put it in his mouth.

It was the same every year. After a few bites, someone with experience would explain: "If it gets too sweet for you, there are always these dill pickles and saltines. After you've had them, you can go back to the sugar on snow. Now you remember, after you go home, if you have a stomach ache you just drink some milk and you'll be all right." We marveled at the stamina of these hardy old timers who could devour a cup or more of maple syrup. And that was the "literary evening."

But of course they were the folk who had made the maple syrup in the first place. Every spring during sugaring season, the town went through a transformation. After the long winter, when the snow might be so deep it buried the downstairs windows, people began to come out into the world. The men couldn't wait to get to the sugarhouses to enjoy a bit of vacation away from their wives.

When we visited everyone's sugarhouses in the 1960s, signs of change were already in evidence. Instead of using a huge woodpile cut during the previous season, they were already burning oil to evaporate the water from the sap. Forty gallons of sap boil down to one gallon of syrup of the officially accepted thickness. That took a lot of oil. Some of the men preferred the ancient appearance of the cordwood burning under the evaporator. At each place, they gave us a spoon and a dish full of warm maple syrup.

At the end of the boiling route was the evaporator, a special container where the syrup was just about done. This was the place where one could break an eggshell and drop the raw egg into the boiling syrup. That was so good we learned to do it at home—an egg poached in maple syrup.

After about six weeks of work to bottle up the spring crop of maple syrup for the markets, the sap ran more rapidly and it was about time to close down. But not before we made another pot of maple syrup coffee. Maple flavor and coffee fit well together, and John's church had a big article about it—but that was his next church.

In a phone conversation with one of the sugar men, I asked how things were progressing as the spring affected the syrup. The sugarer on the phone said, "We're gittin kinda sick of it." And his work changed from evaporating to marketing.

William Christian Bullitt

All these summers in Ashfield, we had finally caught up with Mr. Bullitt, who was a loyal church man. Mr. William Christian Bullitt used to spend his summers in Ashfield in the little old farmhouse Howard Pease had inherited from his own family. Mr. Bullitt bought the house and land from Mr. Pease and rejoiced in the long lane leading to complete privacy and a magnificent view of Mount Monadnock across the valleys.

The summer had barely begun when parishioners began to tell the Reverend John Philbrick, the Vicar, that it was time he called on Mr. Bullitt. John and I were warmly received and Mr. Bullitt could hardly wait to tell us about his latest adventure.

He was furious, boiling angry because the telephone company had sprayed his lane to get rid of the low growing vegetation. "They killed all my wildflowers," he proclaimed vehemently. "I went right to the phone and called their headquarters, and I told them I wanted to see their highest executive officer here in my house at a certain time on a certain date. I would not stand for any excuses." The day arrived and the telephone executive was met by Mr. Bullitt and the judge of the Franklin County Court in Greenfield. Mr. Bullitt sat with his gun across his knees while he presented his case. "In future," he told the telephone executive, "if anyone ever sprays anything on my land, I'll shoot to kill." And Judge Hildreth added, "And he means it, too."

It was not long before we were good friends. He was the soul of hospitality and entertained most graciously many of his former associates, whom he had met in Washington, Paris, and even Russia, where he had been Ambassador. He had a gift for telling stories, sometimes making a big story out of a very small incident. John soon became Mr. Bullitt's beekeeper. Right then and there, John learned a new lesson about bees: Mr. Bullitt's two Chinese "boys" waited on him and kept him constantly supplied with Martinis—a large pitcherful. In those days it was proper etiquette to accept refreshments when they were offered. The beekeeper soon realized to his peril that honeybees are deathly opposed to alcohol, and they caused a great commotion whenever he went near them after drinking alcohol. The result was that the "etiquettically correct" drink thereafter had to be delayed until after his visit to the beehives.

Late in the summer, the hives were heavy with honey. John arranged to come on a certain day to remove the honeycomb. When we arrived with bee smokers and veils and gloves, we found Mr. Bullitt fully prepared to enter into the procedure—from a safe distance. He had made himself a bee veil and hat and gloves, playful replicas, not to be taken too seriously. John went to the foot of the hill to open the hives. Mr. Bullitt and I stayed halfway down the hill at a safe distance. The Chinese boys came and went between us all. John held up the first big heavy frame full of honeycomb.

We could see it dripping with honey, whereupon Mr. Bullitt shouted out, "Philbrick, you are a great man. I always said you were a great man. By God, you really ARE a great man." He loved a joke, or perhaps one should say he enjoyed humor in real life situations, and he had a talent for making a good story out of a very small happening.

One day he suggested that Bei, one of the Chinese men, take us out to see Mr. Bullitt's garden, of which he was very proud. Bei showed us the asparagus patch and spinach and salad greens all planted very close together. "Squeezie," Bei said. "Everything squeezie, squeezie!"

Mr. Bullitt refused to let the arborists prune the dead limbs off a tree near his house because a hummingbird used to light on the dead limb to preen her feathers.

After about fifteen years of politicking and wire pulling, Mr. Bullitt finally succeeded in getting Bei's wife admitted into the U.S.A. from China. Bei explained that they had been separated for many years and they might no longer be compatible. After a month or so, Mr. Bullitt asked Bei how it was working. He couldn't wait to tell us Bei's reply. "Oh, Mr. Bullitt, she is so quiet and so beautiful and so obedient, it is just like having a horse in the house!"

One day Mr. Bullitt called us on the phone to invite us to his house to meet his friends. He said, "I cannot invite you to supper because my little dining table only holds five people. Why don't you come late in the afternoon?" We agreed and arrived in time for the inevitable and unavoidable drinks, served this time by a boy from Viet Nam, who spoke only French. (This made an impression when I heard Mr. Bullitt suggest lemonade for me, "parce qu'elle ne boit pas"!)

The afternoon visit was so much fun that Mr. Bullitt suddenly said John and I must stay for supper. He even rearranged the table settings himself, explaining that he was making extra space for "mes enfants." He placed me on his right and said, "Now I cannot let you eat out of my plate, but . . ." And he proceeded to carve the lamb chops and place them on my plate. (Lamb chops gently broiled with every vestige of fat removed and the tiny bones visible.)

But more important than the food were the guests. Mr. Bullitt introduced Dr. Horwitz and his wife, explaining that "He is my doctor, my friend, my brother, and he has been with me on numerous occasions abroad." They discussed how Mr. Bullitt had left the embassy in the USSR and was immediately appointed to the French Embassy.

"I knew about the appointment before it was formally announced," Dr. Horwitz said, "and my thought was I just hope they repair the plumbing in the Blue Apartment in the Embassy in Paris."

At that, Mr. Bullitt gave him a quick look. "There was nothing the matter with that plumbing."

Other guests at the table were a Chinese lad and his tutor. Mr. Bullitt had brought the boy over from China and found a tutor to give him special help with his education. The conversation moved toward Mr. Bullitt's life as Ambassador. Dr. Horwitz spoke of his unbounded admiration of Bullitt and his diplomatic skills. He insisted that after George Washington, William Christian Bullitt was America's foremost patriot. He expounded at length and we were all deeply impressed and happy that someone had the knowledge and the language to express these deep thoughts. One touching revelation was that Mr. Bullitt had a picture of George Washington over his bed.

Suddenly, as we were moving from the table, Dr. Horwitz said, "I would like to hear Bill Bullitt read us the Declaration of Independence. I would like to hear it from his own voice." A slight pandemonium followed while the tutor and the Chinese student tried to find the Declaration of Independence. Mr. Bullitt roared at them. "Of course you won't find it in the *Encyclopedia Britannica*. They didn't want it in the first place."

At last they located it in *The World Almanac* and handed him the book.

"Do you want my glasses?" someone said.

"I don't need glasses," he said as he began to read, adding his own interpolations, such as "This is only a Bill of Particulars" or "King George was a sick man . . ."

Mrs. Horwitz was a very gentle woman, quiet and appreciative but not very talkative. We were both deeply moved by that evening we were privileged to spend with a truly great patriot, and when we could talk in the Ladies' Room we were both shedding a few tears, we had been so moved.

One day Mr. Bullitt met us in the driveway. "You must come and meet my daughter," he said. "She has just arrived from Ireland where she raises horses that win all the races." She was sitting on a divan with a lapful of press photographs taken at the latest race. They talked with animation about the Arc de Triomphe and Kubla Khan horse races—conversation that hardly related to our New England orientation.

I recall her holding up one picture and saying, "I really thought we had lost the race because the jockey looked so sad." Mr. Bullitt complained to us that when he visited her estate in Ireland, he had to take synthetic vitamins while the horses all had special natural vitamins. Another of his stories was about Anne's horses being terribly nervous and upset, but he prefaced that story by telling us about her estate, which had once been part of an ancient monastery. Nearby and across the country road, there had been a convent. His daughter had purchased the monastery and turned it into a horse farm. The convent across the road was still in operation.

All of a sudden the horses in a certain pasture became unusually skittish and nervous. Something was disturbing their quiet, peaceful existence. Anne and her farm workers set out to solve the mystery (Mr. Bullitt's stories were always at their best if there was a mystery!). They discovered that it was Saint John's Eve, or Midsummer, and that part of the celebration is the Saint John's Fire. Everyone must run and jump over the fire and the yelling and screaming of the convent girls had upset Anne's fillies.

The Reverend John Hatch Philbrick was Vicar of Saint John's Episcopal Church in Ashfield from 1957 to 1962. During that time he was also Pastor of the Ashfield Congregational Church. Mr. Bullitt faithfully came to the eight o'clock service at Saint John's every Sunday. He drove himself in his Simca (one of two identical cars which he kept in his garage at the farm). John and I always enjoyed a short visit with him early in the day when we were all relaxed and free.

One morning Mr. Bullitt insisted that I must ride in his car from the church to the vicarage, a very short distance, perhaps a twentieth of a mile. He wanted to demonstrate what a wonderful car the Simca was, especially for driving on rural roads where sometimes the ruts are deep and the housing might drag on the ground. With his usual aplomb, he instructed me to pay attention to the action of the Simca. Which I did. He touched some lever and the body of the car, right there in the driveway, lifted itself five or six inches straight up. After the demonstration, he graciously accepted our invitation to come into the Vicarage for his usual Sunday morning visit.

There was only one chair in our house that he would sit on. He explained about an old injury to his back. If it ever got out of alignment, his only remedy was to sit in his bathtub full of hot water and ROAR for his Chinese boys to bring him brandy enough to kill the pain. We respected his roar and provided him with a very tall, straight chair.

As usual, there was a story he had to tell, usually commencing with great mystery. "I want to tell you about something I discovered this week when I went down to the farmer's house. I hadn't been down there for a while and what do you suppose I found?"

John was in the kitchen. His voice floated in to us. "Would you like a cup of coffee?"

"Yes, thank you." Mystery again. "The front door was open and . . ."

John called from the refrigerator. "Do you take cream in your coffee?"

"Yes, thank you very much," Mr. Bullitt called back. "I stepped in through the front hall and I just couldn't believe my eyes . . ."

"Sugar?" John again.

"No." Voice lowered, dramatic expression. "You have no idea what skullduggery I am about to reveal."

The coffee arrived, with cream, and the story continued with all dramatic effects enhanced.

"When I looked into the dining room, you won't believe what I saw. *There was no dining room table!* I said to them "Where do you eat?' and they said,

'Oh, we have television trays so we can watch television while we eat.'"

Any great statesman who can make a fascinating story out of nothing at all simply has to be a good storyteller.

Mr. Bullitt was expecting a houseguest and invited us to come and meet her. She was a famous botanist and had given a tremendous arboretum and botanical garden to a great city. He said to us, "She is a lovely person and we have been good friends for years and of course she is an authority on all things botanical. But I must say she has a most detestable quality of always talking about plants by their Latin names. So I wrote her a letter and I said, 'Emma, everyone, just EVERYONE, knows that Heal All is named Heal All and not necessarily *Prunella vulgaris* . . .'"

During the visit he drove her one day to Northampton to show her the Mountain Laurel which was at its prime. He told us afterward that she called it "a magnificent display of *Kalmia Latifolia*. Mr. Bullitt said, "It's nothing of the sort, Emma. It's Calomel and Soda."

One Sunday morning he arrived an hour early for church because he had forgotten about daylight savings time. When he saw us, he was all ready for a story about his life in Paris. He kept an apartment there all the year around, and he liked often to go into the Cathedral of Notre Dame to say his prayers. This was his story:

"I said to the young priests and curates of the cathedral 'You spend too much time on your lunch hour and you are late getting back to the cathedral and I cannot get in.' So they gave me a key. I could go to the west door and unlock it and that let me into the vestibule. Inside the vestibule there was a great closet for their vestments. There was a certain spot in the back of the closet where I could push on a panel and that would open another door and I could step into the great cathedral where I was *alone with God*.

After a while I began to notice that the cathedral was very drafty and my head was cold. I went to my tailor and I told him I needed some kind of hat to protect my bald head from the cold drafts in the cathedral, and he said, 'I know exactly what your problem is because Msg. _____ and the Cardinal have both come to me and I have made them each a hat.' He then made me a hat." Mr. Bullitt then reached into his pocket. "Would you like to see my hat?" As he put it on he added, "This is the only hat in the world that was designed by the Pope himself!"

My sister-in-law tells me of the time she was visiting with us in Ashfield and Mr. Bullitt invited all three of us to come to dinner. There were drinks and conversation and Mr. Bullitt's spellbinding stories. At the appointed time, the Chinese boys announced that dinner was served. Katharine recalls how the rather small and intimate little dining table was properly set in every detail, extremely refined but totally correct. The place settings were neat with silverware and wine glasses all set in the correct order.

Mr. Bullitt invited the Reverend John to ask the Blessing. The Chinese boys commenced the ceremony of serving the dinner. The first boy brought a bottle of wine, uncorked it and poured some into a glass for Mr. Bullitt to taste. Katharine still recalls how shocked she was when our gracious host tasted the wine and suddenly hurled wine and glass and all into the fireplace and shouted, "Rot Gut!" As soon as the imperturbable Bei poured wine he approved, he became the courteous host as though nothing had ever happened.

But in the small town life does not always run smoothly. The clergy, especially, become vulnerable because they have to be "all things to all people." There was a certain man in that town who never got along well with any clergyman and we all understood and accepted the situation. Not Mr. Bullitt. If someone was out of line, he became indignant and threatened to blow up something (a hypothetical threat, of course!) But he kept close watch of all the issues and John kept him informed in his own whimsical way.

If I have failed to give due credit to Mr. Bullitt's experience and his intellectual capacity and his value to our country as a true patriot, so let it be. I only want to share a little of the colorful life of a very dear friend.

The Ashfield churches percolated along at their usual pace. John conducted the eight o'clock Eucharist Sunday morning at Saint John's. He used to explain he would then walk to the center of the road and whirl around so his clerical collar was on correctly and then enter the Congregational church for their eleven o'clock service. The sermons were slightly different because the two churches had some different beliefs.

The Abraham Lincoln Manuscript

Although Ashfield's population was small, it had a handsome library, built by some summer visitor who had shared his wealth with the little town. As the years wore on, the library went through the usual phases that all libraries experience. One of the most common is that the building just gets too crowded and needs to be weeded out. When the Ashfield library was almost at the end of its housecleaning, someone suddenly discovered a document signed by Abraham Lincoln.

In 2002, I received this email message from the current director of the Ashfield library in response to my query about that document:

> The document in question was a copy of the Emancipation Proclamation and was signed by Abraham Lincoln. There were a hundred or so made up and sold to provide the Union Army with ambulance service during the Civil War. There was a framed copy in our library, it was sold at Sotheby's in 1995 for $80,000, with this money and a grant from the state we were able to add a children's room and meeting room and new bathrooms, A great success!
>
> Sincerely,
> Anne C. Judson Director

Silent Spring by Rachel Carson

In the 1950s, DDT had just been "perfected" for general application all over the landscape to kill any troublesome insects. During the years we were in Ashfield, America began to suspect that the newly invented insecticides might not be quite safe. This is putting it mildly.

The first rumblings occurred when planes flew over parts of New York State, spraying for insects. They happened to fly over a corner of western Connecticut where there was a herd of Swiss milk cows. The fabulously expensive lawsuit that resulted proved that the milk produced that day contained poisons, compared with the poison-free milk of the day before, which was protected by being refrigerated. We just happened to be close friends of the owners of the Swiss herd.

Because of our connections with several of the people who were involved in the lawsuit, we were informed because they knew we were opposed to uncontrolled use of poison sprays anywhere. Back in Ashfield, the problem was suddenly close to home. A town-employed worker named Guy Tanner was putting away his spraying equipment when we came close enough to ask what his assignment was. He said he was trying to kill Gypsy Moths "or anything else that we happen to hit." He was wearing no gloves or mask and we wondered if he might be taking some risks. He climbed into his truck and whirled away, spraying right and left and up and down.

The next day John found a dead frog on the lawn. He happened to meet Guy Tanner, showed him the frog. "Do you suppose the stuff you were spraying yesterday could have had an effect on the frog?" John asked.

"No, I don't think so," Mr. Tanner said. "We've all gotta die sometime."

About three weeks later there was a call from the undertaker, asking John to take Guy's funeral. The conversation over the phone: "This is so sudden," John said. "What did he die of?"

The undertaker replied, "The record says he died of an impacted intestine, but I never heard of anyone dying that fast from that diagnosis."

It was shortly after this episode that a friend phoned us at 7:30 one morning in 1962 to tell us that *The New Yorker* magazine was carrying a whole book titled *Silent Spring*, written by a scientist named Rachel Carson, on the dangerous use of pesticides. She wrote about the spray use of DDT over Duxbury, which left many robins dead on the Huckins's lawn right here in Duxbury. It took a long time for America to outlaw DDT, but because of Carson's scientifically documented book, poisonous spraying is more carefully controlled. Unfortunately, some other countries do not recognize the danger. The battle continues to rage. It is a tough fight but it seems that more people are becoming aware of the dangers in the millennium.

Some Thin Spots

The responsibility of ministering to two different denominations in a very small town began to show some thin spots, professionally speaking. One of our weekend neighbors was the former minister and his good family, living in the house they had built when he was minister. During the five years we were there, our good friend Phil Steinmetz, was a faithful neighbor with a big heart for helping every one. He had become a worker for the Massachusetts Council of Churches and every day he drove to Boston. Weekends he returned to his home and family in Ashfield. He knew everyone in town and if anyone had a need, he hastened to fill it. He was really doing John's work, but with such spontaneity and good will that it was not possible to change him.

Mr. Bullitt observed how our clerical friend was interfering, with the best of good will, with the work John could have been doing in the town. One spring when Mr. Bullitt had just come from Washington, we were filling him in on the winter's events in the small town. "Do you still have that Albatross hanging around your neck?" he asked John. That, of course, sent us to the library to re-read Coleridge's *The Rime of the Ancient Mariner*. Albatross became a byword among the few who knew what was happening, and I remember with humor the gift of a set of draperies for our rectory windows that featured an Albatross.

Phil was exceptionally kind and understanding and would go out of his way to be helpful. If anyone was sick, he would go to call on the person. He had lived and worked in Ashfield for eighteen years and it was his skill that had brought the two denominations together. He was likeable and indispensable— and, figuratively, BLIND.

What was there left for John Philbrick to do in Ashfield? The result was that there was often a garden conference in another town or a trip to Spring Valley for a Biodynamic conference of which John had become the president after the death of Dr. Ehrenfried Pfeiffer. Everything was fine in Ashfield with Albatross working so hard. When it gradually became evident that John's work was not terribly important to the town, one of the deacons made the famous statement: "I hope Mr. Philbrick's next church will be nearer his work!" We took it all in good spirits and even now enjoy many friendships started in Ashfield.

Perhaps the people recognized what was happening and perhaps there was a movement among the people. Anyway, one day a friend whispered that there was a movement afoot "to get rid of the minister." The next day we were in the Bishop's office exploring other possibilities. There was a rather backward church down nearer Duxbury that needed some help. We knew that day where the next church would be, but that was our secret for the time being. On a slushy Monday in the middle of the January thaw, we left the mountains of Ashfield and landed near Worcester in the very small old mill village of Wilkinsonville.

"The Gypsies"—Rev. William Kahlert from Saxony, Rev. Focas Stavrianos from Saloniki, and Rev. Spiros Zodhiates from Egypt

The Institute Building in Spring Valley, New York, which served as headquarters of the Biodynamic Gardening Association during the 1940s.

Journeys with a Real Jack in the Pulpit | 203

Parishioners at our church in Weymouth, Massachusetts, staging the story of Saint Francis of Assisi with marionettes.

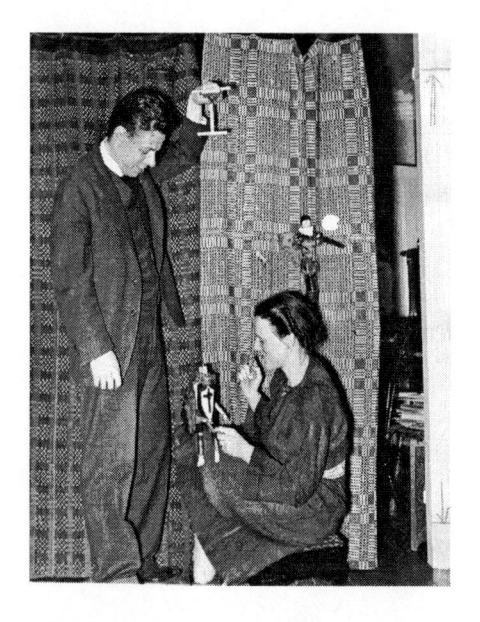

John and Helen behind the scenes with marionettes

Faith Homestead in the early 1940s, when John and Helen bought the house and surrounding ten acres of land. The original house was built in 1772 and the front section was added in 1832.

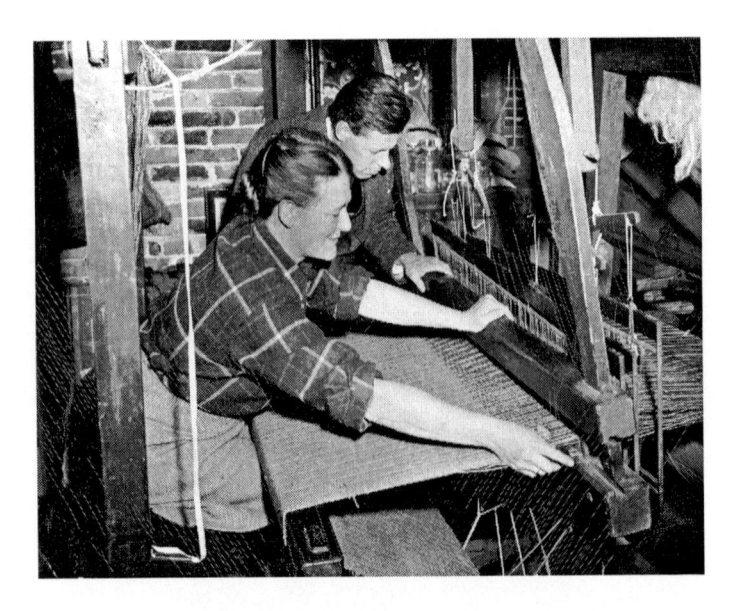

Helen and John weaving on the big loom in the attic and Faith Homestead, late 1940s

Journeys with a Real Jack in the Pulpit | 205

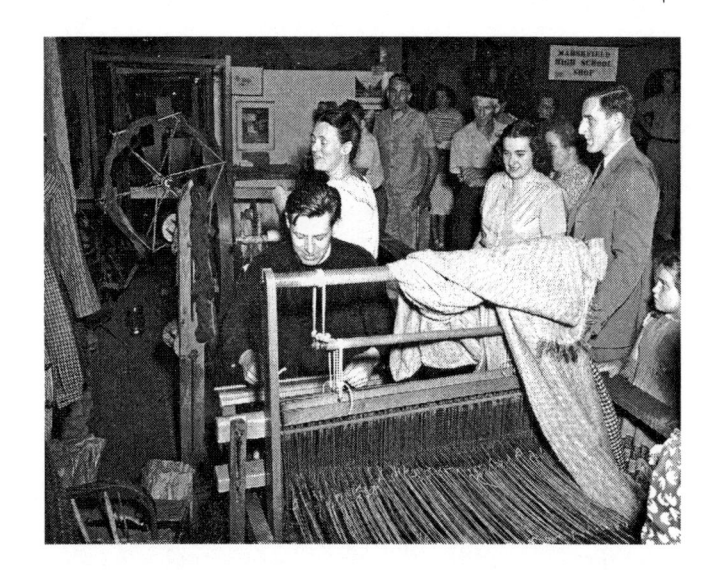

Helen spinning and John weaving at the Marshfield (Massachusetts) Fair, 1945.

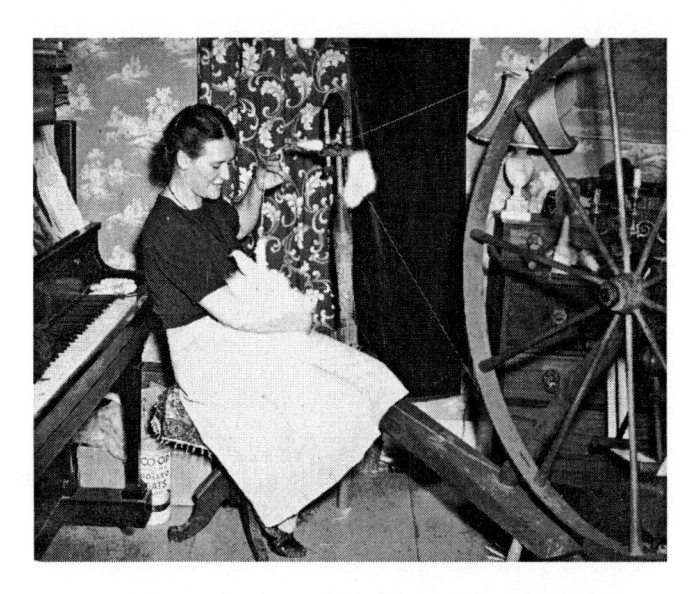

Helen and angora rabbit spinning, late 1940s

The Quartet. From left: Bruno Zangari, baritone; Esther Crowell, contralto; Bea Hunt Iams, soprano; John Philbrick, tenor. In front: Elidae Antonetti, pianist. The group, established in the 1930s, for many years performed evenings of music all across the Commonwealth

Young People's Fellowship of the Episcopal Church meeting with Helen and John at Faith Homestead, around 1945

Helen feeding the goats at Faith Homestead

Chapter 19

Wilkinsonville—Arrival, 1963

It was a day of deep slush and wintry winds when we descended from the mountains of Ashfield down to the valley of Wilkinsonville. We tried to remember the names of the streets as we passed them. Shopping for groceries came first, after we had located St. John's Church and the Rectory nearby. The first grocery store we saw was in Grafton, where we were totally surprised to see a poster advertising a lecture that evening by Carl de Suze on his recent trip to Africa. To attend Carl's lecture was suddenly more important than the groceries, although we did buy a good piece of steak. At the lecture, Carl was as astonished as we had been, and he immediately accepted our invitation to dinner at our new house after his lecture.

By the way, where was our new home anyway? We left the lecture in two cars. It took quite a long time and several false attempts, but we were finally reunited at the address given, the white house beside the white church on the hill. Our reunion with our childhood friend Carl de Suze was a major experience that night.

Midnight meals are always festive, especially when extemporaneous. After that evening, whenever Carl had a lecture within miles of "Wilks," he always came to us. His travelogues covered each country in fine detail, moving as he spoke from motion picture to still photos to one special scene with a monologue. In those earlier days, the equipment for lecturing was still primitive, but Carl had great ingenuity. He used a couple of Coca-Cola boxes to raise the projector to the correct height. He always employed men from John's former seminary as his drivers and his handy men. We rejoiced to have them all come to the late dinner parties at the rectory.

The Place

Mr. Wilkinson built Saint John's Anglican Church within sight of his mill and twelve houses for his workers. Folks from the church took us on walks to explore the wreckage of the mill and the rest of the neighborhood. In front of the church, there was a small park with a flagpole. There was a small restaurant on the street and some houses scattered around. It was not a distinguished neighborhood.

Fabric manufacture was a thriving business for many years and then, as they say, "the bottom dropped out." There were business failures, and eventually the mills were torn down. The church in Wilkinsonville followed the same sequence, except that it was not torn down. There it stood, a stately Greek Revival structure (1832), with a fine big hall but a rather small congregation. The few families remaining were trying hard to keep it alive. This was exactly where we wanted to be—facing a challenge, with some congenial people to be the workers.

The First Vestry Meeting

On our way to the first meeting of the vestry at Saint John's in Wilkinsonville, we talked together about our coming position. We had been told not only by the Bishop but also by friends who knew the parish that there were not many parishioners. They had some earlier problems, which had reduced the size of the membership. We agreed that we had our own ways of attracting people. We would talk gardening with garden enthusiasts and history with history buffs. We had learned to share hobbies with other hobbyists. That in itself is an easily disguised "hobby," one that never fails to make fast friends. Our confidence was in high gear.

The meeting was held in the "front room" of the rectory. The house was pleasant, and the people in the meeting were all agog to find out what kind of characters we were going to be. (They remembered a former minister who had run away with the top soprano). We had agreed in our earlier conversations to soft pedal the crafts, because we didn't want the people to think we would specialize in crafts and neglect the parish. There was to be no word about crafts, especially about weaving, which is much more demanding that the simpler projects like chair caning.

As the meeting evolved and we became better acquainted with our new parishioners, we began to feel an inner sense that this *was* the right community for the Philbricks. After the formalities were over, it was time for informal conversation and quiet rejoicing. Harold Rickards, a Scotsman, took me aside and demanded, "What about your weaving?"

All I could think was Oh, oh, what can we do? He has heard something and we are already in trouble! I was dumbfounded. What did he know? And how did he find out? And did he hate the very idea of weaving? (John was in another room arranging about salary.)

I said, on the verge of tears, "How did you find out?"

He said, with vigor, "My brother George lives in Palmer and he and his wife went to a craft show in Ashfield and saw you weaving. We were all weavers in the woolen mill in North Adams. We loved that mill and felt like the end of the world when it closed."

At that moment, Harold became my best friend. Tears of joy!

The Rug

One sequel was that we together wove a nylon and wool rug for the center aisle of the church. We had made friends with the Stanley Woolen Company in Uxbridge, which generously gave us the material to weave a runner, 40 inches wide and about 45 feet long. Between the warp of nylon and the weft of heavy wool, that rug lasted for about 40 years. We also wove yard goods for winter clothing. Part of the training of an occupational therapist had been weaving. I was never an expert with fancy weaves but my rating as an Apprentice with the Boston Guild of Weavers was of value.

The First Sunday Service

Although the membership list was short, there was a lot of vitality in the congregation, especially in the choir. According to the old custom, our choir women wore the old-fashioned black choir cassock, white choir surplice, and hat, called a "mortar board" (Webster's *Unabridged Dictionary*, 1910, calls that a colloquialism!).

The first Sunday morning, there was a commotion in the choir room as the ladies were vesting. Queenie Oakley said to Priscilla Iverson, "You've got my hat," and Priscilla shot back, "I have not. This is my hat." The dialogue went back and forth until the signal was given for the procession to commence.

The organist, Flora Dudley, was an unforgettable little old lady, who can justly be called a spitfire. She was the youngest child of a large family. She had red hair, and she was well-spoiled by everyone who knew her. A widow, she was small of stature, lived alone, and handled very well the acreage that she had inherited. She created a conservation gift of many acres called Purgatory Chasm, in memory of her only son, who had lost his life in the Second World War.

As organist, she was justifiably and intentionally the center of attention every Sunday—and at all other times, too. She had many brothers and sisters still living and also many cousins. At Christmas time, she laughingly boasted that she was the only one spry enough to fetch all the presents out from under the tree at the Family Christmas Party. Every once in a while, she would "pick a fight" with the Rector and the conversation would regularly evolve as follows:

Aunt Flora to John Philbrick: "You hate my guts!"

The Rector to Aunt Flora: "No, I don't, Flora. Will you please come down to the house for tea?"

The tea party on Saturday afternoon followed a stormy session of preparing the church for Sunday morning. Aunt Flora had become the Altar Guild by scaring everyone else away, except for one faithful member. We always had the tea party ready to smooth out any unexpected wrinkles.

Her greatest joy was to don her graduation dress, which she had made when she graduated from Wellesley College. The dress was beautiful, with lace inserts and flowing ruffles, neat and feminine. But her temperament was more feisty than feminine.

One cherished elderly lady was Mother Colton, who was nearing her one-hundredth birthday. Her devoted family surrounded her with attention, as they lived at Red Farm in Millbury, near Wilkinsonville. There were several sons and their wives, and there were always stories. One day while we were all having lunch together in the parish hall, Georgia, a daughter-in-law, mentioned the Colton dining room. "Someone asked for the sugar and someone else shied the sugar bowl across the table. It landed in Robert Benchley's lap."

Robert Benchley, a Unique Humorist

Robert Benchley! Our favorite minister had read his books to us when we were teenagers, including *Coffee Meg and Ilk*, the story of a shy, nervous man's order at the food counter!

Benchley was the perfect humorist of his time, never mean or off color, but hilariously funny. His humor was never mean or demeaning! His incongruities made us laugh without being hurtful. I was almost in shock to learn he had lived with our beloved Colton family during the war years. It was no wonder the Coltons were all practical jokers, and they had an influence on several members of St. John's Church.

My favorite of Benchley's tales was about the guest who awoke on Sunday morning, hearing no sounds in the house. The family must all be asleep, and he didn't want to make noise and wake them. Little did he know that the family had tiptoed to his door to listen to hear if he was awake yet. Finally, in desperation, he made a ladder of sheets to let himself out of the window and away. Perhaps I had even been in the very same room when I visited Mrs. Colton near her 100th birthday.

Sid Colton told me how he returned from college in Europe without money enough to return home to Worcester. He went to the Hotel Algonquin in New York City, where Dorothy Parker and Robert Benchley and all the rest of that gang congregated. (When someone mentions the name of Dorothy Parker, I recall my favorite of her poems, "Men don't make passes/ At girls who wear glasses.) They were the writers who made the *New Yorker* outstanding, with their own combination of humor and cynicism. This band of friends, lecturers, writers, comedians, and entertainers managed to inaugurate a new kind of humor in American culture. Quick and brilliant and a little mischievous (but never off color), they became memorable. They are still famous today.

One day I asked Jim Colton if he knew how a "figure 4" trap worked. It was a trap sometimes used to kill a small creature, like a mouse. The structure was supposed to be made with stones, fitted together around a piece of bait, with a big stone that would fall and squash the prey when it tried to remove the bait. Jim didn't say he knew about the figure 4 trap. He just grinned and shook his head. A week or so later, he and his wife, Mary, left to go on a summer cruise somewhere. The figure 4 trap was forgotten.

The next December, close to Christmas, a package appeared in the mail, covered with stickers from a post office in Sweden. "Who do we know in Sweden?," we wondered. Inside was an advertisement of a Swedish company which carried a line of "figure 4" traps. The largest was designed to catch an elephant. Next was one to snare a giraffe, then a bear, a bobcat, and so on down the line until the models created to catch smaller and smaller fry, like mice. This line of traps, which was alleged to be made in a factory in Sweden, with special features to appeal to Americans, clearly bore Jim Colton's "maker's mark." As Grace Kilmer said when she saw the production, "I think I see the fine hand of a Colton." The Coltons's cruise the previous summer had been to Sweden. I still have the samples that came in the mail.

Of the Moon and Gold Wire

Cliff Kilmer had a most astonishing job. His company manufactured wire. He and I worked together at the Worcester Craft Center. While I worked on the silver cup (of which more later), he told me that he made wire out of gold. He said it was extremely fine wire, which was used for communications between earth and the first space ship to land on the moon. Gold wire conveys the clearest sounds, he said, and now, many years later,

I know that gold wire is being used to make hearing aids that convey true sound.

Aunt Flora's Flower Ritual

Every Saturday afternoon there was a systematic ritual to be performed. Our elderly organist, of considerable skill on the organ bench, chose also to be in charge of the altar flowers. She had her own system, and woe to anyone who was rash enough to suggest change. The brass vases, with small openings, were polished a bit if necessary. The flowers were laid out on the counter ready for the vases. One by one, the flowers were jammed into the vases. They looked crowded so she would slap at them to loosen them. Oops, there goes a carnation, broken off below the blossom! There was always a final slap just to make sure.

"Oh, dear," Aunt Flora would say. "They just don't grow such good flowers anymore, but I can fix that." A spool of black thread appeared. With a piece of thread, she would tie the broken flower back onto its stem and the altar vase was complete.

The Rectory

When we arrived, the parish had suffered many reverses and was a bit dilapidated. However, there was a nucleus of fine, loyal, loving people. The rectory next door was a big, rambling house with plenty of space for all our hobbies, such as weaving (we called one large room "The Weavery"), with possibly a spot in the cellar for some work with silver.

The parish was growing. New people would come to try it out and the congregation increased. John's ministry was based on the idea that if one shares interests with others, there is a bond that increases friendliness and companionship. This creates loyalty, which is the foundation of every organization. One way to increase membership is to provide activities that attract people. So, in addition to the minister's steady list of house calls and hospital visits, we started a kind of craft session every Monday night in the parish house. Some came to learn how to cane a chair, or brought broken chairs to be mended. Each person brought his or her favorite project. The fellowship was contagious and we had fun. It was not limited to our denomination—all were invited to just come and enjoy creating something. There was no charge for coming and working, but, in response to a request, we placed a small vase on a shelf into which people voluntarily placed contributions to help cover expenses. The output was impressive—caned chairs, knitted afghans, jewelry, dresses, and just the beginning of quilt making. The craze for quilt making was then in its infancy but about to sweep all our sewing machines like wildfire.

We specialized for a while making jewelry, helped by a mineral store where we could buy semi-precious stones, and my apprenticeship to my father, the silversmith, proved useful.

LaSalle House

When spring came, we found time enough when the church-owned LaSalle House in nearby Whitinsville asked us to help with the gardens. The house had been donated to the Diocese as a conference center for clergy. The estate's garden was large—about seventy feet long, perhaps fifty feet wide—and surrounded by brick walls ten or twelve feet high. It was an ideal garden situation. John's reaction was that the special attraction of attending a conference there was the opportunity to work in the garden. He wore his garden shoes.

There was an enormous peony bed in the center, wide brick paths everywhere, and a wide bed in front of the wall on each of the four sides. Because the house was a conference center for the church, it seemed appropriate to plant varieties that would reflect the four major events of the church year—Christmas/Whitsunday, Easter/Spring, Mid-summer/St. John's Day, and Fall/Michaelmas. The red peonies, sometimes called Pentecostal Roses, were featured for the Easter-Pentecost wall, while the fall was adorned with Michaelmas daisies, which in a home garden would be called fall asters. We also relished the opportunity to climb up on the high wall to gather blossoms from the linden tree to make the popular French tea called Tilia.

The garden blossomed and supplied the guests of the conference center with a quiet place for meditation and peace.

The young people enjoyed keeping the wide brick paths in good condition, and the various visitors in the LaSalle House were appreciative. Of course, we had to study botany to keep up with the seasons and do our best for the garden. We found a great resource at the Worcester Horticultural Hall, which housed a botanical library. Over the years, we borrowed so many botany books that we became well-acquainted with the librarians. We happened to ask one day about books on apples. The librarian's face lit up and she began to talk fast.

Her father had spent his life studying apples, beginning in the town of Danvers. I jumped at that. He must be the Mr. Davenport I used to know when I was very young and thought he had been named for a sofa. That name closed a circle of coincidences in my life. We touched base with him, and learned he had assembled all the ancient varieties, which were in danger of disappearing from the markets and from the orchards.

We learned from that garden at LaSalle House that amateurs should never undertake advanced horticultural operations. The apple tree we tried to make into an espaliered tree became totally impossible, and we were too unskilled to make it put out branches like a ladder. (*Espalier* is the French word for the supporting trellis or ladder.) After months of trying to make it conform to our idealized vision, we dug it up and planted it in the middle of a field in Duxbury. There it is happy to bloom and grow apples where it chooses. No ladder design for its branches. A few other transplants successfully found their way into the ground at Faith Homestead, our place in Duxbury, namely a crabapple, *Malus bacata*, and a small linden tree. We brought them down when we went to visit our long-term tenants, the Benjamin Aldens, who had moved in when we went to Missouri in 1949.

Mrs. Alden and Mrs. Badger

One day Mrs. Alden was visited by her cousin, Mrs. Badger, from Quincy. The ladies sat in the dining room, exchanging their thoughts and opinions. Mrs. Alden mentioned that she had received a visit from the local policeman, who had been very kind and helpful to her as an elderly lady living alone in a house on a busy road.

She said, "And he even gave me this to use if anyone should want to get in." She held up the object to show Mrs. Badger, who was much interested. She asked Mrs. Alden, who was known as Susie, how the thing was supposed to work. Whereupon Susie pointed it at her friend and said, "See, he told me to just point it at the intruder and press this little button . . ."

"Do you know, Mrs. Philbrick, she just coughed and coughed and coughed. Why, I had to get her a glassful of water to help her stop coughing!"

(This isn't really my autobiography, it is only reminiscences of my very favorite people. I have tried to record their actions and reactions as I observed them.)

One of the best features about Wilkinsonville was that it was nearer our house in Duxbury, which we rented to Mr. and Mrs. Benjamin Alden, as I've mentioned. As soon as possible, we made a trip to Duxbury to gather apples from our ancient trees to show to our newly discovered Mr. Davenport. He not only identified each apple but he gave us a set of sketches, which showed the features of each variety, from Andrew Jackson Downing, the famous landscape architect and authority on apples. It was fun to renew acquaintance with the old names, including Baldwins, Greenings, Pippins, and Porter apples. The list continued with Blue Pearmain and Sutton Beauties, and, of course, the "best favorite McIntosh."

It was also a happy coincidence that Wilkinsonville was very close to the city of Worcester, where the big All Saints' Church and the four satellite churches named for the four Gospels—Matthew, Mark, Luke, and John—provided us all with many friends and ecclesiastical good times. At a meeting of clerics, John met a gentleman of color whom he had invited to have lunch with us the following Sunday. We were congenial and the luncheon was a success. Later in the week at some top-notch church gathering, all the clergy were putting on their vestments for the service when John noticed his friend across the room.

The gentleman was so tall that he looked down on John. Taken by surprise at John's greeting, he said: "Do I know you?"

"Of course you do," John said. "You and your wife had lunch with me and my wife just last Sunday."

The man laughed a friendly chuckle. "You know, all white people look alike!" he said.

Chapter 20

Holy Humor—From the Bulletin of the Sutton Historical Society—About John's Ministry

During the turbulent 1960s the nation was experiencing social and political upheavals. It was a time of protesting human rights, LSD, Rock and Roll music and Flower Children. While St. John's remained a calm and peaceful house of prayer, we were blessed with our own version of a 'Flower Child' in the person of the Rev. John H. Philbrick, our Rector, a man of God and a true lover of nature.

Father John as he liked to be called was an avid gardener and naturalist. He spent much time with St. John's children teaching them about flowers, trees and gardening and even letting them extract sap from the maple trees surrounding the church grounds. With Father John's enthusiastic encouragement his wife, Helen, penned a book about organic gardening. Such was his love of things in nature, plants, flowers and astronomy that these topics often times found their way into his Sunday sermons.

Father John and his wife were both very active in the activities of St. John's women's groups. Helen was a silversmith and taught jewelry making to them.

Along with textile weaving done by Father John and Helen these newly learned skills served as very successful ways of earning money for the various St. John's Fairs. Having such an involved couple as our Rector and his wife it was no surprise that they are well-remembered by many of our older parishioners.

When they left in 1973 they left many happy memories behind.

Accompanying this gracious description of our ministry is a photograph of Evelyn Newton's oil portrait of Father John tapping the sugar maple by the church to get maple sap, which he used to make coffee for the Sunday morning refreshments. The newspaper in Worcester also sent a man to interview Father John about how and why and with what tools one would tap a maple tree during the early spring, when the sap first begins to flow. More about this later.

Silent Spring, continued

But Wilkinsonville was not all fun. There was serious work to be done and there was a new mimeograph in the church office. As I have mentioned previously, when Rachel Carson's book *Silent Spring* was published in 1962, it had a tremendous on us and confirmed our intuitive sense that chemical sprays could be very harmful. Suddenly, there was scientific research to confirm what many people had suspected for years: that the use of chemical poison sprays for controlling pests was doing an equal amount of damage to our human population and to our domestic animals. We knew many people who experimented with simple and harmless insect controls. We, ourselves, in our organic gardening experience had tried a number of household substances. A fairly comprehensive literature about familiar kitchen-type substances that would help to control some of the insects began to develop.

Inspired by Rachel Carson's book and disgusted that Guy Tanner in Ashfield had died from his spraying of DDT, I collected all the insect controlling substances I could find and wrote the text, even producing a few clumsy attempts at illustration. We decided to type them all out in a systematic collection, with application directions for each substance, and print them on the new mimeograph machine in the church office. Perhaps someone would like to know about them. With advice from a friend who knew about such things, we wrote a book that we called *Harmless Insect Controls,* which later became the subtitle of the published version, *The Bug Book*. By using colored paper, we could make one list of the insects involved and with a different color we could list the remedies. Down in the Rectory, I was kept busy writing the directions while the new minister cut the stencils for the mimeograph.

The Bug Book

John patiently cranked the mimeograph after I had typed each page. It wasn't long before people began to ask for copies. Soon, they sold faster than we could print them. An old friend, who had a print shop in the cellar below his house in Northampton, welcomed the job and offered to add binding. In time the book emerged with green covers and a green plastic comb binding, ready for sale. Another friend, who had long experience with libraries and bookstores, advised us to name it simply *The Bug Book*. We opened a special "Bug Book" account in the local bank and forgot about it.

We were also advised to keep the book big and bulky to prevent it from getting lost in a bookcase. Soon, we were running a small book business, not on the side but right out in the open, trying to spread the message far and wide that DDT and all the other poison sprays not only kill insects but also kill or hurt people and animals. This was our new Gospel and we took it seriously. The book was printed by the hundreds, and the demand continued. When the publisher paid for the original book, John went to the Millbury Bank and deposited the check.

Our friends in New York State, whose milk cows had been sprayed during an aerial spraying, continued to be involved in a big lawsuit because the spraying had affected the milk, which carried evidence of the poison sprayed down on them. This was serious business, worth publicizing.

The original bug book was published in 1963. Thirty-four years later, in 1997, a publisher, Garden Way, bought our book and published a "revised edition" named *The Gardener's Bug Book*, which brings the information up to date. Since then, Garden Way has been taken over by another publisher. I can hardly recognize my own creation. It now has better drawings and a plethora of new harmless substances. I sometimes miss the old, simple homespun appearance, but it is good to know that there is a fast-selling book on how to safely control insects without poisoning people or animals. There was also an edition in Spanish directed toward the Central American countries.

Biodynamic Farming and Gardening Association

As the years unfolded and work in the parish in Wilkinsonville expanded, we still found some free time to work on other responsibilities. John traveled now and then to Spring Valley, where we were learning about Biodynamic gardening. Dr. Pfeiffer, our mentor, had died, and the Biodynamic farmers were in the process of creating the Bio-Dynamic Farming and Gardening Association. They selected John as their president, and we spent our holidays driving to Spring Valley, New York in an effort to get the newly formed organization in shape. It only needed a steady hand and the loving understanding that John could supply, with some useful references to Robert's Rules!

Companion Plants

There was one meeting at which someone suggested that the BD Association should publish a book about the relationships between plants. Someone suggested the work already written on that subject by Richard Gregg, a member and old friend. It was finally approved by the Association that I should work with Gregg to revise his pamphlet.

Suddenly, I was in the process of writing another book! Richard Gregg had already made a study of which plants liked each other and which plants were incompatible. We produced *Companion Plants*. It was published in 1966, thanks to the steady urging of a member of the board of the Association, who phoned the publisher faithfully once every day. It has remained in print over the past 36 years and has, I hope, helped backyard gardeners. It is now in its 17th printing. *Companion Plants* was published in England simultaneously. Not long after, we received copies published in France, Holland, and Japan. There were never any royalties for *Companion Plants*, but *The Bug Book* after all these years still brings in royalties twice a year. Since their Central American edition appeared, the royalties have gone up to the astounding sum of about thirty dollars a year.

The Growth of the Parish

The small parish in Wilkinsonville grew, as we had been confident it would. New people were attracted by this unexpected, unpious clergyman, who invented activities that brought people to the church. The *Worcester Telegram* kept a weather eye on him, so as not to miss anything worth reporting. The church, with its spacious hall, was in constant use by many people of different backgrounds. The French neighbors came to play whist. The Native Americans made teepees and held educational meetings and pow wows. A square dance club met regularly. There were also Polish friends from Grafton, who learned to cane chairs.

Winter was weakening, and the mercury was beginning to rise. As we thought back to spring in Ashfield, we remembered it was almost time to tap the maple trees. We noticed that the wind had blown hard, the twigs were broken way up high in the tree, and there was a tiny icicle. The sap was already running in the tree and was dripping in tiny drops out of the broken twigs. If only one could reach the twig, one could suck on a maple-flavored icicle. We had learned in Ashfield that this is the signal that maple syrup makers watch for.

In Wilkinsonville, we could not go carry out the full-blown process of making syrup, but there was the sap and we were excited. The first thing John did was to bore a hole in the huge maple tree near the Rectory and insert the metal pipe that would drain the sap into the bucket that he hung below. We had all the equipment that had been presented to us by our friends in the sugar bush part of Ashfield. By the next Sunday, there was enough in the bucket to make Sap Coffee for the congregation after the service. Next, we poached eggs in maple syrup for the Ladies Guild. The word spread.

News does travel fast. Soon, we had the inevitable visit from the Worcester newspaper. The photographer knocked on our door. "I'm not quite sure why I am here but they told me to go up to Wilkinsonville to take a picture of a man boring a hole in a tree," he said. John was delighted. He invited the man to come in, we filled a kettle with maple sap from the bucket, and we made coffee with the boiling sap. Did you ever drink Sap Coffee? The best coffee this side of Heaven!

The photographer had a long visit and photographed John, wearing a red shirt, tapping the big maple with the church in the background. The photo appeared in the *Worcester Sunday Telegram*. When I visited St. John's Church in the year 2000, a handsome oil portrait of John tapping the maple tree near the church still hung near the entrance. It had been painted by a beloved friend, who was an experienced and skillful painter.

It takes 30 gallons of maple sap to be boiled down to one gallon of syrup, but even with just the sap one can enjoy poached eggs or sap coffee and a happy welcome to the coming of a new spring.

The Paul Revere Cup

This is a true story, every angle of it. As a preface, I want to tell about my friend, whose young daughter wanted to make an apple pie. Her mother gave her some instructions, the little girl followed the rules, and the pie was baked. When it was cut and served to the family, it was warmly accepted and highly praised. Father, the ultimate critic, pronounced it "The Perfect Pie." Whereupon, Mother, who had been teacher and guide throughout, announced in an authoritative voice, "Now, never make another apple pie. If you have reached perfection, it is time to stop." My adventure with the Paul Revere Cup ended in a similar way.

As I've said, we were near Worcester and its fine Craft Center when we moved to Wilkinsonville. Our friend was the teacher in the metallurgy department. Just the smell of the silver shop made me eager to go back to my early training from my father. Very quietly, we assembled the hammer and anvils for silversmithing in the basement of the Rectory next door to St. John's Church. John had his church work, and I presided over a very small "foundry." We kept it pretty quiet because silver and gold sometimes attract unwelcome visitors.

One day there was a phone call from Mr. French, the new minister of the Congregational Church in Sutton. He had recently arrived from the Midwest and was naturally taking stock of the possessions of the church. He noticed a small silver cup hanging on a nail in a little cupboard in his church hall. On one side, it was engraved with the name of the church and the minister's name. He wondered if it was anything worth studying and what would be the right thing to do with it.

At my suggestion, he took it, in a brown paper bag, to the Museum of Fine Arts in Boston, where they told him it had probably been made by Apollos Rivoire, who later changed his name to Paul Revere. He was the father of the more famous Paul Revere of the Revolutionary Era. The elder Apollos Rivoire was a Huguenot who had been sent on a ship to America when he was a lad—to escape a difficult combat situation in the Old World. He was apprenticed to a respected pre-Revolutionary goldsmith and silversmith. The experts at the Museum couldn't identify the cup definitely, but told him to keep it in the paper bag and to hold onto it. New to eastern colonial history, Mr. French was astounded.

He called to ask if I could make a copy of the cup. He knew I had been my father's partner in silversmithing in the old days. "Sure," I said to Mr. French. "I'll be happy to make a copy." Then I hung up the phone, wondering what kind of a mess I was getting into. He brought it to me in the paper bag, and I was enchanted. The initials "PR" appeared in two places—on the rim and on the bottom. I immediately wrote to a woman who was an authority on early colonial silver. Her reply was brief and negative. It was a sad mistake, she said. It could not be a Paul Revere piece because there was no record of it. (The original cup was now in the process of creating its own record.)

By this time, I had already ordered a sheet of sterling silver— the "blank"—and made sketches of the dimensions. I also signed up at the Worcester Craft Center, where our old friend taught. The companionship of other silversmiths helped to lighten the really hard work of "raising" a cup, with rounded bottom and flaring sides, out of a flat piece of sterling silver. The handle was an S curve with half-round strips soldered on before it was bent, known as a "fluted handle." The bottom was set into a round base. Before it was shaped, I enjoyed the silversmith's experience of stamping it with my mark—"Handwrought Philbrick Sterling HLP." It took many trips to the Craft Center and many hours of hammering, but finally the fluted handle was soldered onto the cup and the bottom rim was finished.

The cup was presented and dedicated to an overflowing church. Like my young friend who made the apple pie, I stopped right there and never made another one! The church now has a full record of the original Paul Revere Cup, which was the first piece the very young Apollos Rivoire, silversmith, made after arriving in America. That cup is now safely in the Worcester Art Museum, and the value of the original little cup is now fifty thousand dollars.

The Snapping Turtle

Across the street from the Rectory there were several houses. We were slightly acquainted with the residents of each. One afternoon, a huge snapping turtle crossed the road from one back yard to the swamp down behind our house. While I was watching the turtle cross the road, an automobile drove up. The driver jumped out and snapped a picture. The next day the picture was in the Worcester newspaper. This was 1967 or 1968. When I visited St. John's in 2000, the Rector told me that the same turtle comes along that same route every spring—more than 30 years later—to lay her eggs in the local swamp.

Some Old Customs I Can Remember

In my childhood, life in a small town was just plain simple. There were no automobiles. People walked or, if they were a little more sophisticated, they might ride in a horse-drawn carriage.

Practically every home had a henhouse and a small flock of hens to provide eggs. The milkman kept a barn full of milk cows, and he delivered milk every day in his small horse-drawn carriage. Many people cultivated their own gardens, where they grew the year's supply of potatoes, which they kept in a cold cellar with a dirt floor. The several apple trees produced a barrel of apples, which also were stored in the cold cellar, where they would not freeze. (It was important not to store the apples too close to the potatoes or the apples would lose their flavor.)

Every year old friends would vie with each other about the quality of their apples. The best credits went to the man whose apples kept the longest. If he could keep his apples until May or June, he would win the informal admiration of his neighbors. Of course, his wife would be making apple pies all winter—and she had only to go down cellar to come back with an apron full of apples. She did not have to go to a store, choose from among many apples, or pay money before proceeding to bake her pie.

If a family had a barn and kept a cow, they naturally set the milk in the pantry for the cream to rise, and the wife made her own butter and sometimes cheese. This was the accepted custom and we all took it for granted.

For mince pie the recipe was:

> 1 cup minced (chopped) meat
> 1 1/2 cup raisins
> 1 1/2 cup currants
> 1 1/2 cup brown sugar
> 1/2 cup molasses or 1 cup granulated sugar
> 3 cups chopped apples
> 1 cup meat liquor
> 2 teaspoonfuls salt
> 2 tablespoonfuls cinnamon
> 1/2 teaspoonful mace
> 1/2 teaspoonful powdered cloves
> 1 lemon (grated rind and juice)
> 1/4 piece citron
> 1/4 cup wine
> 3 teaspoonfuls rose water

These ingredients were simmered together until the apples and raisins were soft. "Do not add the wine, brandy and rose water until the mixture is cooked."

These cooked ingredients were stored for the winter in the cold cellar in a great crock, and the housewife would go down to get enough mincemeat to fill the crusts whenever she made pies. Between the cold climate of the cold cellar and the presence of brandy and wine and the spices, the mincemeat ingredients blended together and mother's mince pies were welcomed on special occasions.

To make soap, she had only to keep bacon fat and other meat fats. On her infrequent visits to a store, she could buy a can of lye. It was not difficult to make enough soap to supply the family at a very small monetary cost. Twentieth-century housewives could consider themselves lucky to be able to buy the lye in cans. The early pilgrims had to drain the lye out of the ash from their fireplaces.

There was always a pantry near the kitchen in those days and every pantry held two barrels: the sugar barrel and the flour barrel. Women baked their own bread and cakes and, of course, pies. The spring favorite was the rhubarb pie, which led the housewife to go out into the garden.

Both men and women grew vegetables. An old cookbook lists twenty-five ways to cook potatoes, including one method of preparing southern sweet potatoes. The rest of the vegetable section does name eighteen other vegetables, but omits some of today's favorites, like lettuce, kale, and broccoli. Those old back yard gardens were managed according to old traditions and to neighbors' observations of each other's successes.

Another old custom I can recall, as established as the Rock of Gibraltar, has been superseded by the washing machine and dryer. In the old days, when we carried the big clothes basket outdoors to the clothesline (which incidentally, we sometimes had to "put up" or rewind or otherwise prepare for its next assignment), we were ready to go to work.

Hanging up the wet clothes aroused a combination of thoughts: first, what was in the wash anyway? Was there a sheet big enough to hide the wash from our next-door neighbor? If there was, we were safe and could hang everything else—in order, of course. The largest pieces first and, finally, Father's handkerchiefs and Mother's pretty embroidered hankies. Now we would use Kleenex. My first employer almost fired me, because I hung her wash as it unfolded from the laundry basket. I can hear her laughing now, because all the family underwear was on the "front line."

I Led Three Lives

While the Reverend John Philbrick and I were developing the church in Duxbury and our very small farm on the outskirts of town, we had no knowledge that John's cousin Herbert Philbrick was, as he called it, "living three lives."

During the nine or ten years of his undercover assignment during the 1940s, Cousin Herbert worked in an advertising business in greater Boston. His wife Eva and their four little girls, and later a fifth one, were living in Wakefield, which he reached every night by train. His family life was a happy one—his number one life.

By an unexpected turn of events, his second life commenced when his former membership in a special youth organization gradually involved him with a branch of the Communist party, which was active around Boston. That work kept him so involved that he looked upon it as his second life. His third life developed when he began reporting information on Communist activities to the Federal Bureau of Investigation. This third life had to be kept secret, of course. His advertising business became associated with the media and with the motion picture industry. That is why "I Led Three Lives" became one of the most popular screen stories at the end of the 1940s. That film was so popular that wherever we went, when people heard the name Philbrick, they would eagerly quiz us about the cousin who could attend an evening meeting and next morning make a report in code to the FBI.

In our branch of the family, he was always known as Cousin Herbie. After the whole story became public and the communist leaders went through the court, he was acclaimed as a hero. The book he wrote tells a lively story of his constant uncertainties and his wife's unswerving loyalty through those nine or ten desperate years. After the excitement calmed down, he spent the rest of his long life keeping a store in Rye, New Hampshire.

A Casual Visitor—Punxatawny Phil

Sometimes funny little coincidences seem to have little or no significance in our real lives. February second in old church custom was always known as Candlemas, because on that day the year's supply of candles was blessed. Today, it has become Groundhog Day in Punxatawny, Pennsylvania, when Phil sees or does not see his shadow to predict whether or not we will have six more weeks of winter.

A young clergyman told John that he was taking a new position in a new parish. Naturally, John said, "Whereabouts?"

The clergyman said, "It's way down in Pennsylvania and the name of the town is Punxatawny. But you wouldn't ever have heard of it."

Whereupon John asked: "Is the Senior Warden named Barclay Jeffries Woodward the Third?"

The man was astonished and said, "How in the world do you know?"

"Because in the 1940s in Duxbury I baptized Barclay Jeffries Woodward the Fourth. That was the baptism that the BJW's four-year-old sister ran away from—but she came back many years later from Smith College with a crowd of girls who used our house for a study retreat in Ashfield."

She was the sprightly girl who stood at the foot of the steps and called, "Mr. Philbrick, do you remember me? I'm the one who ran away from being baptized."

"Yes," said John "even though I hardly recognize you after all those years. I certainly do remember you running all the length of the church driveway."

Barclay J. Woodward the Fourth was duly baptized along with another brother and sister, who did not run away. The next day their mother, who was my dear friend, called to say to the minister, "Please do it again. It didn't take!"

Chapter 21

Duxbury II—Retirement 1972

After we left Wilkinsonville, we were now back in our old house, with time to devote to anything that would catch our attention. An early encounter combined surprise and appreciation. On the street one day, we met a woman we knew only by her success as author of her first book. She had attended a class in writing taught by our friend Russell Gordon Carter, known to us as the Thin Man (see his poem under *Brightwater*.)

Her name was Cid Ricketts Sumner, and she had just written her first book, *Quality*. It was about a southern family that had a black slave. The book enjoyed quick recognition and was immediately made into a motion picture, with the new title of *Pinky*, with Ethel Barrymore. Of course, we congratulated her on her achievement (it was her first book).

Mrs. Sumner said to John that sunny morning, "Although I am not of your denomination, I always attended your church to listen to the prayer you gave before you started to preach the sermon." She then graciously took her departure.

The prayer is "Oh God, our great Companion/Lead us day by day ever deeper/ into the Mystery of Thy Life and ours/ and so help us to be interpreters of Life to our Fellows."

Based on what we had learned about retired clergymen returning to their former churches, we steered away from St. John's in the flesh. Of course, we still cherished memories. We landed in the Church of the Pilgrimage in Plymouth, in the choir, of course, and that led straight into the Pilgrim Bell Ringers again. John rang the two heaviest bells, and the concerts continued here and there.

Back at Faith Homestead, there was work to do. Our gardens were planned, using the Biodynamic system of non-chemical cultivation. Several neighbors and friends were also using the same method, and we naturally became an active group to meet and study and help each other. In the meantime, John had replaced Dr. Ehrenfried Pfeiffer as president of the Bio-Dynamic Farming and Gardening Association in America. With John president of the Association, our gardens must be worthy of inspection by visitors. At last, this was his real work.

The visitors multiplied, because everyone wanted to learn more about Biodynamics. At one big conference meeting, one young woman stood up and hollered, "You aren't telling us everything." That was in the 60s, when there was new vitality and a totally unexpected urge among young people, who intended to become farmers and wanted to understand the deeper implications of the changes they were witnessing.

Faith Homestead suddenly became a center for weekend conferences of people coming to learn about gardening. We learned how to prune an apple tree. In fact, one day as John went out the back door he heard a rather pleading voice emanating from the top branches of an old apple tree. "Father John, have you got a ladder?" His wife had climbed up and up, but down was different.

We also invited Dr. Hal Williams to teach a weekend course every year on Homeopathic First Aid. Heinz Grotzke taught botany. One weekend conference included Dr. Koepf, who came from England, where he was professor of Biodynamics and Earth Sciences at Emerson College. The visiting scholars even brought their own macrobiotic cooks. We enjoyed learning new facts about healthy foods, while our two Philistines, John Philbrick and his "Swamp Yankee" friend Leon Handell, escaped to Howard Johnson's for chocolate ice cream sundaes.

A most faithful attendant at every conference was a father who brought two little boys. As the years went on, the little boys grew, but in 1998 one of them returned. More of that in a later chapter.

One day someone said, "We need more space. We ought to build a building." As luck would have it, John had recently visited an old bank looking for a friend who had retired. One of the tellers said to him, "Do you remember that you have an old account in this bank?" It was the old Bug Book account, and it had increased enough to pay for a cement floor and walls big enough for a building 24 x 36 feet square, which Owen McBride designed for a lecture hall on the upper floor. The cement floor was suitable for a garage and for farm implements. The notice went out, *Omnium Gatherum,* below.

Omnium Gatherum
June 11 and 12, 1974

"Let every structure needful for a farm arise in Castle semblance."
Sanderson Miner, an amateur 18th century architect

You are all heartily invited to a community bee and old fashion barn raising.

Date: June 11 and 12
Place: The Philbricks', Duxbury

We are now ready to proceed with the stages shown at left on the new lecture-studio. We will be starting at 7 a.m. on Saturday morning and will need all the hands that can help us then. Because of the need to coordinate succeeding operations we will be needing assistance as early on Saturday morning as you can make it.

Food will be provided so please let us know by return mail if and when you will be joining us.

We hope you will be able to come together with us for this genuinely elevating occasion.

Gratefully,
John and Helen Philbrick

[But it really was composed and written by our friend Owen McBride.]

So, for awhile, the weekend conferences changed to construction work. With Owen's experience and everyone's enthusiasm, the building slowly took shape and was used by many groups of different interests. We even had a small food co-op. Pine DuBois, Peggy Gallagher, and Helen Oshima engineered a truck. They went into Boston very early in the morning once a week to buy two thousand dollars worth of food, which they brought back to the building (which never did have a name.) They placed large boxes around the circle of the parking lot and filled each box with a customer's order. Items which required water were handled in the house cellar. By afternoon, the customers would come to collect their produce. The whole procedure worked so well that it outgrew everyone's energy to keep it going.

Duxbury 1971: The Second Whole Earth Exposition.

The Exposition was to be on Commonwealth Pier in Boston, the old exposition hall. They asked our group of Bio-dynamic gardeners to create a demonstration garden. They would give us a 30 foot circle without charge, if we would create the garden. From a historical point of view, I believe this was the first public acknowledgement that organic gardening was real and important and worthy of publicity.

Our group was led by Helen and Bill Oshima, well known in Massachusetts for their Herb Garden. For weeks, the radio repeatedly played the theme of the "New Earth Exposition which will include a 30 foot Organic Garden." The program included all the practices many of us now include as part of our daily lives: yoga and tai chi, therapeutic massage and Reiki, homeopathy and acupuncture and hypnosis, and, as they always say, "much more."

Gene Thomas built a gazebo and three wooden arches, with pathways to the center. The garden included the staples of any organic garden: a compost pile, a specially treated manure barrel, and a sundial to represent our constant study of the sky-borne elements that influence every garden. Among us all, we assembled dozens of herbs and familiar garden plants. Hundreds of people came and asked questions and told us about their gardens.

John Philbrick, retired by now, was known as one who could deliver a lively lecture about gardening—always with a deeper spiritual connection, too. He lectured several times in Canada and in California. When lecturing nearer to Duxbury, we also included a spinning wheel and an angora rabbit, while Helen spun the yarn.

After the Whole Earth Exposition, the gazebo and the arches were set up in our garden, where they still stand. The garden now belongs to the Wildlands Trust of Southeastern Massachusetts, the organization to which I have given our land and house. I still live in the house under a "reserved life estate."

Volunteering in Plymouth for Betty Ford's Visit—1974

Living so close to Plymouth, the constant repetition of the Pilgrim's landing began to influence my imagination, so I volunteered to put in a few hours' work at Pilgrim Hall. There were several congenial volunteers, and we were ready to do whatever we were asked to do. It so happened that the next big event was to be a visit by Mrs. Betty Ford, the First Lady, wife of the President of the United States.

There was an undercurrent of excitement, locally and nationally. Many people were involved, especially the members of the Press. Pilgrim Hall, where the news reporters were expected to gather, had to be ready to receive the onslaught. We volunteers were assigned to several different aspects of the preparations.

Experience had revealed that persons without passes sometimes tried to sneak in to a crowded place without being authorized. We volunteers were assigned the job of making identification badges, which could be used by only one identified holder. The identification badge was a large, heavy green card hung around the person's neck by a strong green string. Everyone with a green card would be admitted—and no green card could be passed underhanded to anyone else.

We spent the morning cutting the cards to size. Someone went out and purchased lots of green string, which was carefully cut and circulated to all of us to be tied through holes in the corners of the cards. When many people work separately on the same assignment, there are likely to be many variations. Some of the knots were big and some were small. Some strings were long and others were short. It took special skills to be sure every one would fit the expected guests. We spent the whole afternoon on making these cards.

The great day arrived, and with it came the members of the Press. Everyone was eager to be in on the excitement. For that morning, we volunteers were to be the ones to pour the coffee and to distribute the goodies. I felt scared to have to speak to all those exotic strangers from big cities.

The atmosphere came alive, and we were inundated by dozens of extremely lively and demanding press people and photographers. After my comparatively quiet and sedate surroundings, this sudden turmoil took me by surprise, and I had to adjust somehow. All of a sudden I thought: "Ask him what network he works for." It worked. People like to talk about themselves. In my old age, I had learned a new trick.

That was all I had to do. The answers came back like a shot, and I handed coffee to reporters all the way from the *New York Times* and the *Wall Street Journal* to the *Boston Globe*. Of course, they had all come to see the First Lady, and to write the details for their papers.

One of the reporters just couldn't contain his enthusiasm about the event. While I refilled his coffee cup, he was bursting with all his new discoveries. He was proclaiming, "I'm a photographer for _____ Magazine and I've just seen Jacqueline Kennedy for the first time. I'd heard how beautiful she is and now I know."

Betty Ford was not expected to arrive for an hour or two, but we volunteers had more assignments. Mine was to walk down to the Hedge House, where the visitors were to visit and inspect the historical building. I had been told to observe the guests as they returned to the limousines to go to the Plymouth Yacht Club. I was supposed to make sure no one who was ineligible would get in the cars. How could I tell?

Besides, I felt it was important to stand close to a wire, which held up a tree—an inconspicuous wire which could trip up an unsuspecting visitor. Being that close to the excitement gave me a chance to see Nancy Kissinger and several other celebrities without ever having to speak to any of them.

By the time the crowd had sped away to the Yacht Club, our assignments had been accomplished and we were free to assemble again at the old Woolworth Store on Main Street for a cup of coffee and the inevitable conversation.

Plymouth County Wildlands Trust (now The Wildlands Trust of Southeastern Massachusetts)

What to do with Faith Homestead when we were old? We read in the newspaper that there was a Trust being founded to protect land from being sold or divided into house lots. We asked for information. We met the founders, and before we knew it we were on the Board of Directors. Our Lecture Hall was useful for Board Meetings. The weaving studio became an office for the Plymouth County Wildlands Trust. Eventually, I gave the five acres of Faith Homestead, including the lady slippers and all the buildings, to what is now the Wildlands Trust of Southeastern Massachusetts.

But that is not the end of the story. In March of 1998, I received a phone call from Mr. Byron Shepard, the father who had always brought his sons to the agricultural conferences. He would come the next day with his son, he said. I enjoyed a warm reunion with Byron and Mark. Mark is now the owner of a hundred-acre farm in Wisconsin. He is a pioneer in a new kind of agriculture called New Forest Farming. Instead of plowing to sow row crops, they now specialize in tree crops—apples, hazelnuts and grapevines.

But there is still more. That day, Mark walked out to those same old apple trees. From each tree he cut five long branches of clean new growth. He brought them in and we tied them in bunches with the right names and closed up the ends with grafting wax. Back in Viroqua, Wisconsin, he went to the Waldorf School, where they have many apple trees. He gave everyone scions to make grafts, so that in years to come the school children will have the experience of eating apples from the trees they have grafted.

And so, some of Faith Homestead's apples will continue into the future the work that started here many years before we came.

Apples

From the *Boston Globe*, Thursday, August 24, 2000.

> The Davenport Collection of 119 antique apple varieties, propagated a decade ago from trees previously maintained at Old Sturbridge Village, is growing into a handsome and important orchard. Tasting tours on Columbus Day weekend, October 6-9, will give visitors an opportunity to experience varieties their great-grandparents loved and that have never seen the inside of a supermarket.

The apple collection of our old friend Mr. Davenport has become a public tradition. Back in the so-called "good old days," when apple trees seldom needed to be sprayed, many of our neighbors had bearing trees in their backyards. In those days, when the subject of conversation was apples, one heard many names like Baldwin, Rhode Island Greening, McIntosh, and Porter (these were yellow apples). There were several named varieties of Russets, referred to by Jo in Louisa May Alcott's *Little Women* as "some leather apples," which she carried to her attic hide-away.

Some varieties, which ripened more slowly, had to be stored in the cold cellar until they were ready to eat. All winter long, Mother would go down cellar to get enough apples for a pie or for two or three, if there was a big anniversary coming along. If there were any apples with spots, she would take those first. Otherwise, the spotted apples would contaminate their neighbors. This is the origin of the saying that "no conscientious New Englander ever eats a perfect apple." If you ask, "Why not?" the answer is: "Because if you don't eat all the spotted ones first, the perfect apples will all become spotted."

When all the leaves fall off the tree in the autumn, the tree reveals another facet of its existence. Look at the apple tree as an example. Even a well-formed one resembles an apple. The trunk looks like the stem of the apple and the branches resemble the outline of the fruit. The pear tree grows tall like the shape of a pear. Can we notice in the towering spruce the tapering shape of a spruce cone?

Obituary

Like everyone else, I have my own interpretation of the meaning of the phrase, "the Grace of God." Over and over again, when something appears to be difficult and one anticipates a problem, something comes up to relieve the threat, to change one's outlook, and to make living feel adequate again.

This can happen while one is contemplating the seriousness of grieving. When Father John passed over, we needed a gravestone. A fine granite stone in the wall of the graveyard of Saint John's in Duxbury looked adequate, and I told our Interim Clergyman about the stone. He came to see it, approved it, and with the help of several men, he put it into the back of his very small automobile.

He then drove to the home of the young woman he was courting. As he drove along her driveway, she said to him, "Alex, what in _____ have you got in the back of your car?"

"A_____, that is not a very proper way to speak of Father John's tombstone."

Humor may often become a revelation of the Grace of God.

John Philbrick sugar mapling near Saint John's Church, Wilkinsonville, Massachusetts.

From left: Helen, Connie Vulliamy, and John at Faith Homestead, after an excursion to Edaville Railroad, Carver, Massachusetts. Connie died in 2004 at age 100.

Journeys with a Real Jack in the Pulpit | 241

Helen with Scollay outside the gazebo transplanted from the Whole Earth Exposition to Faith Homestead.

Building the Schoolroom at Faith Homestead, October 1976. Back row from left: George Chamberland, Ken Holt, Owen McBride, Bill Oshima. Center from left: John Philbrick, Jim Barrett, Roxanne Coombs. Front from left: Sonni Chamberland, Helen Philbrick, Robert Ladd.

John in his homespun jacket with Scollay in the early 1970s

Helen with a young friend, Becky Dusek, who fights fires in the west.

Thanksgiving at Halfway Pond, 1998. From left: Ruth Briggs, Helen, LeBaron Briggs, III.

Helen on a return trip to a log cabin at Brightwater in the early 1990s.

At breakfast on the lawn of the Bradford House, Kingston, Massachusetts. Clockwise from left: Ursula Traenkle, Terry Bremer, Linda Hewitt, Helen Philbrick, and Inghilt Traenkle.

Helen with compost silo, 1990s.

Helen at the Cushman Preserve with Jean Stewart and Reed Stewart

Cushman House, 1988

The day when the Plymouth County Wildlands Trust suddenly inherited the house willed to the organization by Miss Lura Cushman, it was a day of change. Miss Cushman was a descendant of John and Priscilla Alden, and she had been President of the organization named Alden Kindred. This organization was founded when the John Alden House was sold by immediate members of the Alden family. Now the house is in the possession of the Aldens forever.

John and Priscilla had arrived on the Mayflower. They landed in Plymouth but soon moved to Duxbury, where they built a small dwelling, which later was moved and enlarged to accommodate their famous family. It is the only house now in existence built by Mayflower passengers.

Because Miss Cushman's family were all Alden-related, her house contained many objects which had belonged to Aldens. In addition, her house also contained many objects brought to

Duxbury by her grandfather, Captain David Cushman, whom she had never met because he died before she was born in 1895. Miss Cushman's fondest wish was to have her house and land become a memorial to Captain David, who was famous in his own right, even though he had only married into the Alden family.

The Wildlands Trust was alerted of Miss Lura's death. Members of the Trust immediately made sure the house was secure, because there were many stories about her—that she kept money in the books she was reading, and that the house was full of treasures brought from foreign lands.

For me that was a period of déjà vu, or perhaps it was a mirror reflection of childhood, when my family were resident docents of the Judge Samuel Holten House, owned by the Daughters of the American Revolution. With other volunteers, I studied and sorted and eventually placed the contents of the house. Members of the Trust were assigned to examine and sort one room at a time. The house itself had been built in the early nineteenth century, according to plans Captain David had drawn up during one of his "viages." The Trust inherited the house in 1988.

In an old house in New England, nothing is ever thrown away. There were small scraps of paper everywhere, identifying special items. The oil paintings done by Chinese artists were immediately removed to a safe place. Neighbors told us how Miss Cushman had hidden money in magazines. We carefully searched every copy of the *National Geographic Magazine* and found several hundred dollars. A more spectacular find was a little basket in the corner of a horsehair sofa in the family parlor, which contained a thousand dollars.

There were volumes of photographs from Miss Cushman's own voyages around the world three times, following in her grandfather's footsteps. There were books and books of stamp collections. There was a huge bookcase so deep that it contained two layers, front and back, of the classics. The books were carefully identified and arranged on tables, ready for the book dealers to bid on. In the attic, there were thousands of ephemera (I almost wrote anathema), including whole series of newspapers and other periodicals printed before photography was common.

Added to the ancient ones were complete years of magazine like the *Woman's Home Companion*, from its first edition to almost its current issues. These covered the floor of the room where we sorted them. They were of great attraction to the booksellers, who came and bid and eventually brought their trucks to collect. Miss Cushman had stipulated that anything saleable could be sold, but that no public sale was to be held on her property.

Things bought by the Captain were of the highest interest, and there were three or four auctioneers visiting and evaluating and making bids. Mr. LeBaron Briggs was the "director of operations" and the hardest worker in the months it took to empty the large house.

Mr. Briggs was always ingenious in his treatment of the inevitable problems that kept coming up. Miss Cushman had been an ardent dressmaker, and she made all her own dresses for her career as a teacher in the Boston School of Cookery. In addition to her dresses, she also took a course in Millinery and made all her hats. We needed some way to sort and evaluate clothing. Mr. Briggs used lengths of gas pipe to make rods, sloping but adequate, to hang garments for auctioneers to see and bid on. We finally had an auction, presided over by Joan Caddigan, who handled the clothing situation admirably.

There was also a superabundance of fabrics, which we sorted for the garment auction. The fabrics went all the way from sheets and pillowcases to, well, anything one can imagine made of cloth. That auction was scheduled for an evening, but Ruth Briggs and I dropped in at the auction hall in the afternoon. The auction enthusiasts were already studying the stock and deciding what they would bid on. We had done the work, and the entire wall of the auction room was lined on all four sides by large cardboard boxes filled with all kinds of cloth.

To our surprise and delight, we saw that the auction enthusiasts were happily exchanging stuff in this box for equal amounts of stuff in other boxes. At the auction, the 500 dresses and the 400 homemade (and very neat) hats were bid for and bought and carried away. Even the two top hats went. The boxes of fabric all around the four walls of the hall were sold down to the very last scrap, and we all went home that night happy with a very adequate reward!

At one of the bigger auctions, when the valuable Chinese paintings were on the auction block, there was a telephone call and a long wait. Later, when the details were revealed, the story went like this: someone bidding for a person in England was not sure how much he or she was authorized to spend. The bidder had to call England and, eventually, China, so that the transaction could be completed and the auction could continue.

The treasures brought back by Captain David from Asia were beautiful and valuable. Their sale at auction helped the Wildlands Trust to save more of the special places of Southeastern Massachusetts. The records of his voyages and his connection with the wars in China have added to the history of those times, especially in the shipping industry, when Duxbury's "King Caesar" had more ships on the seas than any one else.

The legend is that the Cushman House was the second house in Duxbury to have indoor bathroom facilities. The old bathroom still has the ancient metal bathtub, with a wooden frame around it. There is also the usual marble around the washbasin.

When the Trust team finished clearing out the house, we went on to empty the boathouse, where Captain David and his son Walter built small boats after the Captain retired in 1860. Walter had a fine reputation for his boat-building skills, which Duxbury sailors still praise. He also built a fascinatingly complete dollhouse, ordered by the Wright family, which had a large estate in Duxbury. When the Wrights left town, the dollhouse came back into the Cushman House. Probably the last equipment added to the dollhouse was a tiny pink telephone, purchased by Miss Cushman on one of her world tours. She placed the miniature telephone in the upstairs guest room in the dollhouse. Proceeds from selling the dollhouse and the multitude of other things at auction gave The Wildlands Trust an opportunity to hire staff and to expand its land-saving activities.

The one noteworthy component of the Cushman House is no longer there. It was the outdoors bathroom, probably engineered by Walter, the builder.

In 1853 Fowler and Wells published a popular book entitled *A Home For All, or the Gravel Walk and Octagon Mode of Building.* Mr. Orson Fowler was "a true innovator." He advocated that building in a circle would create the greatest amount of space. He refined the circle to the octagon, considering that shape more practical for building with sawed boards. His book resulted in many octagonal houses being built—even one in nearby Kingston and another in Pembroke. One of the best features of the octagonal house was that the builder could use scrap lumber in the construction of the eight sides, and construction required no corner posts because the sides fitted together.

Walter Cushman was another innovator, who could build boats and dollhouses. Walter, influenced by the Fowler book and having in the boat shop a quantity of scrap wood, had the necessary materials to build a smaller building for the family privy. An octagon would have been too big. Therefore he reduced it to a hexagon.

Another virtue of a building of this type was that it required no insulation, because the scrap wood pieces were cut to fit flat in the straight sides and thus the smallish building already had five solid wood sides with the sixth side serving for the door.

When the Trust acquired the Cushman Estate, the hexagonal privy stood close beside the boat shop. The door hung well on its hinges, and the windows had not been broken. The little building contained the usual equipment universally to be found in any privy. The whole structure could have been restored with a minimum of expense and labor, except that the roof had rotted and caved in. It was a sad day when this small architectural gem was demolished (especially since the historical societies all around us had been restoring their own local examples of antique architecture).

However, not all has been lost. Now one sees at the edge of the trees, a beautiful hexagonal frame of cement, which surrounds and sets off the beauty of the spring bulbs in full bloom. This is my loving memorial to a charming and historically valuable little building built by the Captain's son. One could go on to add, most enthusiastically, that the Plymouth County Wildlands Trust, nurtured by funds from the Cushman operation, has gone on to become the Wildlands Trust of Southeastern Massachusetts and expanded its successful efforts to save land.

The Hydraulic Ram

Working with the actual artifacts of such a house was an education in how people lived in the early days of our country. One of the most fascinating and mysterious discoveries deserves description here. In the early days, our ancestors had to go to the nearest spring or perhaps a brook or a river to get a drink of water. There was no such thing as a faucet or a plumber. Our local Native Americans undoubtedly knew where to find water, because they lived close to nature all day, every day.

Within a few years, when the early settlers had established their homesteads, they usually started with some kind of a kitchen sink. The sink at the Harlow House in Plymouth is a hollowed out stone, which came from abroad as ballast in the bottom of a ship. Collecting the water was an important task in those ancient times. Using the local bog iron, the settlers manufactured anchors and tools and eventually pitcher pumps, which would lift water about 25 feet.

Then someone invented an automatic water pump that would run constantly and would lift water from the brook down in the hollow up to a cistern in the house itself. This "machine" was called a hydraulic ram. Someone said it was—and still is—the invention nearest to a perpetual motion machine. The principle of the hydraulic ram is now used in all kinds of big machinery, such as petroleum oil wells.

Chapter 22

Memory—1985

Nature provided the fireworks. The lightning flashed and the thunder rumbled.

It carried me back to the roof of 200 Beacon Street in Boston on the Fourth of July 1985. We practiced ascending to the roof in daylight, learning to maneuver a missing step in the stepladder, which served as a staircase.

Once on the roof it was a different world. We were up there among Boston's "skyscrapers," beyond the chimney pots and the clotheslines of our neighbors. Just below us flowed the Charles River, and in the near distance we could see the "Shell," where the orchestra would sit to play. People were assembling. They walked along the roadway, now devoid of automobile traffic. They were carrying blankets and chairs and babies and picnic baskets in a never-ending procession, which increased and thickened as the hours passed. A few pitched tents. There were no fires. There was no alcohol. Sailboats on the blue water found their desired locations and set anchor.

We found the roof too distant. We had to go into the crowds of vibrant holiday people. Descending from the rooftop, we saw reminders of what Victorian living in Boston at its formal best must have been like. There was red carpeting on the five flights down. Each floor was cluttered with family treasures, like a disorganized museum. There was Rose Medallion china here, a Shaker chair there. The descent still went down by the elegant stairs to the formal dining room. Then we passed into the servants' domain, the butler's pantry and the plain, narrow uncarpeted stairs for the servants, into the kitchen.

The padlock on the wrought iron gates of the parking lot were unlocked, and we were unceremoniously caught up by the surge of people moving steadily toward the Esplanade. In the Hatch Shell, the musicians were already tuning their instruments. We heard the mellow notes of the English horns and the colorful notes of the flutes. Sometimes they would play an overture, or, setting the tone for the Fourth of July, a John Philip Sousa march.

Living alone in a rural atmosphere had made me aloof from any crowd. Back in Duxbury, six people in the Post Office was too many. But this multitude of 725,000 people relaxed in the sunshine, carefree, laughing, enfolding or perhaps engulfing the hot dog stand suddenly became my friends, a part of me. I was a part of each one. We smiled and laughed and dogged each other, totally given up to the magic of the sparkling river, the green grass, and the music. It reminded me of an old hymn describing Heaven as it was pictured in the nineteenth century. "The pastures of the blessed are decked in glorious green."

We had to seek out the six Howitzers, which traditionally provided the boom of the cannon at the climax of the 1812 overture (also a Boston tradition). At the Bell Tower nearby, a troupe of bell ringers were already practicing for the peal of bells they would unleash when the battle is won in the Overture. Memories from childhood welled up in my mind, as I recalled gentlefolk who felt strongly that the 1812 Overture was the absolute zenith of musical invention to celebrate even America's Fourth of July. They wore out the phonograph record!

Dusk. Back again to the roof. The fireworks barge floated in the river close below us. Back into the twentieth century. Increasing darkness as the band concert and the crowd's enthusiasm climbed in an ascending pitch, bells, cannon, applause, and bombs.

That evening I learned fireworks are not a waste of money. They are an artistic magic. Boom, flash, smoke, then another flash. Brilliant lights and color against the gray smoke to heighten the colors—and people ecstatic over the beauty and mystery of the show.

The crowd was moving again back to parked cars and the real world. The streets were washed and swept clean. The next morning, the barge was gone and there were two or three white sailboats at rest on the quiet river.

"Eightieth"

Doggerel* for a very special octagenarian
(at times in the manner of W.S. Gilbert)

H.L.P. 2/23/90

A charming young woman of eighty
Whose talents are varied and weighty.
If you think I am daft,
(Who was that who just laft?)
She has "done" every craft.
She's grown fruit trees from graft,
She's worked silver, caned chairs,
Preserved apples, spiced pears,
Baked bread and made pies,
And produced home-made dyes.
She's made candles from wax,
Carded wool and grown flax.
She can spin it and weave it
(You may win it or leave it),
Make baskets, grow herbs,
On a farm in suburbs
With Tuffy and Tiger,
(Orange fiend from the Niger). [cat]
She moved from ceramics
To biodynamics,
Makes music, daubs paint;
Stout heart, never faint,
With the warmth of a saint.
Overstated? That ain't.
Deeply immersed in research that's historical,
Cushman and Duxb'ry by class categorical,

Often intrigued by a question rhetorical.
As keeper of herds she once worked with biology;
But can now process words with computer technology.
The nineties (her eighties) are at last underway—
And she'll ne'er go to Hades for her work or her play.

*Doggerel—a sort of loose or irregular verse. Undignified; trivial.

This was presented at a surprise birthday party for me with the Plymouth County Wildlands Trust, written by Mr. LeBaron Briggs, Secretary of the Trust. It tells you all my news and I send you greeting and all best wishes this Christmas—1990.

—Helen

Ruth Briggs

Ruth Briggs is my dear friend, and we have had many good times together. The Harlow House was such a good example of preservation of the old that it won my admiration, and we often worked there together. We also enjoyed many different excursions, following various trails, but one of the best was our favorite thrift shop. It was very large and the variety was enormous. One of the best features was that it worked both ways. We could bring things, and we could buy other things.

One day I said to Ruth, "Winter is coming and I really need some good warm woolen pants." Ruth was skillful in finding the best things available. After awhile she brought me a pair of heavy woolen pants. I looked them over and said to Ruth, "Look, somebody else had the same idea I had. They cut the ankles off without having to sew bulky cuffs. I'll buy 'em." I brought them home and reached into the closet where pants were hung. There were no pants there because I had taken them to the thrift shop last August. Now I had bought them back!

We go to Church—Johnny Cat

Parishioners who have an understanding of cat nature show a certain inner satisfaction that Johnny Cat has made his place in our "Faith Community" at Saint John's. There must also be beloved people who are not cat lovers but who show admirable patience and forbearance, and a bit of tongue in cheek tolerance for a comedian feline.

Anyone coming to visit the Church of Saint John the Evangelist in Duxbury is likely to be met in the parking lot by Johnny Cat, a former stray of Siamese background. He has been a self-appointed welcomer for almost 20 years. He greets everyone with equal dignity and enthusiasm, and leads them into the church.

At choir rehearsal, he goes around the circle, recognizing anyone who will reach down a hand. He would like to attend church services and sometimes evades the ushers, walking down the aisle toward the chancel. The day the Rector's wife was directing the Junior Choir, Johnny Cat walked within her reach. The music was directed by Johnny Cat's paw in her right hand, to the great delight of the Junior Choir.

One Sunday, while the Rector was preaching about serious matters from the pulpit, the congregation was spellbound as it watched Johnny Cat climbing the Rood Screen until he was rescued by an usher.

One could marvel at the gentle influence exerted without speech by one of our (perhaps) lower beings. Children are exuberant with pure delight, which Johnny Cat shares.

Musings of a Nonogenerian

Once someone asked an old Quaker how he managed to live so long. His answer was, "Perhaps it's the peppermint I put in my whiskey every day." To tell the truth, it is easier, even, than that. Much simpler. A big smile and a good laugh will save a day. One does not have to be sentimental or even let on why one is trying to care. It can be one's own inner secret, and it really works.

Recently someone said, "That villain is beyond forgiveness. I'll never speak to him again." This attitude never hurts the bad one, because he is way over there and never knows he is being threatened. But the one who resents and lets resentments build up, can and probably does lose a night's sleep now and then.

The only way to close this meditation is, "Don't hold resentments or put peppermint in the whiskey. Just make an effort to remember to love and to forgive."

I don't claim to have any authority, but someone ought to be expressing some deeper thoughts in these rather troubled days of the twenty-first century.

This is What I Have Really Been Intending to Write

Our twenty-first century world is so filled with marvelous inventions that take care of all our needs with such skill and precision that we are being lulled to sleep. It is time to look deeper to discover that there are invisible values that demand our attention to save our spirits. It seems to me that the only way we can survive the problems that stem from our materialism is to look for deeper spiritual values, which are right there for us to discover. Instead of being bored by a new route that seems less alluring, one may suddenly find that there is infinite joy and love and freedom to be found in the life of the spirit.

By the life of the spirit, I don't necessarily mean any church. There are infinite interests in education and creative skills in every direction. With an eye for creative skills, one can discover a whole new world of satisfaction and joy, which are every day being drowned out by our fascinating and indispensable material inventions.

Our early ancestors had no such "benefits". That is why the spiritual world was constantly available to them. Just think about it. Aren't we missing something?

Index

Symbols

4-H Club 157, 158

A

Abramoglu, Afanazi 171
Abramoglu, Anastasia 171, 172
Adams, Faniel 133
Aggie 108
air-conditioning, introduction of 146
Albrecht, William A. 173, 175
Alcott, Louisa May
 Little Women 238
Alden, Benjamin 104, 133, 216
Alden, John 133, 245
Alden Kindred 245
Alden, Mrs. 216
Alden, Priscilla 245
Alden, Susie 133
Alden, Thomas 133, 134
 *Book of Recipe Article*s 134
Alden, Willard 104
Alice in Wonderland 77
All Saints Church 217
Altar Guild rooms 55

Ames, Fisher 98
Anastagoras, Philoxynos 167
Angora rabbits 113, 127
Anthroposophic Press 114
Appeal to the Great Spirit (Dallin) 42
Appleby, Jonathan 103
apples 217
Appleton, William Sumner 43, 47, 48
Aramaic 78
Arc de Triomphe 194
Artificial Limb and Brace Company 20
Ashfield 184, 187, 230
 library 198
Atlantic Monthly 40
Aunt of Dr. Clifford Samuelson 142, 143

B

Back Wards 61, 62
Badger, Susie 216
Baldwin 39

257

Baldwin, Dr. 26
Baldwin, Letty 161
Bamford, Christopher 114
Banner, Earl 112
Bard College 78
Barrymore, Ethel 231
Bartow, Archdeacon 101
Basin 65
Bates, Frances 39
Bath 71
Bath Iron Works 86
bayberry bush 84
Beacon Hill 43
Beaver Brook Lane 100
Bei 192, 197
Bell Ringers Beta Quartet 138
Bell Tower 55
Bellas Hess 172
Benchley, Robert 212
    Coffee Meg and Ilk 212
Benton, Thomas Hart 182
Berry, Gordon 85
Berry, John 65, 72, 73, 85
Berry, Katherine 65
Beston, Henry
    The Outermost House 33
Beverly Jog 32, 48
Bible 19, 83
Bigelow, Francis Hill
    Historic Silver of the Colonies and Its Makers 46
Bigelow, Maude 99
Biodynamic Farming and Gardening Association 222, 232
Biodynamics 114, 115, 222, 232
Bitteroots 144
Blaha, Mr. 96
Blaha, Mrs. 95

Blood and a Plank (Helen Philbrick) 36
Boak, Miss 49
Book of Common Prayer 46, 94
Book of Recipe Articles (Thomas Alden) 134
Boston 14, 41, 179
Boston Globe 39, 236, 238
Boston Guild of Weavers 210
Boston Museum of Fine Arts 36, 42, 225
Boston Pops Orchestra 48
Boston Public Library 54
Boston School of Cookery 247
Boston School of Occupational Therapy 60, 61
Boston Sunday Globe 112
Boston Transcript 40
Boston University 20, 21
Boulevard 65
Bourne 108
Bourne's Wharf 125
Bowker, Howard 82
    as leader of a road-repair endeavor 83
    relationship with the Philbricks 86
    sharing private telephone with the community 87
Bowker, Mrs.
    relationship with the Philbricks 87
    sharing private telephone with the community 87
Bowles, Tizzy 90
Boxford 23
Bozeman 143
Bradford, Laurence
    Historic Duxbury 134

Bradner, Bill 81
Bremen 126
Brig Leander 43, 45
Briggs, LeBaron 247
   Eightieth 253
Briggs, Ruth 254
Brightwater 65, 66, 70, 82, 84
Brink, Mrs. 161
Bristol 14
Bristol Ferry 13, 14
Brock, Malcolm 129
Brockton 65, 109
Brookings Institute 70
Brown, Allen 161
Brown, Ethel 42
Brown, Leo Maxwell
   Vision Fulfilling 161
Browne and Sharpe 46
Bug Book, The (John and Helen Philbrick) 221, 223
Bulletin of the Sutton Historical Society 219
Bullitt, Ann 194
Bullitt, William Christian 187, 190
Butter and Eggs 28
Byron, Lord 178

C

Cabot 111
Caddigan, Joan 247
Cambridge 74
Candlemas 230
Canham, George 139
Cannon, Bill 163, 164
Cannon, Opal 164
Cape Cod 33
Cape Cod Crocker 36
Carmen 156
Carson, Kit 182
Carson, Rachel
   Silent Spring 199, 220
Carter, Russell Gordon 88, 231
   Poem by the Thinnish Man 87
Cathedral of Notre Dame 196
Cather, Willa 144
Cats Hell 93
Cedar Street 93, 98
Ceylon. *See* Sri Lanka
Champion Lamp Factory 20, 28, 31
chapatis 170
Chapin, Mr. 20
Charles River 251
Chautauqua 27
Chestnut Dormitory 145
Chestnut Street 43, 47
Chicago Grand Opera Company 156
China 192
Christian Register 40
Christmas 215
Church Militant 91
Church Missions House 139
Church of the Holy Spirit 139
Church of the Pilgrimage 231
Church of the Redeemer 145
Civil War 134, 161, 182, 198
Clark, Talkative 29
Closer Look at Your Garden, A 174
Cobbler Shop 113, 127
Cochel, Wilbur 140, 148, 149, 171, 181
Coffee Meg and Ilk (Benchley) 212
Coffin, Gertrude 93

Coffin, Jane 111
Coffin, Winthrop 111, 131
Colorado School of Mines 143
Colton, Jim 213
Colton, Mary 213
Colton, Mother 212
Colton, Sid 212
Columbus, Christopher 133
Commonwealth Pier 234
Communist Party 229
Companion Plants and How to Use Them (Helen Philbrick and Richard Gregg) 173, 188, 222, 223
Compost (John and Helen Philbrick) 154
Conant Street 21
Concord 37
Congregational Church (Ashfield) 184, 194
Congregational Church (Sutton) 225
Connecticut River valley 189
Continental Congress 31
Corey, Eva D. 38
Cornerstone Masonic Temple 133
Corriedales 111
Cottrell, Arlo 147, 149, 153, 169, 175
Cousin Herbie. *See* Philbrick, Herbert
Cove Street 104
Croom, Letitia 160, 161, 163
Croskey, Wyman 176
Cross, Paul. *See* Stavrianos, Focas
Cunningham, Emily 98, 99
Cunningham House 93
Cushman, David 246, 248

Cushman House 245
Cushman, Lura 245
Cushman, Walter 248, 249

D

Dallas, Bishop 55, 56
Dallin, Cyrus 42
   Appeal to Great Spirit 42
   Samoset 42
Damrosch, Walter 60
Dana, Mrs. 24
Danvers 19, 20, 27, 60
Danvers Herald 48
Danvers Highlands 31
Danvers Historical Society 49
Danvers Insane Asylum 61
Danvers State Hospital 60, 63
Danvers Womens Association 28
Dardanelles 178
Daughters of the American Revolution 31, 32, 33, 40
Davenport 39, 216
Davenport Collection 39, 238
David (Michelangelo) 57
Davidson, William 161
Davis, Jerome 57, 58, 59, 64, 65, 71
Davis, Mildred 71
Davis, Patty 59, 64, 71
Davis, Wilfred Grenfell 59, 64, 71
DDT 198
   hazards as described in *Silent Spring* by Rachel Carson 199
   incident in Connecticut 199
   subject of *The Bug Book* by John and Helen Philbrick 221
   sudden death of Tanner Guy 199

de Suze, Carl 119, 120, 121, 184, 208
   poem by 122
Declaration of Independence 193
DeCoursey, Annette 98
Delano, Judah 104, 105
Delano, Lydia 105
Delano, Philip 106
Demeter 115
Demonstration Homestead 147
Denver 143
Diocesan Board for the Women's Church Service League 100
Directory of American Silversmiths 46
Dobson, Michael 114
Dorchester 74
Dragons Blood 77
DuBois, Pine 234
Dudley, Flora 211, 214
Dunstans, Saint 34
Duxbury 86, 87, 93, 110, 116, 125
Duxbury Beach 125
Duxbury Clipper 110
Duxbury Home 39
Duxbury Rural and Historical Society 120
DWA Glee Club 29

E

Early American Homes 33
Easter 215
Easy Street 40
Ecuador
   minister of agriculture of 169
Eddy, Netty 130
Edinburgh 61
Egypt 75

Eightieth (Briggs) 253
Emerson College 232
Emma 111
Encyclopedia Britannica 193
England 167
Episcopal Church 37, 98, 148, 154, 171
Episcopal Prayer Book 153
Episcopal Theological School 74, 81
Episcopal Triennial Convention 179
Erickson, Leif 133
Essex County 29
Essex Institute 48. *See also* Peabody Essex Museum
Estes, Miss 42
Europe 16, 18, 40
Ewin, Dr. 25
Excelsior Springs Church 161

F

Faith Homestead 94, 101, 104, 111, 113, 120, 232
Falconi, Cisneros 169
Farley Church 162, 176
Farragut, General 186
Faust (Gounod) 156
Federal Bureau of Investigation 229
Ferber, Edna
   So Big 144
Field Guide to Salem's Architecture, A (Lorenz) 32
Filinos, Alex 172
Filinova 172
First Church 128
First World War 12, 16, 18
Five Cent Savings Bank 16
Flannery, Florence 93

Fogg Museum 77
Foote, Mrs. Norman 168
Foote, Norman 151, 152, 154
Forbes, Alan 73
Ford, Betty 235
Ford's Store 125
Fourth of July 18, 71, 251, 252
Fowler and Wells 249
Fowler, Orson
   A Home For All, or the Gravel Walk and Octagon Mode of Building 249
Fraiser, Mrs. 167
France 223
Francis, Saint 91
Frank (adopted by Lynches) 26
Franklin County Court 191
Frazier 153
Free Deeds 174
French, Mr. 225
Friendship Hall 187
Front Wards 61

G

Gallagher, Peggy 234
Gandhi, Mahatma 188
Garden Way
   The Gardeners Bug Book 221
Gardeners Bug Book, The (Garden Way) 222
General Electric 20
Germany 95, 114, 171
Gilbert, William S.
   Pirates of Penzance 60
Gorham Silver Manufacturing Company 12
Gounod
   Faust 156

Grand Tetons 143
Grange 17, 188
Great Depression 46, 56
Greek sculpture 57
Gregg, Richard
   Companion Plants and How to Use Them 188
   The Power of Nonviolence 188
Grotzke, Heinz 232
Groundhog Day 230
Groveland 81
Guinness, Alec 146

H

Hallet's Drugstore 71
Hamilton 35, 51
Handell, Leon 232
Harlow House 250, 254
Harmless Insect Controls (John and Helen Philbrick) 221
Harvard University 59
Haverford 85
Hawkes, Benjamin 45
Hawthorne, Nathaniel 43
Hedge House 236
Heifer Project International 154
Hellespont 178
Henderson 19
Henderson, Alice 110
Herb Garden 234
hermit (in Boxford) 24
Hero 179
Herreshoff Boat Yards 14
Hildreth, Judge 191
Historic Duxbury (Bradford) 134
Historic Silver of the Colonies and Its Makers (Bigelow) 47
Hobart College 96

Holland 223
Hollywood 16
Holten House. *See* Judge Samuel Holten House
Holten Street 31
Holy Humor 219
Home For All, or the Gravel Walk and Octagon Mode of Building, A (Fowler) 249
Horwitz, Dr. 193
Horwitz, Mrs. 193
Hotel Algonquin 212
Hotel Essex 76, 77
How to Know the Wildflowers 24
Howes Hill 18
Howland, Frances 100
Humphrey, Walter 163
hydraulic ram 250

I

I Led Three Lives 229
Improved Order of Red Men 17, 188
India 166, 170, 178
Ingalls, Jimmie 110
Ingersoll 108
Irish 21, 22, 23, 25, 26
Italy 91
Iverson, Priscilla 211
Ives, Hilda 178

J

J. B. Thomas Hospital 25
Jackson Hole 143
Jacobs, Allen 92
Jacobs, Mrs. Allen 92, 100
James, Jesse 182

Japan 65, 223
Johnny Cat 255
Johnson, Howard 232
Jones, Rufus 85
Judge Samuel Holten House 29, 31, 44, 45, 47, 49, 246
Judson, Anne C. 198
June Bug (Frazier) 156
Junior Guild 100

K

Kahlert, Willie 126, 127, 173
Kalgourlie, Bishop 168
Kansas City (Kansas) 146
Kansas City (Missouri) 144, 145
  centennial celebration 181
Kansas City Airport (Missouri) 150
Kansas City Music Hall (Missouri) 155
Kansas City Star 147
Keep the Home Fires Burning 17
Kelley, Tom 83
Kent, Anne 130
Kent, Beulah 130
Kent, Jack 130, 132
Kerans, Mrs. 21, 23
Kerans, Rachael 21, 22
Kerans, Rebecca 21
Kilmer, Cliff 213
Kilmer, Grace 213
Kimball, Florence 138
Kimball, John 30
Kimball, Maria Grey 29, 30
Kimball, Richard 138
King Caesar House 120
King, Connie 98
King of Siam 51
Kline, Reamer 75, 78, 79

Kline-Tyler Codex 75, 76, 77
Koepf, Dr. 232
Kubla Khan 194
Kuleratnam, Dr. 167

L

Labrador 64
Ladies Guilds 92, 224
LaSalle House 215, 216
Lathrop, Helen Saunders 11, 12
Lavender Hill Mob, The 146
Lawrence 14
Lawrence, Frederick 110
Lawrence, Katharine 110
Lawrence, W. A. 97
Leadville 143
Leander 179
Leiden Lantern Light 109
Leiden Lassie 109
Lewes, Bishop 167
Liebestod 59
Lincoln, Abraham 198
Little Saxham Church 54
Little Women (Alcott) 238
Lizzie 108
loess soil 149
Long Bridge 125
Longview 142
Lord, Elinor 178
Lords Prayer 11, 12, 19
Lorenz, Mark
   A Field Guide to Salems Architecture 32
Loring, Oliver 129
Louisburg Square 43, 48
Lovelace, Mr. 28
Lowell 111
Lowell, Howard 75

Lucy, Aunt 12
Lund, Jo 103
Lynch, Mrs. 22
Lynch, Timothy 21

M

Magnolia 31
Mahatma Gandhi 178
maple syrup 189
Marblehead 35
Maria G. Kimball Peace Fund 30
marijuana 147
Marsh, Francis 28
Marsh, Jasper 28
Marshfield 125
Marys, Saint 34
Masons 188
Massachusetts 139, 141, 146, 184, 235, 237, 248
Massachusetts Council of Churches 200
Massih, Inaiyat 166
Mathematical Curiosity 136
Mattakeeset Hall. *See* Sprague Hall
Mayflower Society 40
McBride, Owen 233
McCarthy, Joseph P. 40
Memorial Eucharist Set 54
Merrill, Virginia 19
Merry, Hortense E. 106, 111
Merry, John 106
Metropolitan Museum of New York 48
Metropolitan Opera 155, 156
Michaelmas 215
Michelangelo
   David 57

Middleton 14, 16, 19
Millbury Bank 221
Mills, Marjorie 120, 121, 184
Miner, Sanderson 233
Ministers Vegetable Garden, The
    (John and Helen Philbrick)
    154
Miriam, Aunt 82
Mississippi River 144
Mississippi Valley 149
Missouri
    thundershowers 149
Missouri River 142, 143, 146, 182
Mizzenmast 186
Mohawk Trail 187
Monadnock, Mount 190
Moriarty 26
Morse, John 83
Mother Earth News 169
Mount Hope Bridge 14
mountain laurel 196
Mullen, Charlie 120
Myopia Hunt Club 51

N

Nameless Group 110, 111, 112
Nancy 111
Nantucket 121
Nash, Dr. 74, 76, 77
Nathan 116, 117
National Cathedral 54
    Resurrection silver 36
National Council of the Episcopal
    Church 133
National Geographic Magazine
    246
National Town-Country Church
    Institute 148, 150, 154

Navajo 42
Nazis 126
Nearing, Helen 112
Nearing, Scot 112
Nelson, Dorothea 95
Nelson, George 95, 96
Nelson, Margaret 92, 94, 95
Nelson Memorial Forest 97
New England 35, 40, 246
New England Forestry Foundation
    97
New Haven Commercial High
    School 57
New Testament 74
New York City 114, 169
New York Times 236
New Yorker 99, 199, 213
Newport 13
Newton, Evelyn 220
North Hill 105, 106
North Hill Brook 105
Northfield School for Girls 49
Nova Scotia 133

O

Oakley, Queenie 211
Obst, Miss 27
occupational therapy 60, 61
Occupational Therapy School 43
Odd Fellows 17, 188
Odd Fellows Hall 100
Oklahoma! 146
Old Crow Whiskey 151
Old Sailors Home 93, 107
Old Stone Bridge 106
Old Sturbridge Village 39
Opportunity Class 118
Orleans 138

Orrs Island 71
Oshima, Bill 234
Oshima, Helen 234
Outermost House, The (Beston) 33

P

Packet 125
Pansy Petunia 110
Park College 145, 150
Parker, Dorothy 212
Parkville 144
Partridge Manuscript 74, 79
Partridge, Wilfred J. 75, 76, 78
Paul Petersons Drugstore 129
Paul Revere and the World He Lived In 38
Peabody Essex Museum 35, 51
Peabody, Joseph 45
Pease, Howard 190
Penney, J. C. 152
Pennsylvania Turnpike 141
Pentecostal roses 215
Perkins, Alfred 15, 16, 17, 18, 36
Perkins, Ethel 14, 15, 36
Perkins, Frank, Jr. 15, 16
Perkins, Frank, Sr. 15, 16, 18, 36
Peterson, Paul 110, 129
Peterson, Thaddeus 104
Petrushka (Igor Stravinsky) 17
Pfeiffer, Ehrenfried 201, 222, 232
Pfeiffer, Mr. 17
Philbrick, Helen 48
 as an infant terrible 22
 as schoolteacher 116
 Blood and a Plank 36
 Companion Plants and How to Use Them 173

Compost 154
concept of gardening 124
concept of life of the spirit 256
describing the simplicity of life in her childhood 226
Harmless Insect Control 221
high school 36
making a replica of the Paul Revere Cup 224
poem for John 158
summer youth conferences 37
The Bug Book 221
The Ministers Vegetable Garden 154
Thoughts from Brightwater 71
thoughts on longevity 255
Philbrick, Herbert 229
Philbrick, John 24, 37, 55, 64, 74, 81, 92, 93, 96, 97, 110, 111, 112, 116, 125, 140, 164, 185, 190, 192, 232, 235, 239
 Compost 154
 Harmless Insect Control 221
 The Bug Book 221
 The Ministers Vegetable Garden 154
 traits as a clergyman 186, 219
Philbrick, Katharine 81, 197
Philbrick, Ralph 93
Philharmonic Music Society 155
Phippsburg 86
Phoebe 73
Pikes Peak 142
Pilgrim Bell Ringers 187, 232
pilgrims 125
Pilgrims Progress 79
Pink Bishop. *See* Anastagoras, Philoxynos

Pinky 231
Pirates of Penzance (Gilbert and Sullivan) 60
Platte City 158
Platte River 162
Plymouth 125
Plymouth Harbor 42
Plymouth Yacht Club 236
Poem by the Thinnish Man (Carter) 88
Porter Collection 51
Porter, Edward 20, 27, 57, 59, 81
Porter, Ethel 13, 18, 24, 28, 29, 82
Porter, Franklin 13, 19, 20, 23, 27, 28, 30, 35, 42, 48, 50, 82
Porter silver 48, 51
Portland (Oregon) 30
Portsmouth Navy Yard 55
Power of Nonviolence, The (Gregg) 188
Pratt, Ms. 59
Providence 12, 46, 74
Psalms 46
Punch and Judy 90
Punxatawny Phil 230

Q

Quaker 83, 85
Quality (Sumner) 231
Queen of Siam tea infuser 51
Queen Victoria 41

R

Rabbit Castle 127
Rambai Barni, Queen 51

Reineke, John Marion 157
Religion and Labor Foundation 57
Remey, Charles Mason 55
Remey, George C. 55
Renaissance 57
Resurrection Chapel 36, 54, 55
Revere, Paul 35, 48, 53
Revolutionary War 86
Rhode Island Greenings 39
Rhode Island School of Design 46
Rickards, Harold 210
Rime of the Ancient Mariner, The 200
Rivoire, Apollos. *See* Revere, Paul
Roanridge 140, 145, 165
Roanridge Demonstration Homestead 148
Roanridge Rural Training Center 141
Roanridge Rural Training Foundation 148
Roanridge Rural Training Center Cattle auction 180
Roberts Rules of Order 222
Rockhampton 168
Romans, the book of 74
Roxbury Russets 39
Rural Workers Fellowship 38, 183
Russia 17, 58, 193
Russian Bear 48

S

Saint Andrews Boys School 20
Saint Giles in the Woods. *See* Seaview-Humarock Church
Saint Johns Anglican Church (Wilkinsonville) 208, 209, 224

Saint Johns Church (Duxbury) 92, 98, 100, 107, 110, 112, 128, 239
Saint Johns Church (Portsmouth) 55
Saint Johns Day 215
Saint Johns Episcopal Church (Ashfield) 185, 194
Saint Johns Eve 194
Saint Johns Fair 100
Saint Johns Mission 93, 97
Saint Lukes Hospital 172
Saint Margarets Convent 48
Saint Margarets Hospital 111
Saint Marks Church 81
Saint Pauls Boys School 37
Salem 16, 30, 35, 43
 250th anniversary 35
Salem Custom House 43
Salem Spoon 54
salt box 31
Salt Lake City 38
Samoset (Dallin) 42
Samson 111
Samuelson, Clifford L. 139, 140, 142, 176
Samuelson Hotel 144
Samuelson, Justin 142, 143
Samuelson, Tamar 142
Seamans Library 30
Seattle 142, 144
Seaview-Humarock Church 94
Second World War 30, 101, 115, 171, 211
Senior Guild 92, 99
Setter Room of the Duxbury Library 118
Shepard, Byron 237

Shepard, Mark 237
Sherrill, Henry Knox 141, 152
Shurcliffe, Mrs. 43
Siam 51
Silent Spring (Rachel Carson) 199, 220
silversmithing 19, 20, 35
Sisters of Saint Margaret 43
Smith College 185, 230
Smith, Herman 119, 120
Smugglers Cove 73
So Big (Ferber) 144
soap making 166
Society for the Preservation of New England Antiquities 43, 47, 48
Society of Biblical Literature and Exegesis 78
Soule, Addie 128
Soule, Mrs. 99
Sousa, John Philip 16, 252
Spirit of Missions 91
Spofford, Bill 145
Sprague Hall 100
Sprague, Seth 100, 105
Spring Valley 114, 115
Sprouse, Dean 180
Sri Lanka 167
Standish Hotel 178
Standish, Myles 133
Stanley Woolen Company 210
Stavrianos, Focas 126, 127
Steiner, Rudolf 25, 114
Steinmetz, Phil 200
Stiles 19
Stiles Pond 23
Stone Bridge 105
Stoney Brook Road 66, 87

Stravinsky, Igor
   Petrushka 17
Suffolk 54
Sullivan, Arthur S.
   Pirates of Penzance 60
Sumner, Cid Ricketts
   Quality 231
Susie 111
Swampscott 30
Swansea 82
Sweetheart Tea Room 187
Sylvan Street 28
Sylvania 28
Symphony Hall 48
Syringa Bush 22

T

T Wharf 30, 31
Tanner, Guy 199, 220
Taylor, Ray 127
Ten Nights in a Barroom 22
Terwiliger 130
Thisby 73
Thistle 73
Thomas, Charles 106
Thomas, Gene 234
Thoughts from Brightwater (Helen Philbrick) 70
Tiffany Springs Church 161
Tilia 215
Tinkham, Grace Wright 61, 187
Tituba 29
Toggenberg 109
Tolman Sweet 39
Tool Shed with a Past, A 33
Topsfield 33
Tosca 155

Town Hall 17
Tremont Street 41, 46, 125
Trinity Church 92
Tristan und Isolde 60
Trusties 61, 62
Tyler, Barrett 75, 78

U

U.S. State Department 170
Union Chapel 160
Unitarian Church 40, 110
University of Missouri 173

V

Vandalia 141
Vicks VapoRub 63
Victorian era 12
Viggers, Dizz 145
Viroque 39
Vision Fulfilling (Leo Maxwell Brown) 161
Vulliamy, Constance 145, 161

W

Wadleigh, Frances 36
Waldorf School 39, 238
Walker, Donald 128
Walker, Percy 103, 133
Wall Street Journal 236
Waltham 40
War Chapel 107
Washington, George 31, 193
Washington Street 99
WBZ 120, 121, 184
Weber-Fulops 119

Webster, Daniel 99
Wenham 35, 51
West Main Road 13
Weston, Ezra 120
Weston, Thomas 105
Wheaton 49
Wheaton Female Seminary 56
Whitehead, Macy 72, 82
Whole Earth Exposition 234
Wildlands Trust 235, 237
Wilkinson, Mr. 209
Wilkinsonville 39, 208, 217
Williams, Hal 232
Winsor Lane 99
Winsor Street. *See* Winsor Lane
Woburn 127
Wolf of Gubbio 91
Womans Home Companion 247
Womens Educational and Industrial Union 41
Woodward, Barbara 111
Woodward, Barclay Jeffries 111
Woodward, Barclay Jeffries, III 230
Woodward, Barclay Jeffries, IV 230
Woody. *See* Woodward, Barclay Jeffries, III
Worcester 72, 217
Worcester Art Museum 226
Worcester Craft Center 213, 226
Worcester Horticultural Hall 39, 216
Worcester Sunday Telegram 224
Worcester Telegram 223
World Almanac, The 193
Wynburg 65, 87
Wyoming 143

Y

Yale Divinity School 57, 59
Yale University 59
Yale University Gallery of Art 36
Yellowstone National Park 143
YMCA 70
Young Mens Hebrew Association Building 58

Z

Zwingle 145

BVG